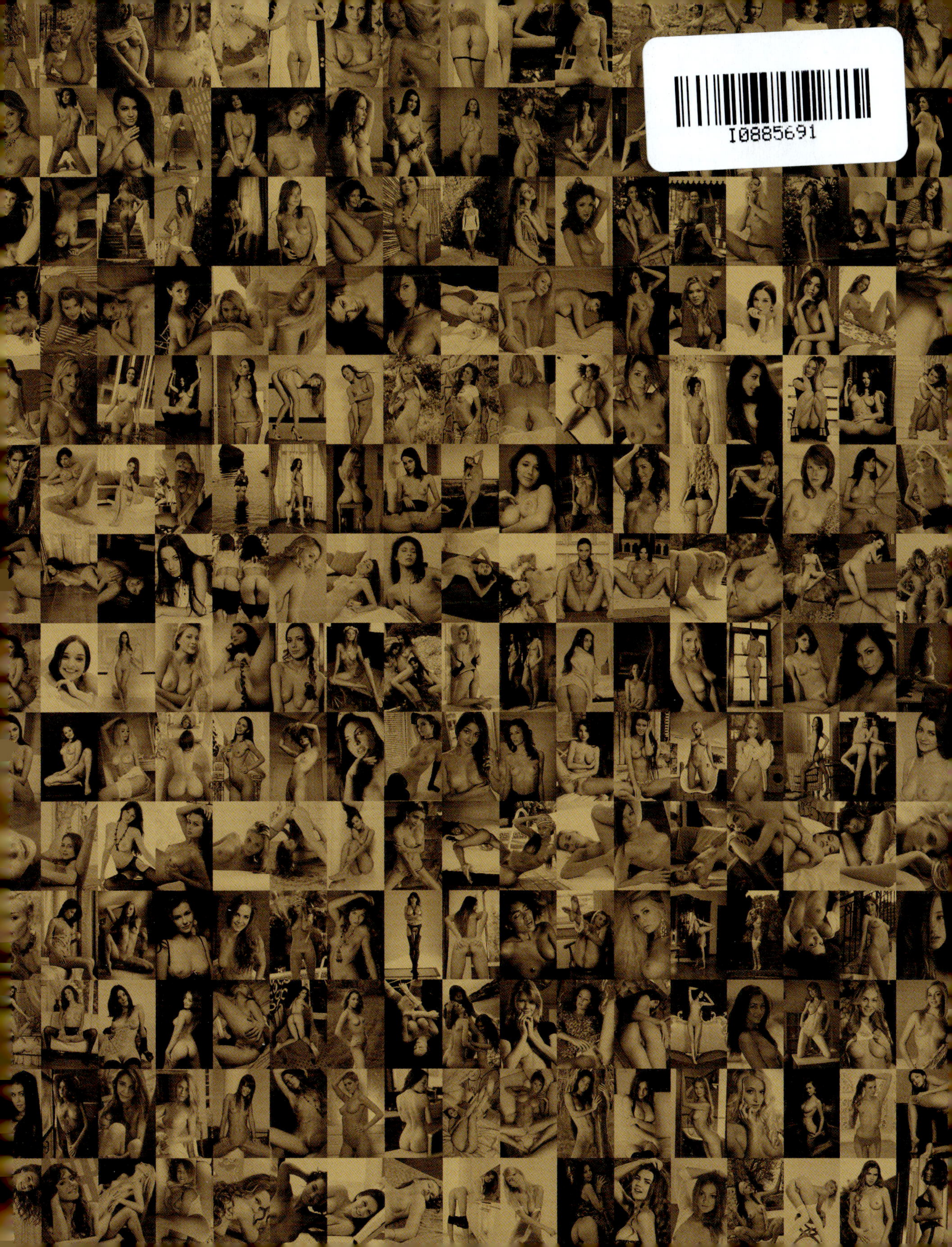

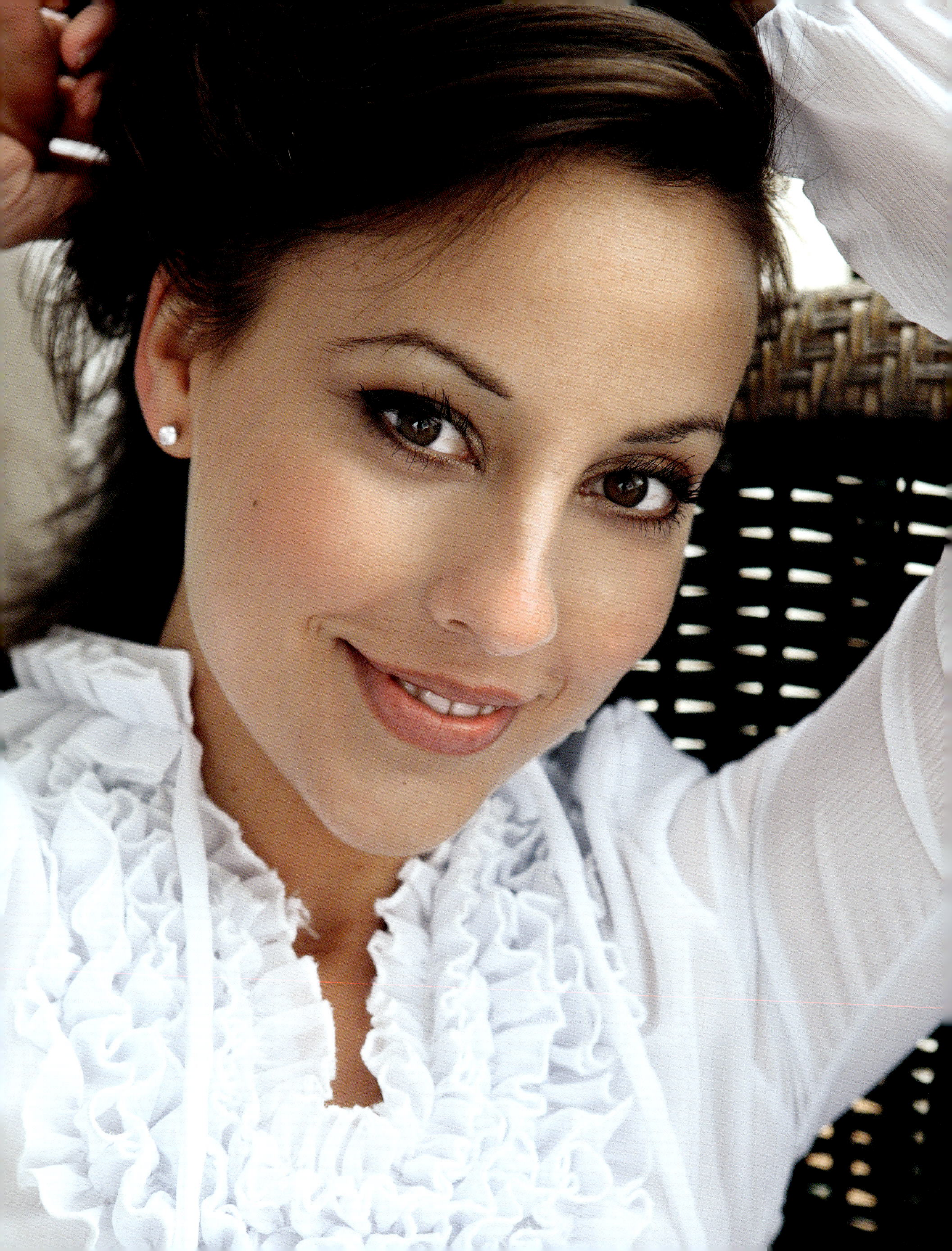

TOP MODELS OF

METART.COM

WHERE FLAWLESS BEAUTY MEETS ART

LORENA B

COLLECTED AND EDITED BY ISABELLA CATALINA

EDITION Skylight

First edition 2026

EDITION SKYLIGHT
Rosengartenstrasse 13B
CH-8608 Bubikon / Zürich
Switzerland
info@edition-skylight.com
www.edition-skylight.com

ISBN 978-3-03766-716-3

Bibliographic information published by Die Deutsche Bibliothek
Die Deutsche Bibliothek lists this publication in the
Deutsche Nationalbibliografie; detailed bibliographic data
are available in the Internet at http://dnb.ddb.de.

Printed in Bosnia and Herzegovina

“I LIKE PASSION, TO PLAY ... AND YET I DO LIKE IT WHEN IT IS FIFTY-FIFTY.“

Lorena B is a stunning Spanish beauty, and was born in Sevilla on 16 September, 1986. She has big brown eyes, a perfect slim body and thick, brown, luxurious hair. She has a firm bottom, and her perky breasts, tipped with sensitive brown nipples, make perfect handfuls. You will love her sensual smiles and her slender, all-natural body.
In the world of beautiful girls, Lorena B is once seen, never forgotten! This Spanish sweetheart is not only spectacularly gorgeous, with a smile that's radiant and a body that's irresistible, but also possesses an energy and charisma that make every one of her appearances memorable and worth treasuring. Lorena is one of the most enduringly popular girls on the MetArt Network, with dozens of appearances on our flagship site MetArt, as well as featuring in some superb girl-girl movies on SexArt and also on VivThomas.com, our sister sites. She seems to become more and more stunning every day, and after seven years at the top of her game, members still clamour to see more of her. She brings an authentic sweetness and sexuality to the screen that make her seem less like an unattainable goddess but more a type of ideal girlfriend! I've been lucky enough to interview Lorena on more than one occasion, and she's always been a great pleasure to chat with. Her answers are so genuine, natural and warm!
Lorena is studying to be a masseuse. Her dream is to live close to the beach in a hot country. In one MetArt interview she says "Being watched turns me on and also watching who I might be with and feel something for. Looking deeply into their eyes is a good way to arouse intimacy." Lorena's warm welcome gives us a special thrill when we see her and dream about her.

„ICH MAG LEIDENSCHAFT, ICH SPIELE GERNE ... UND DOCH MAG ICH ES, WENN ES FIFTY-FIFTY IST”

Lorena B ist eine atemberaubende spanische Schönheit, geboren am 16. September 1986 in Sevilla. Sie hat große braune Augen, einen perfekten, schlanken Körper und dichtes, üppiges braunes Haar. Ihr knackiger Po und ihre frechen, kleinen Brüste sind perfekt geformt, mit sensitiven braunen Brustwarzen. Wir alle lieben ihr sinnliches Lächeln und ihren schlanken, natürlichen Körper. In einer Welt voller schöner Frauen ist Lorena B auf den ersten Blick unvergesslich. Die spanische Schönheit ist nicht nur umwerfend schön mit ihrem strahlenden Lächeln und ihrem unwiderstehlichen Körper, sondern besitzt auch eine Energie und ein Charisma, die jeden ihrer Auftritte zu einem besonderen Erlebnis machen. Lorena ist eine der beliebtesten Frauen im MetArt-Netzwerk und war bereits dutzende Male auf unserer Hauptseite Metart sowie in einigen hervorragenden Lesbenfilmen auf unseren Schwesterseiten SexArt und Viv Thomas zu sehen. Sie scheint mit jedem Tag noch atemberaubender zu werden, und nach sieben Jahren an der Spitze ihrer Karriere wollen die Mitglieder immer noch mehr von ihr sehen. Sie bringt eine authentische Süße und Sinnlichkeit auf die Leinwand, die sie weniger wie eine unerreichbare Göttin, sondern eher wie die ideale Freundin wirken lässt! Ich hatte das Glück, Lorena schon mehrmals zu interviewen, und es ist immer ein Vergnügen, sich mit ihr zu unterhalten – so authentisch, natürlich und herzlich in ihren Antworten.
Lorena macht eine Ausbildung zur Masseurin. Ihr Traum ist es, in einem warmen Land in Strandnähe zu leben. Und in einem Interview mit MetArt sagte sie: „Es erregt mich, beobachtet zu werden und den Mann zu beobachten, mit dem ich zusammen bin oder für den ich Gefühle habe. Jemandem in die Augen zu schauen, ist eine Möglichkeit, Intimität zu erzeugen." Mit dieser Einladung wird es für uns natürlich besonders spannend, Lorena zu sehen und von ihr zu träumen.

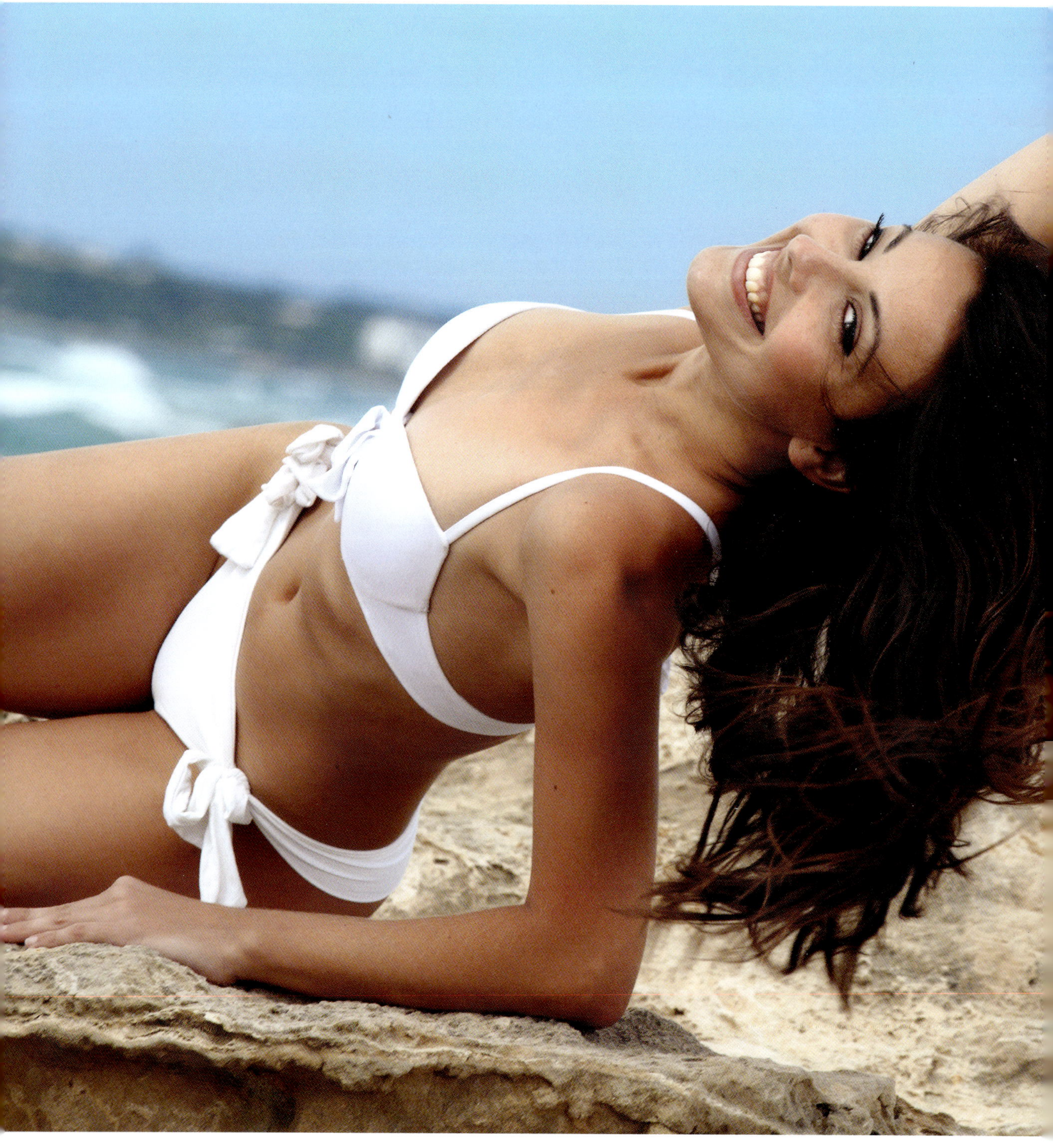

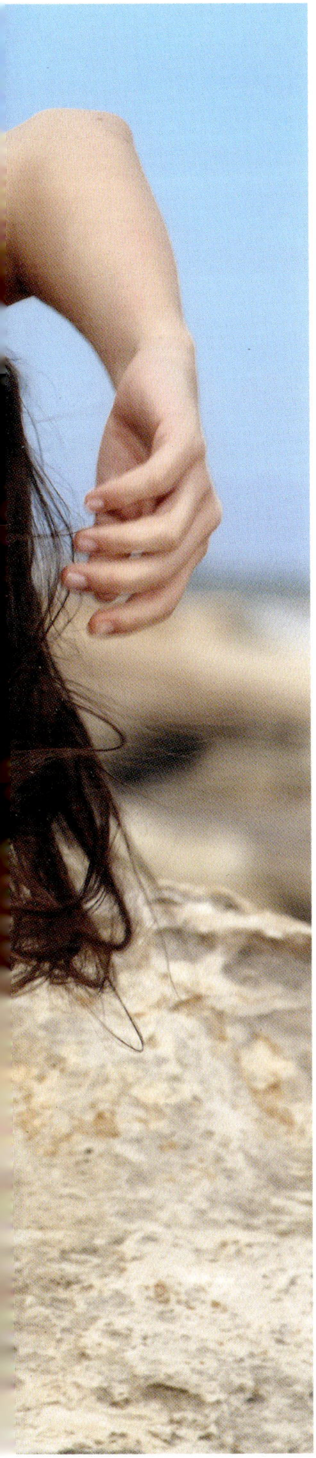

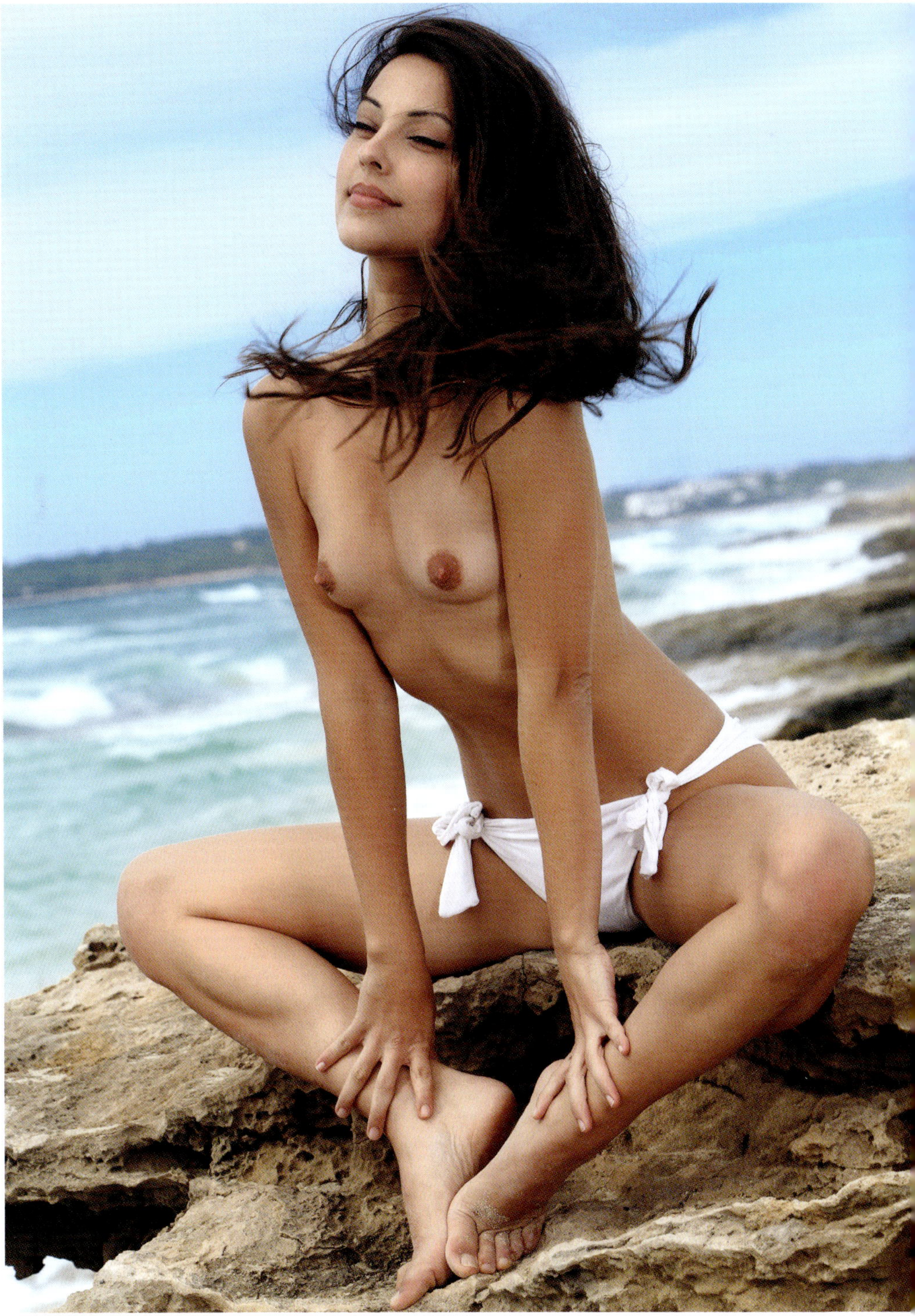

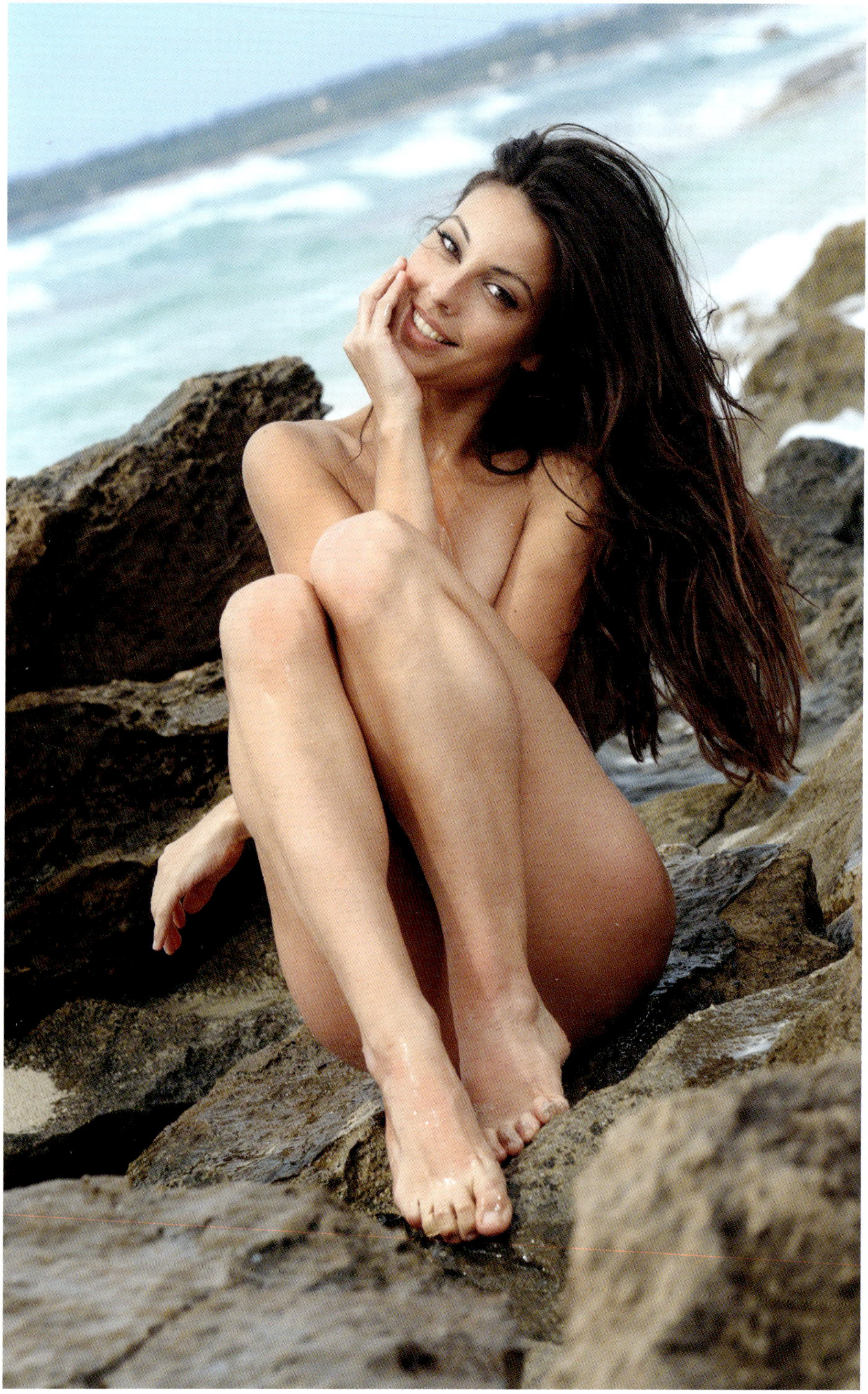

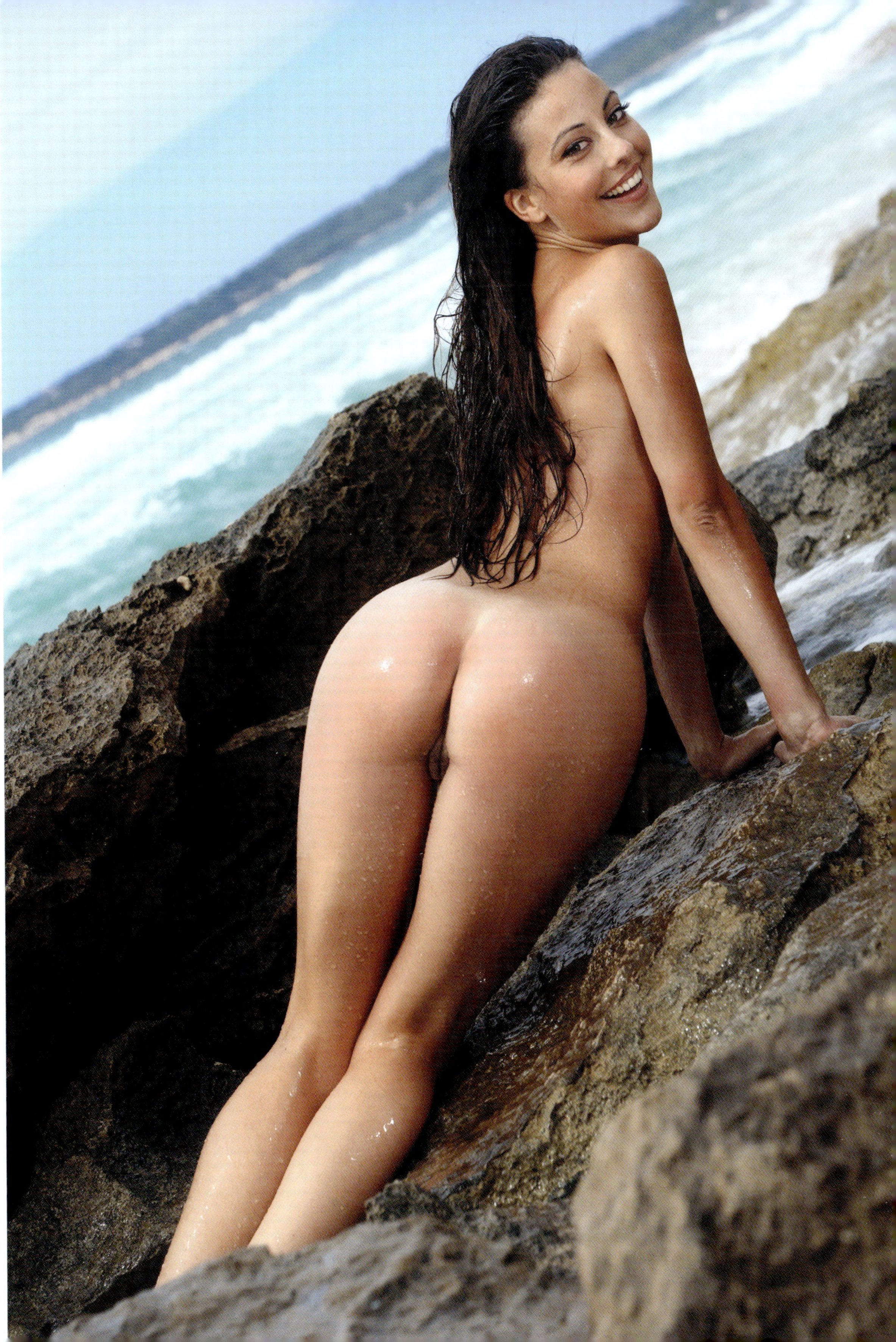

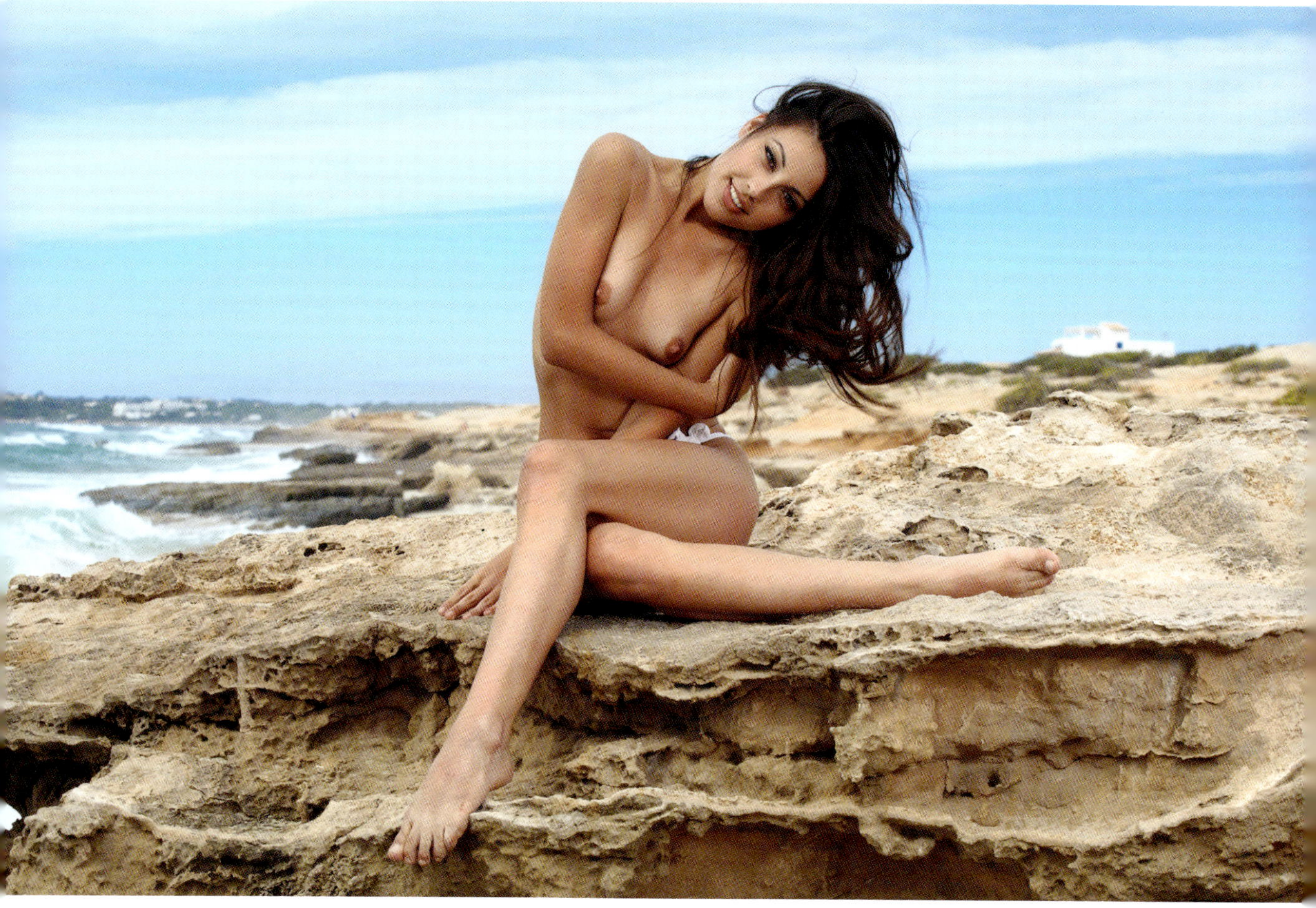

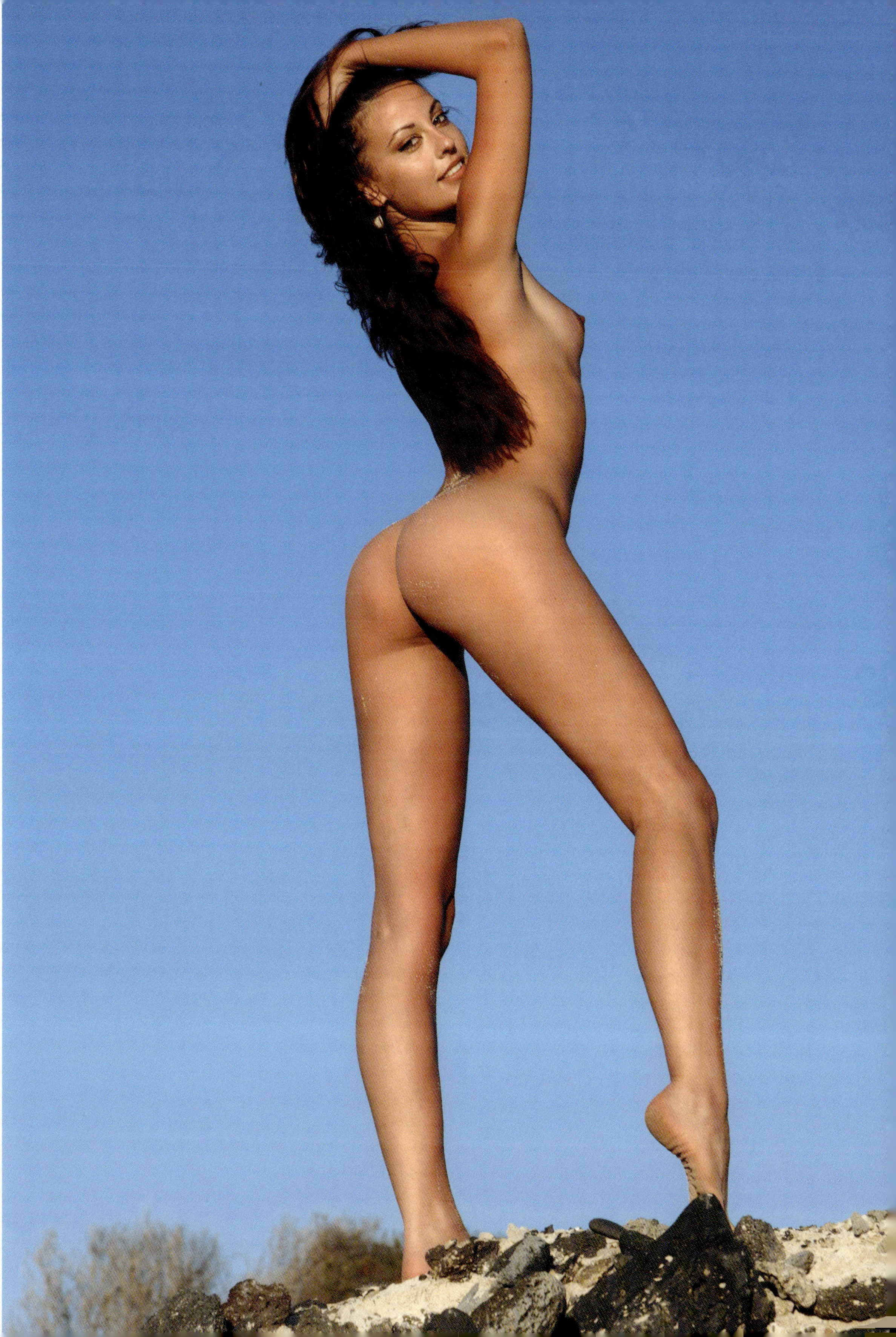

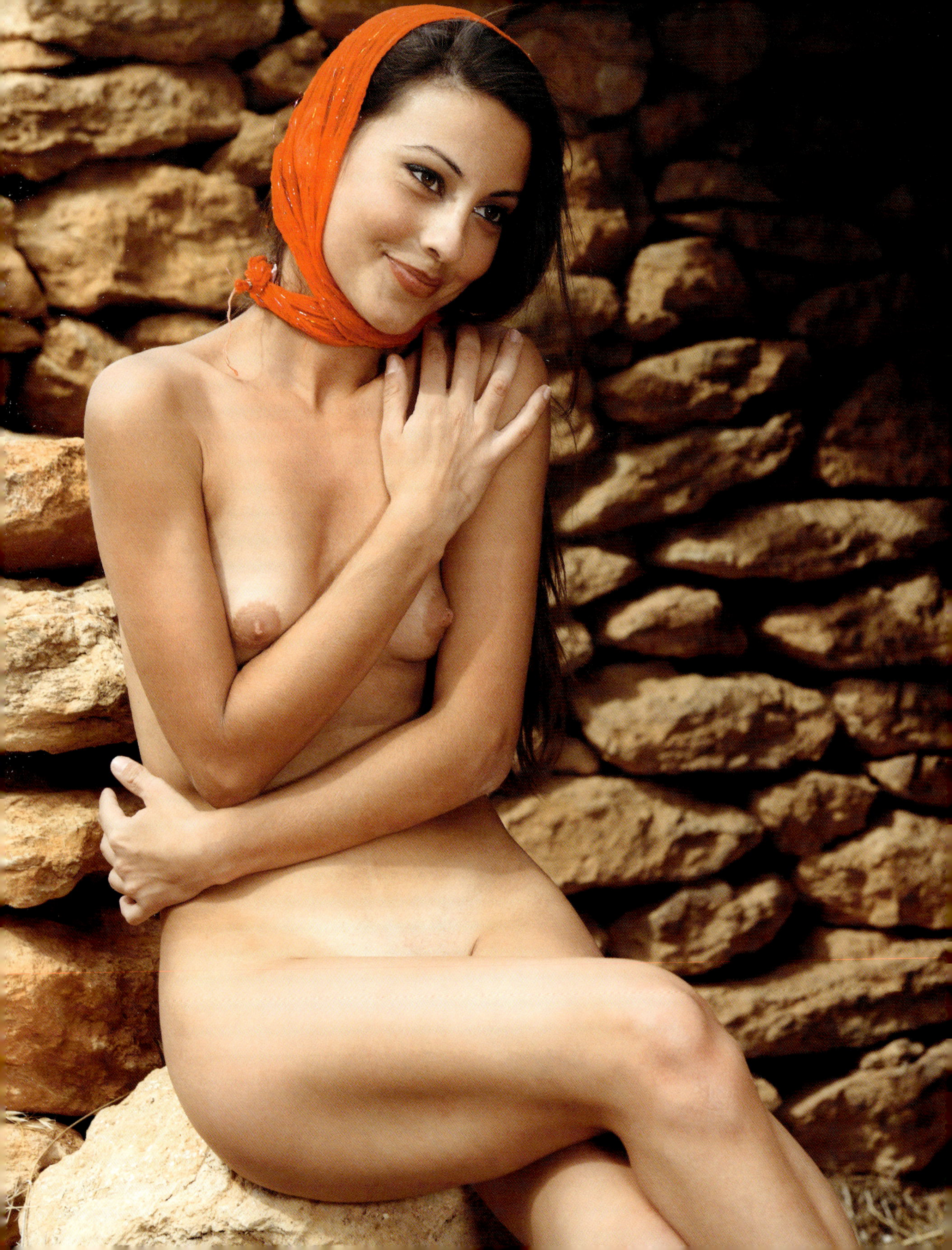

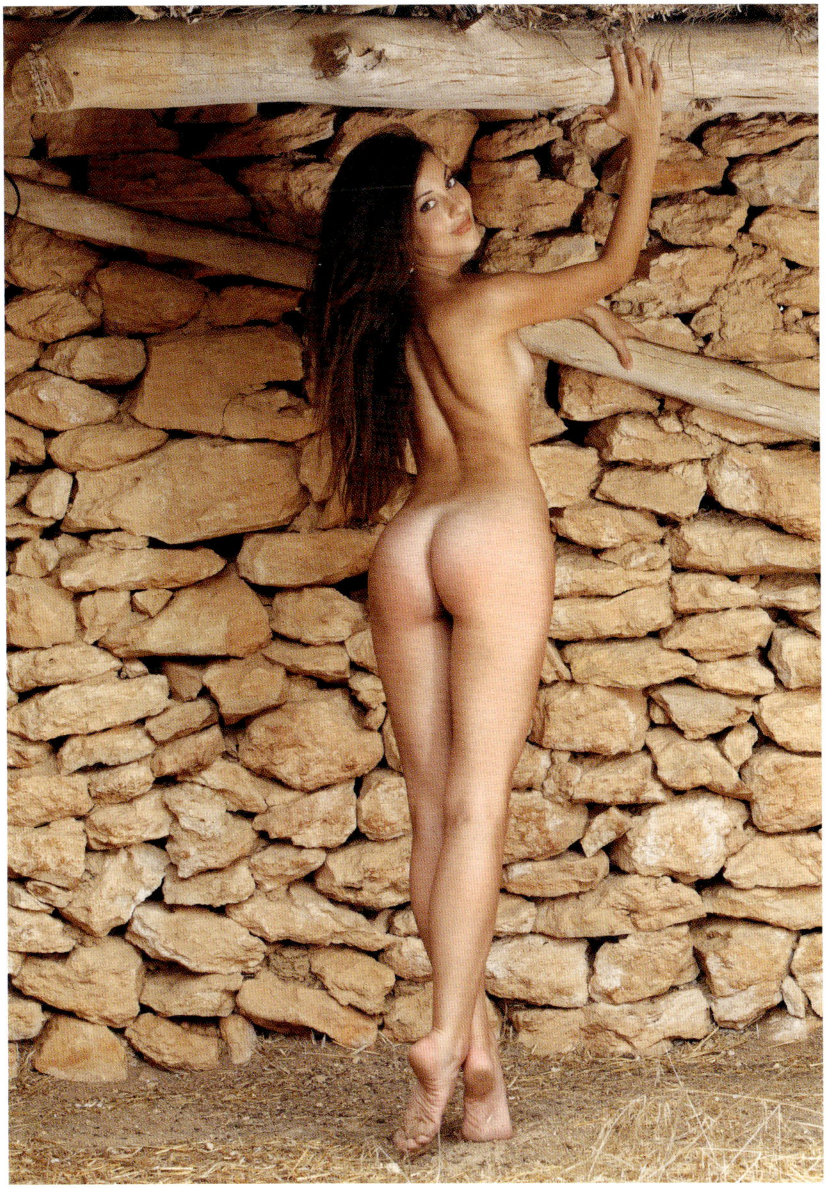

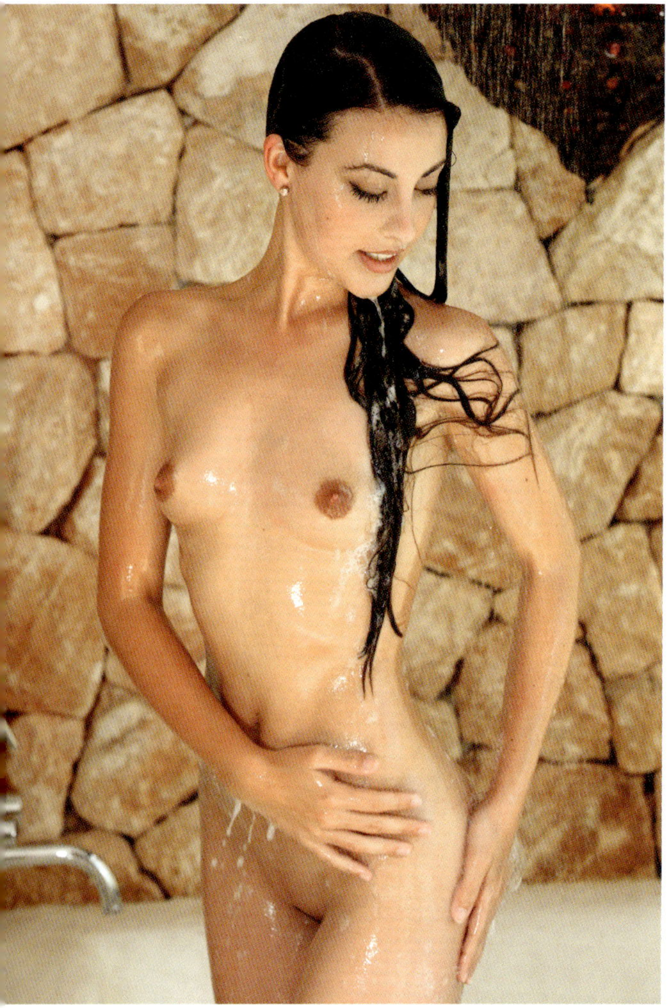

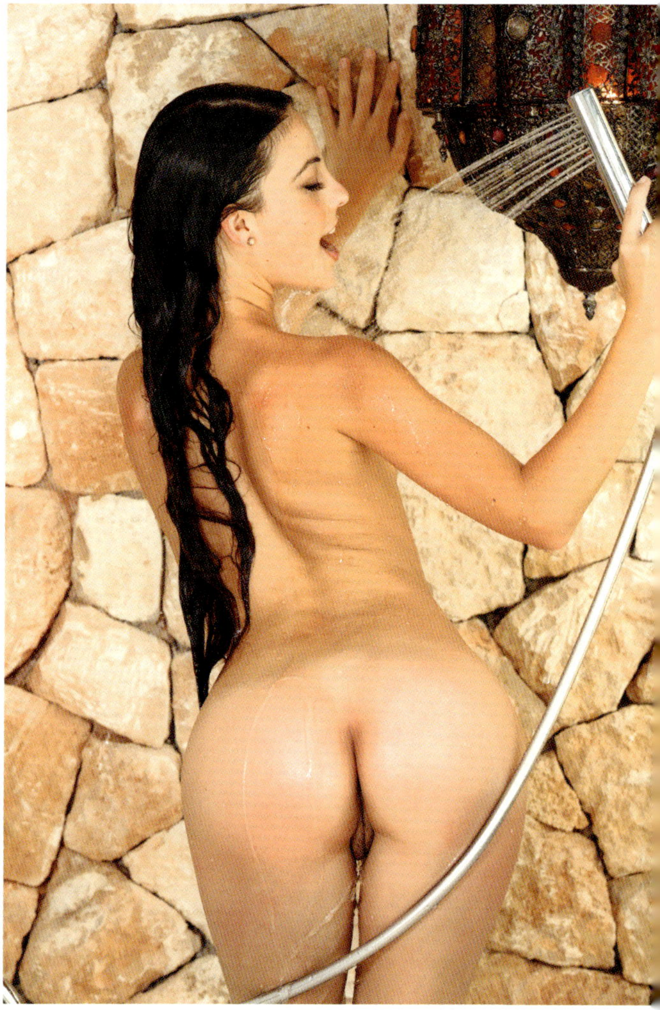

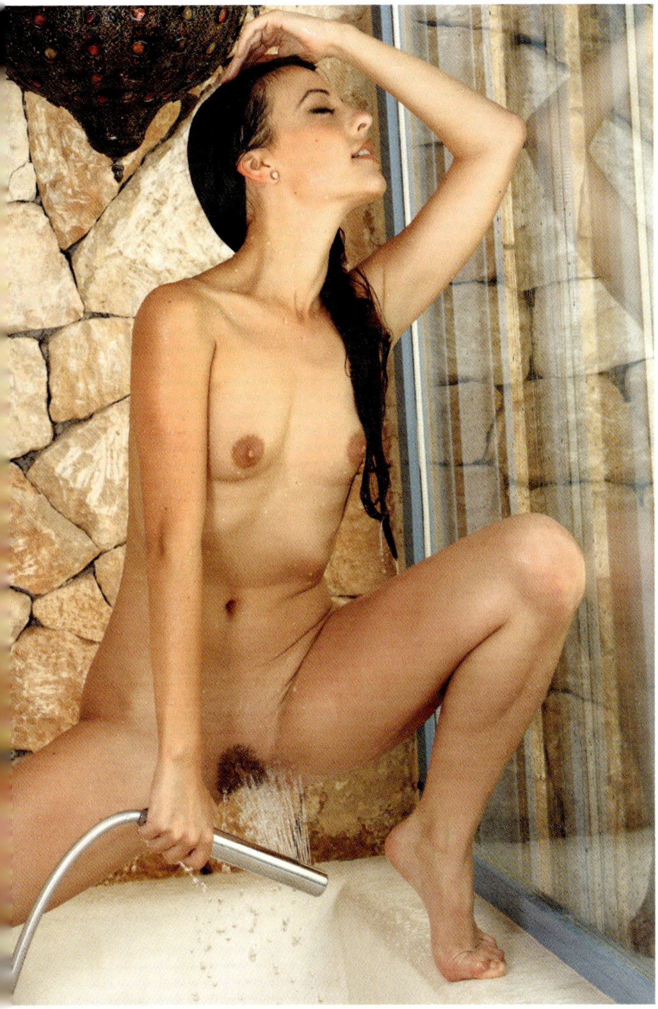

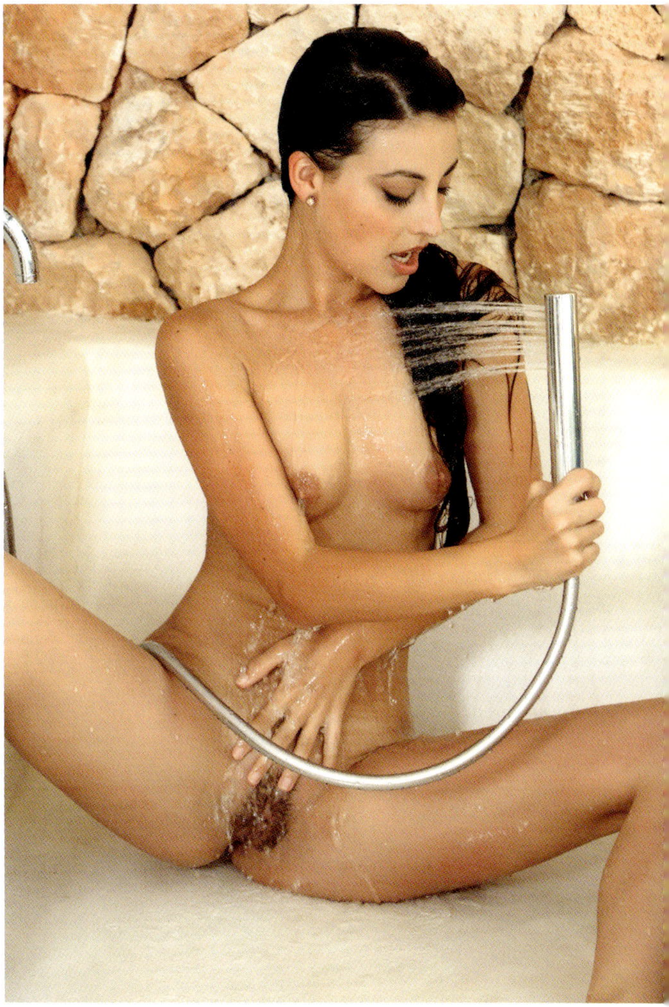

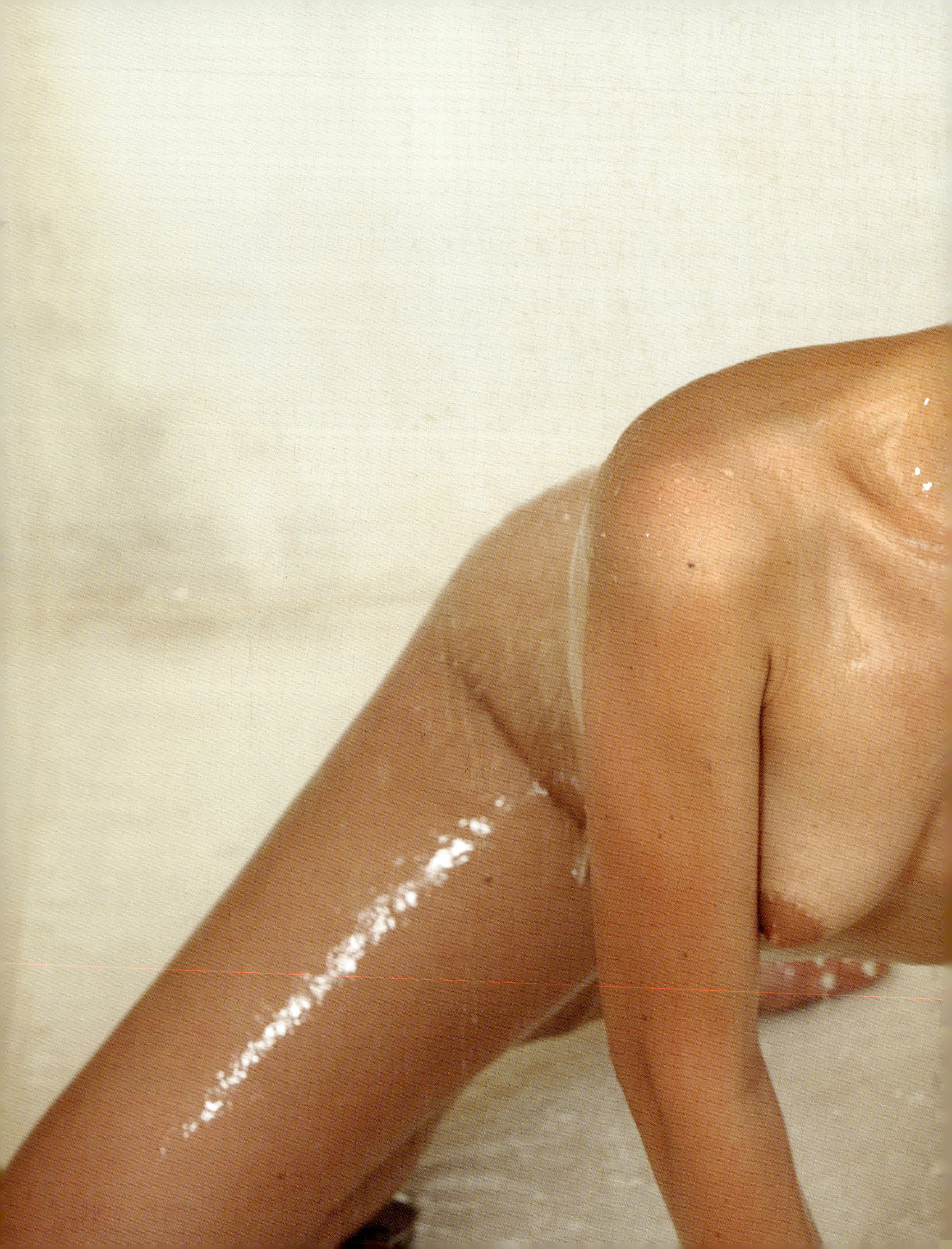

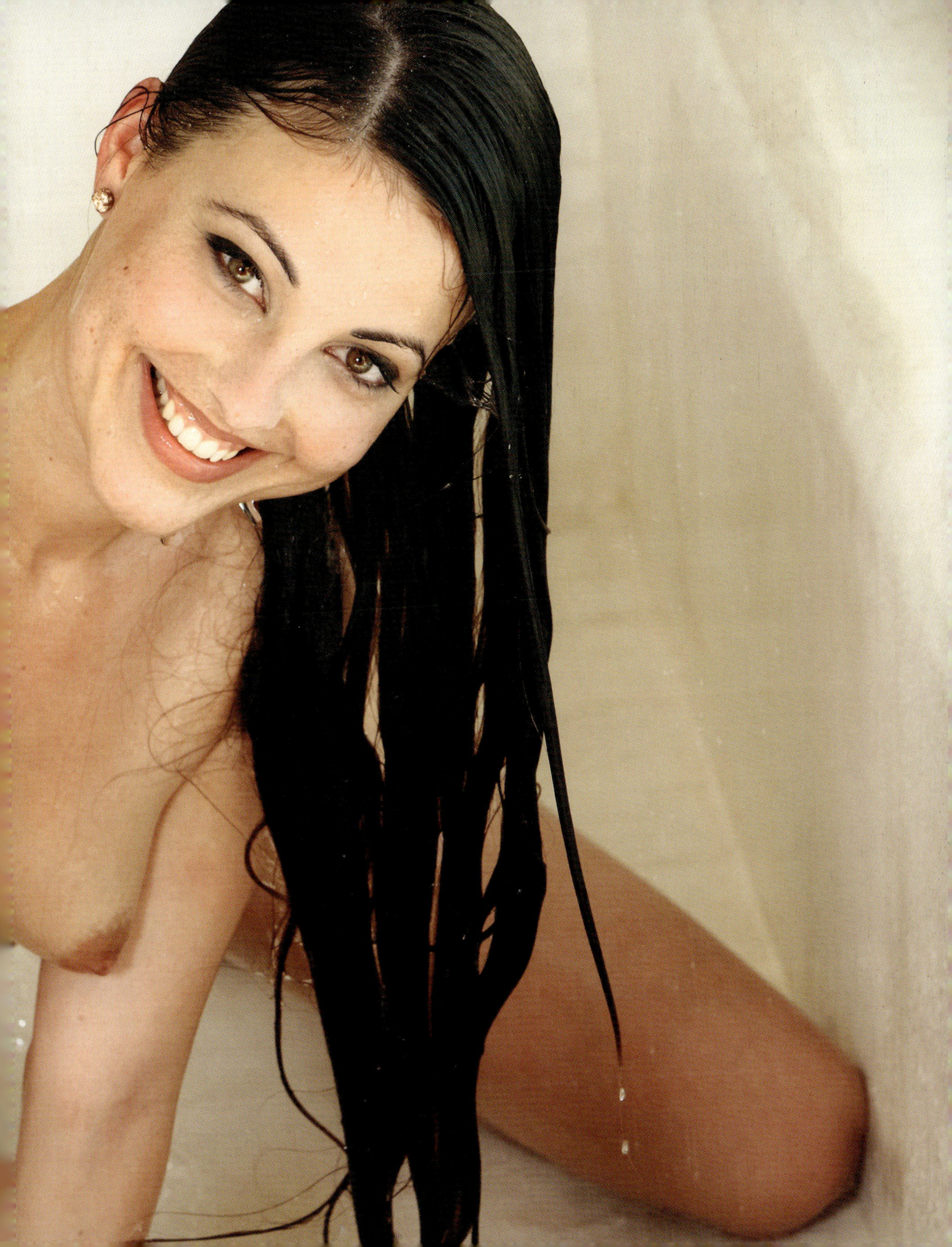

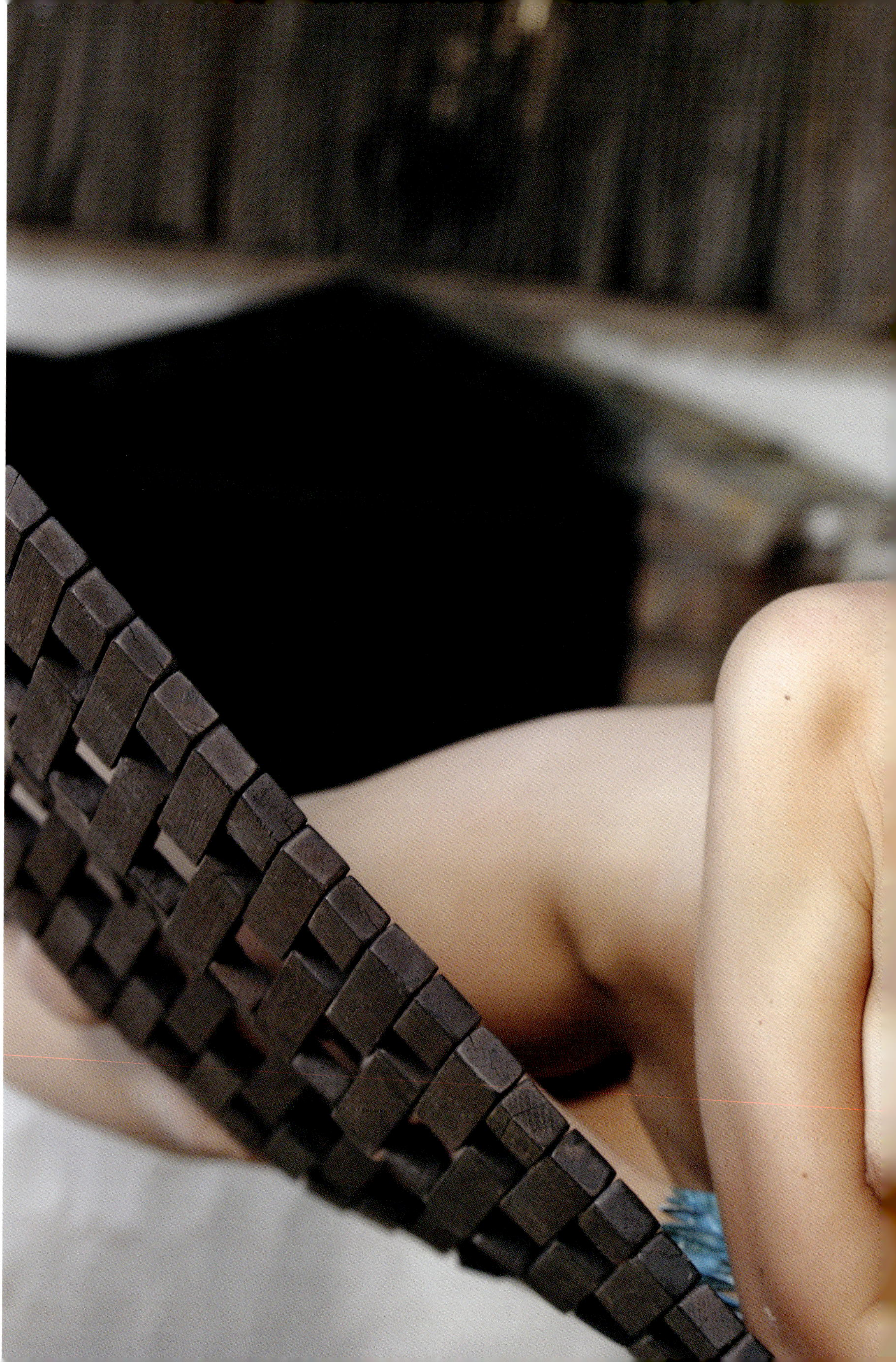

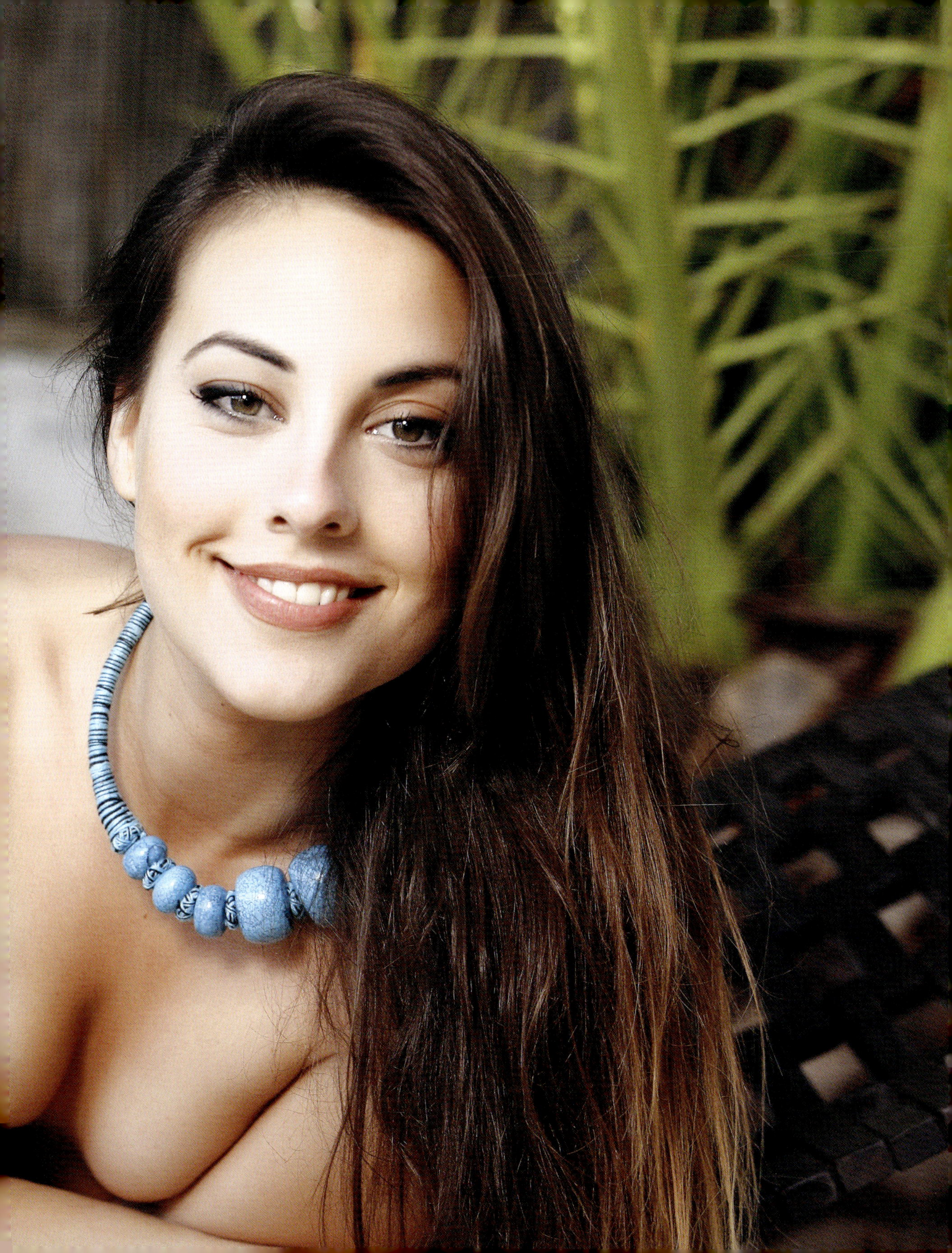

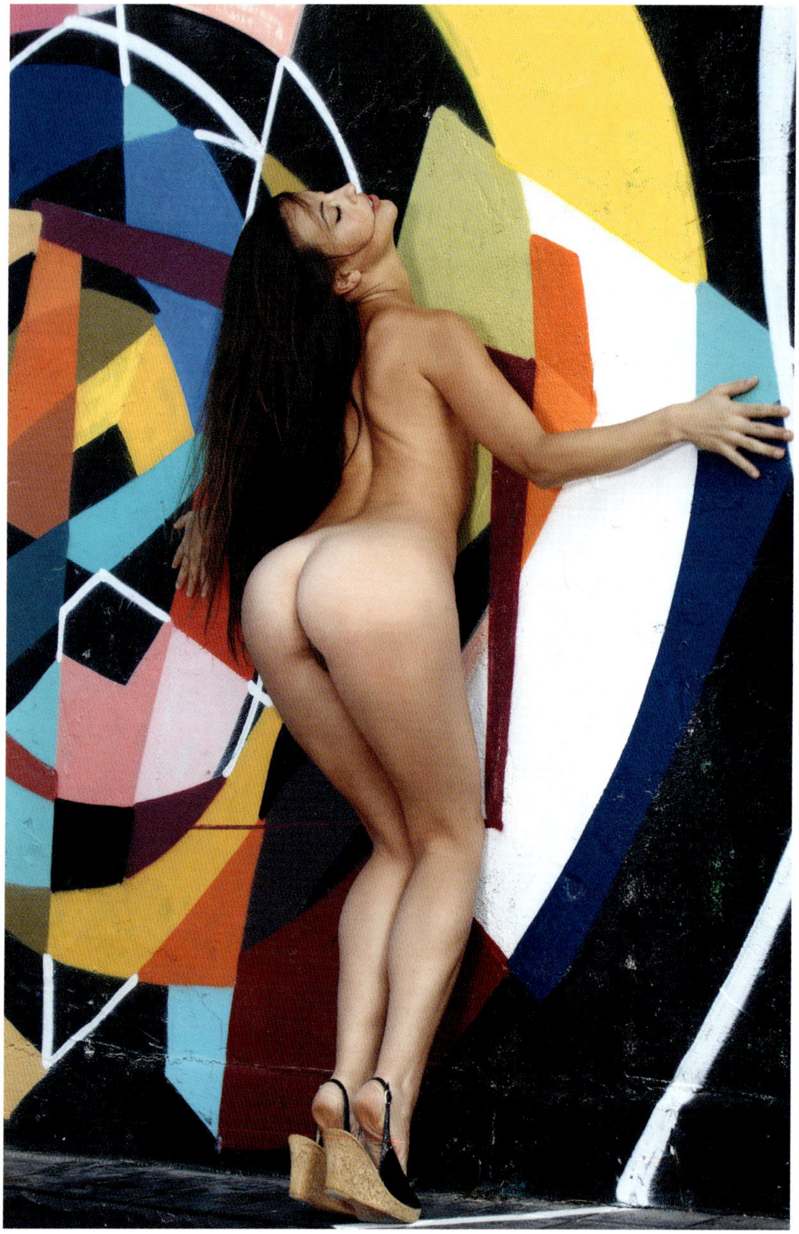

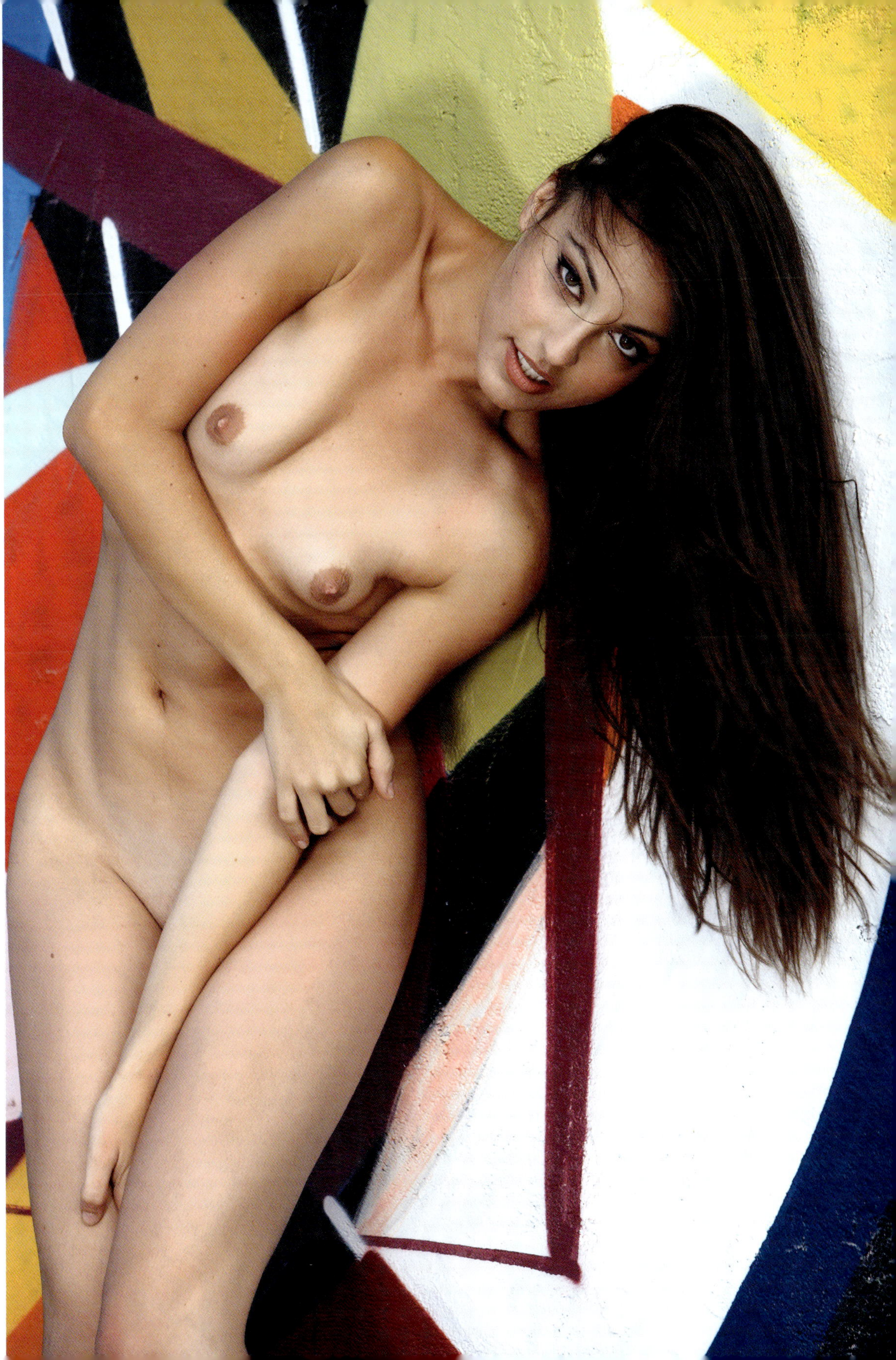

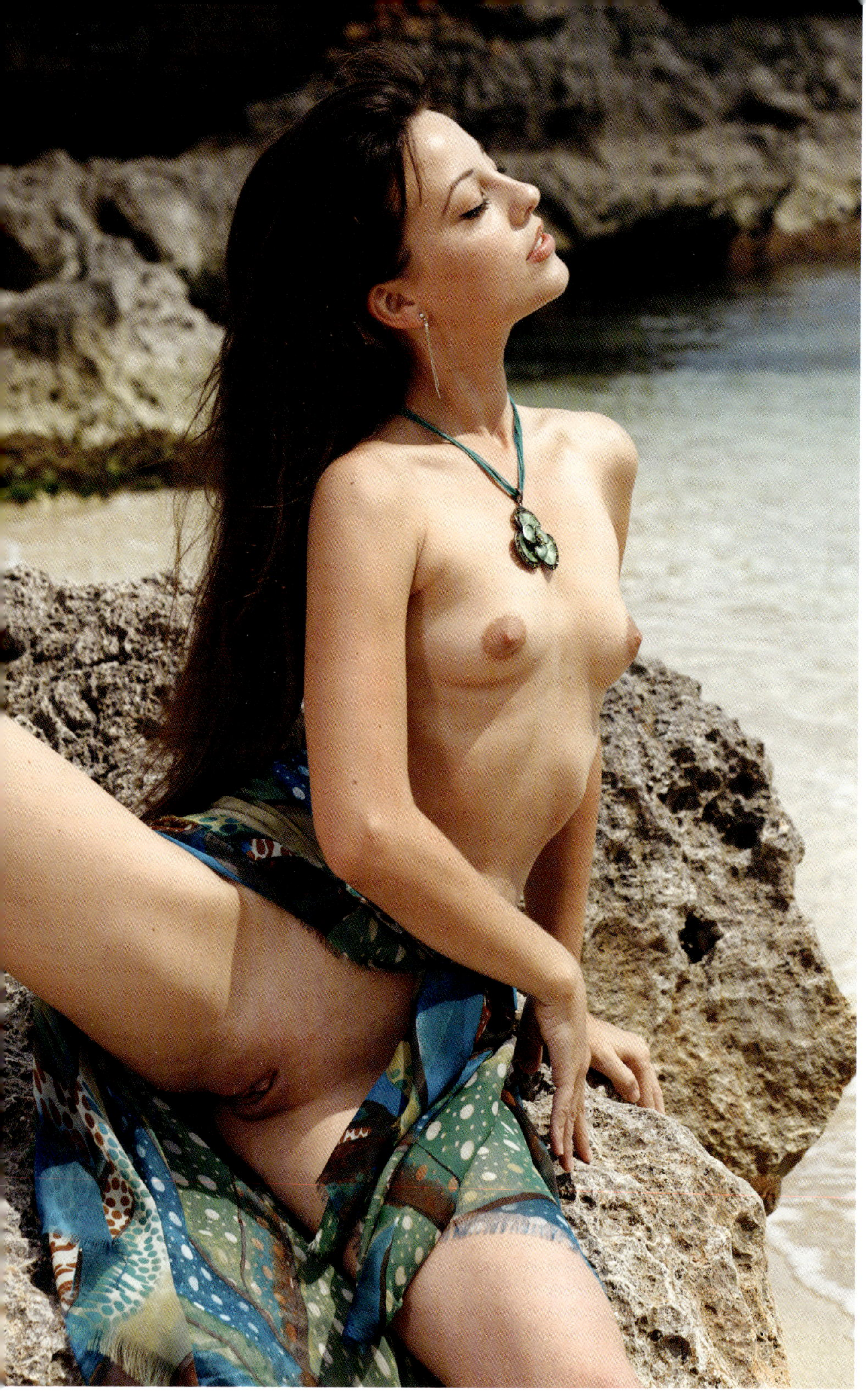

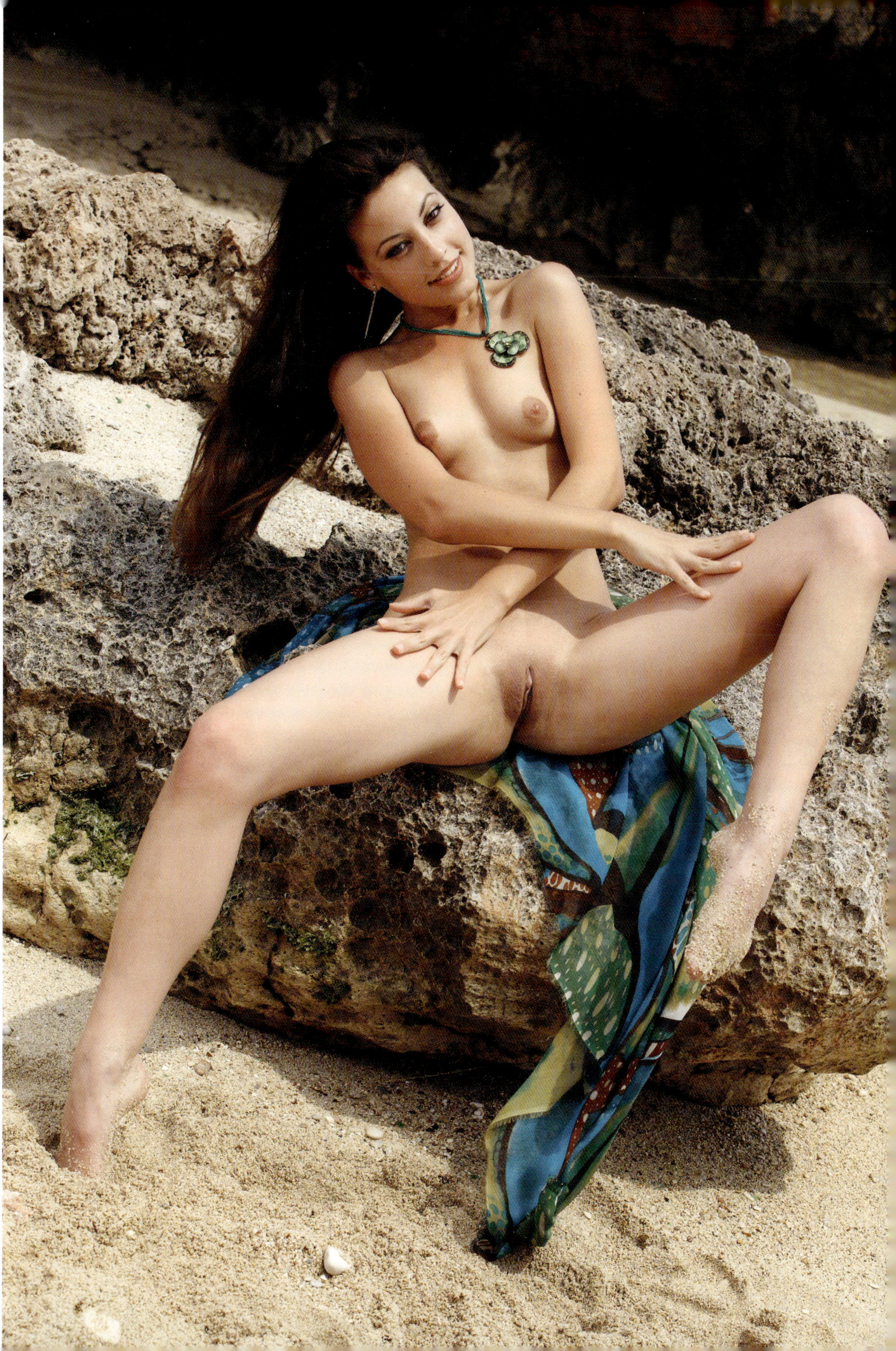

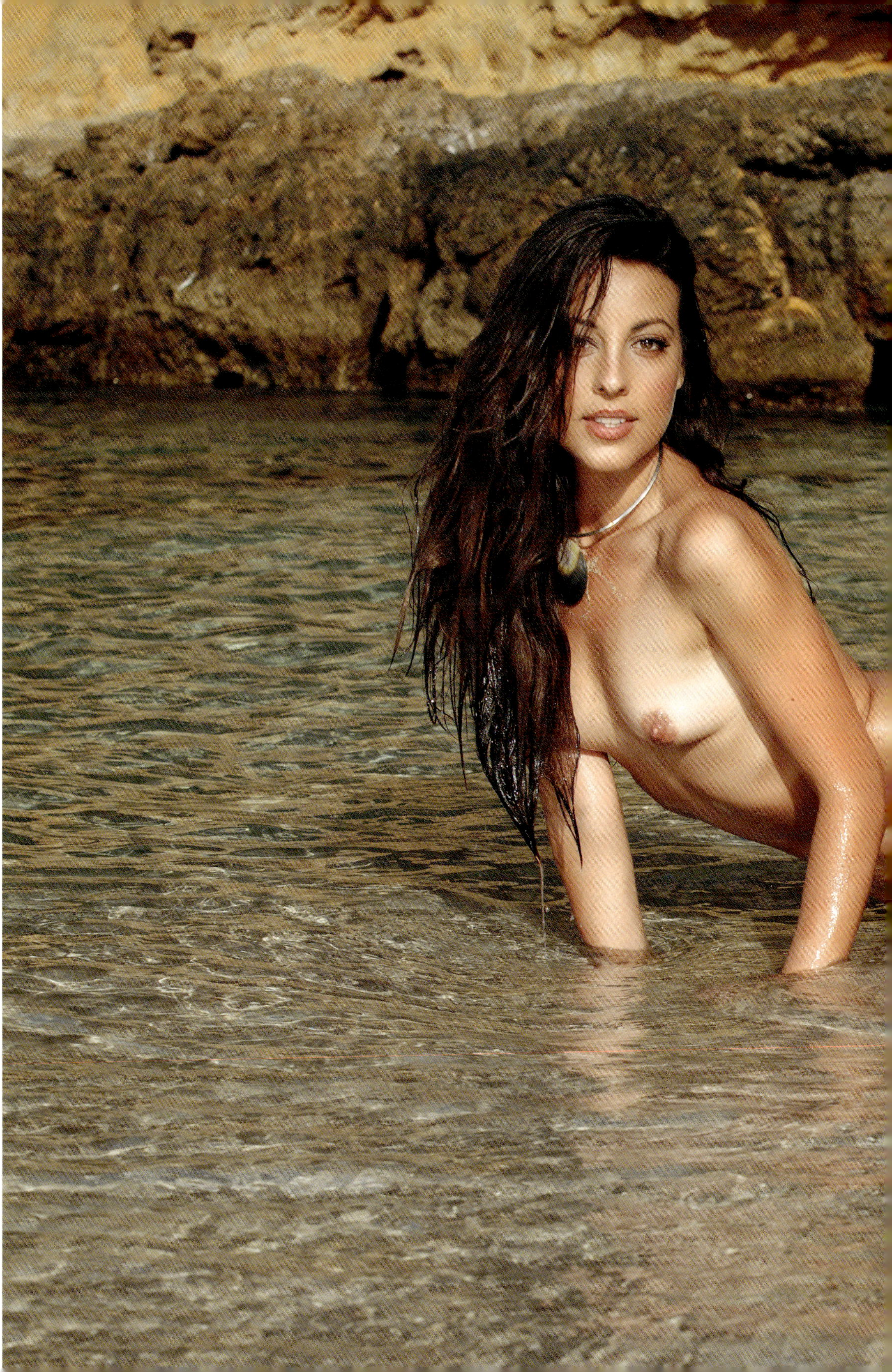

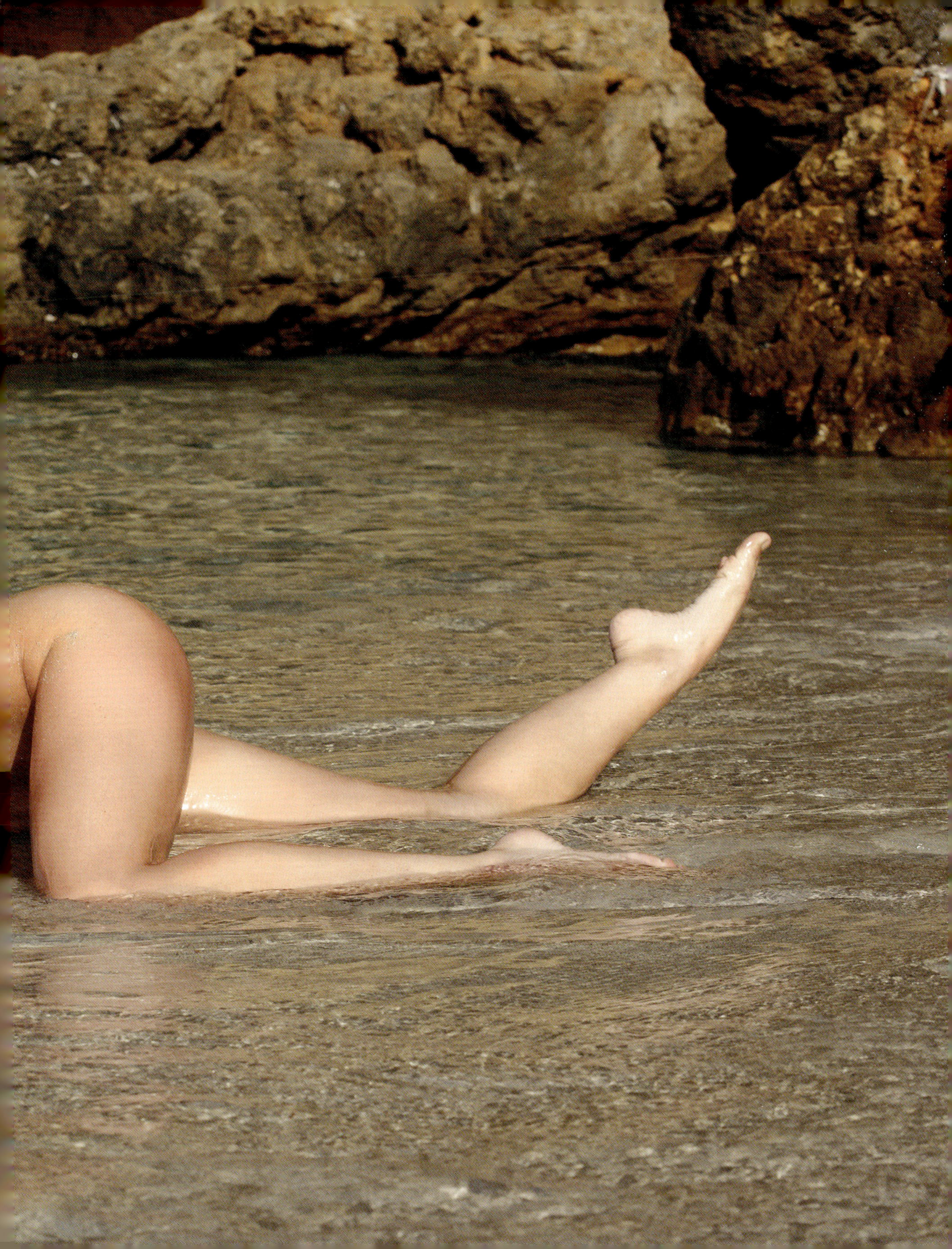

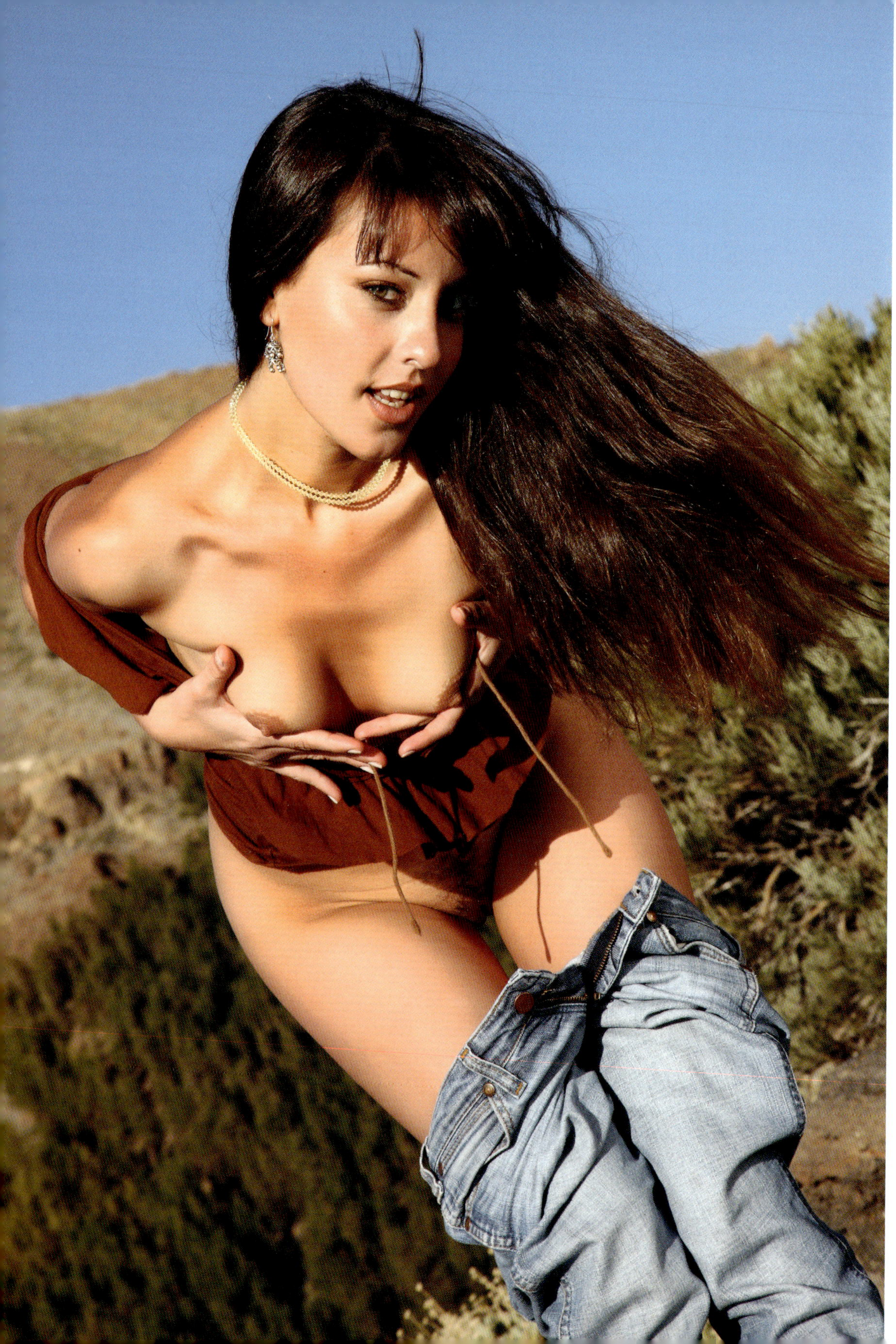

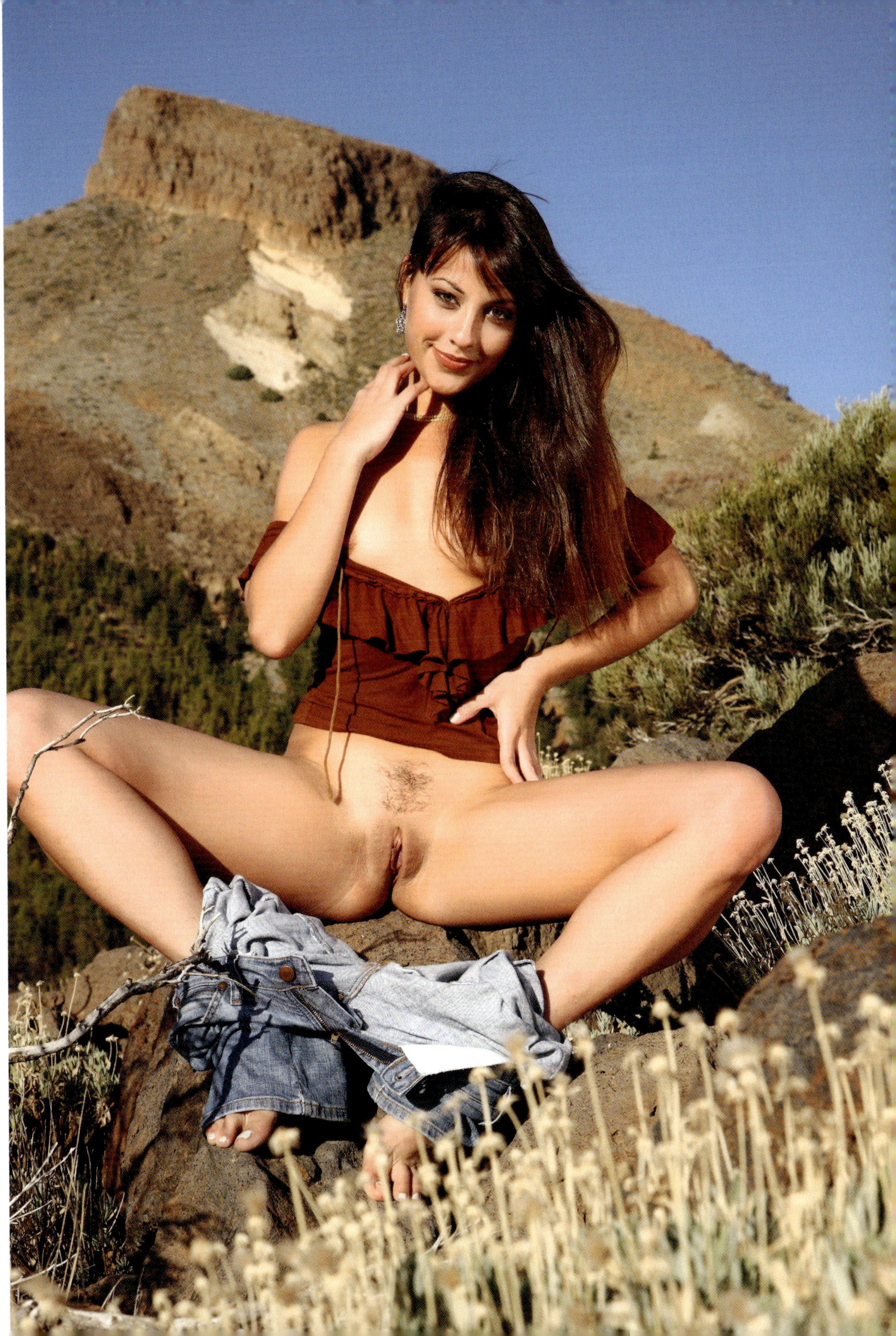

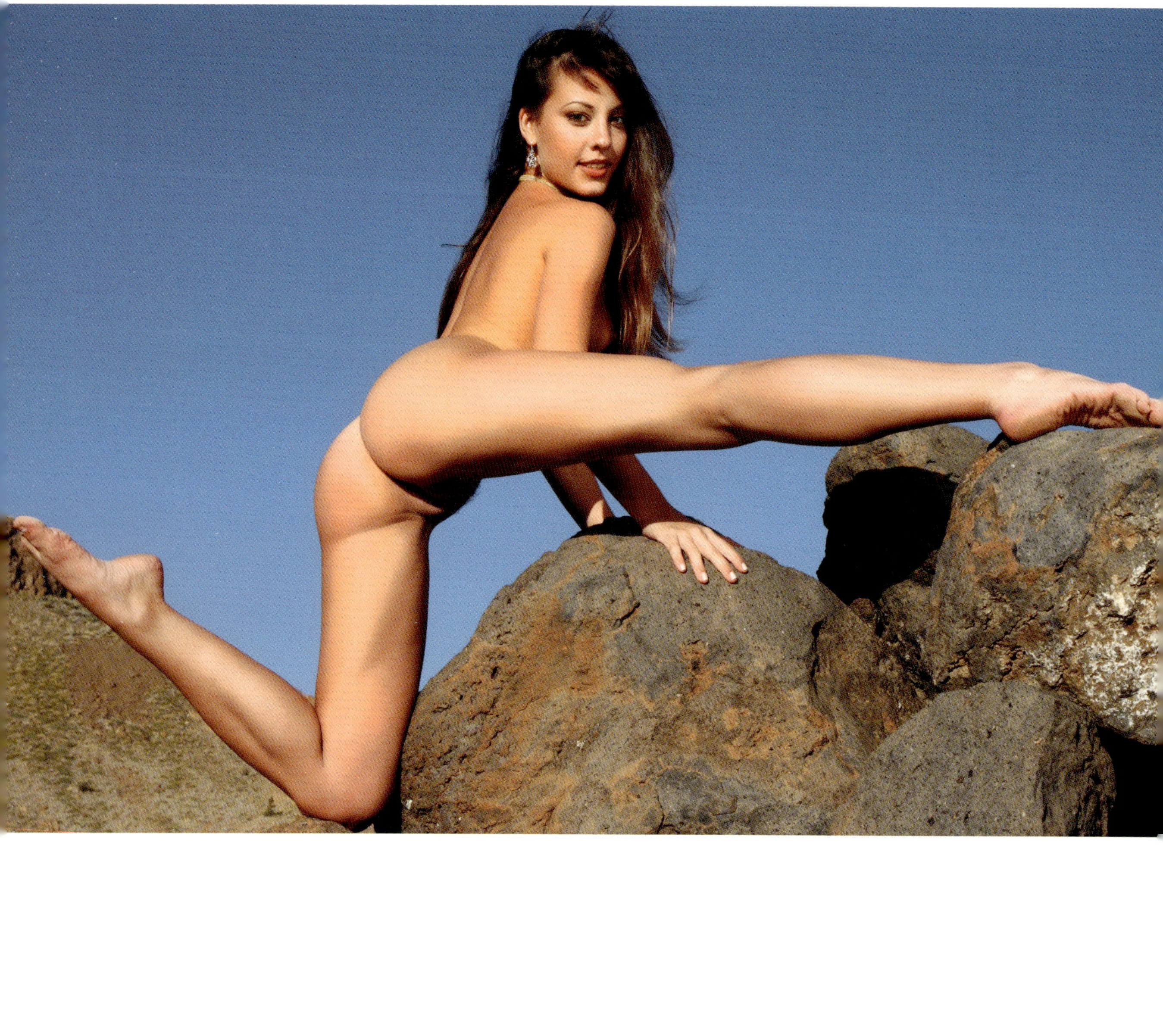

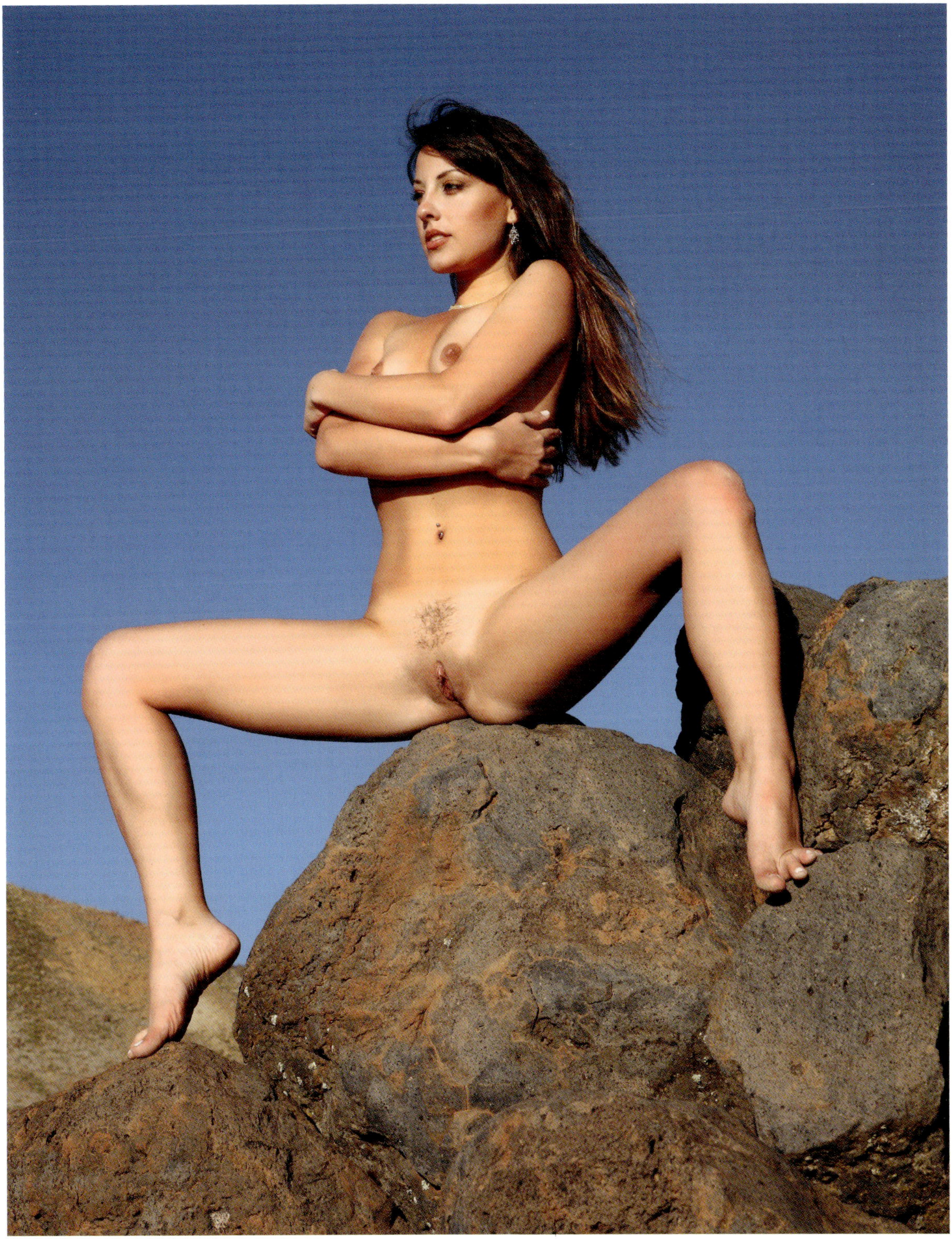

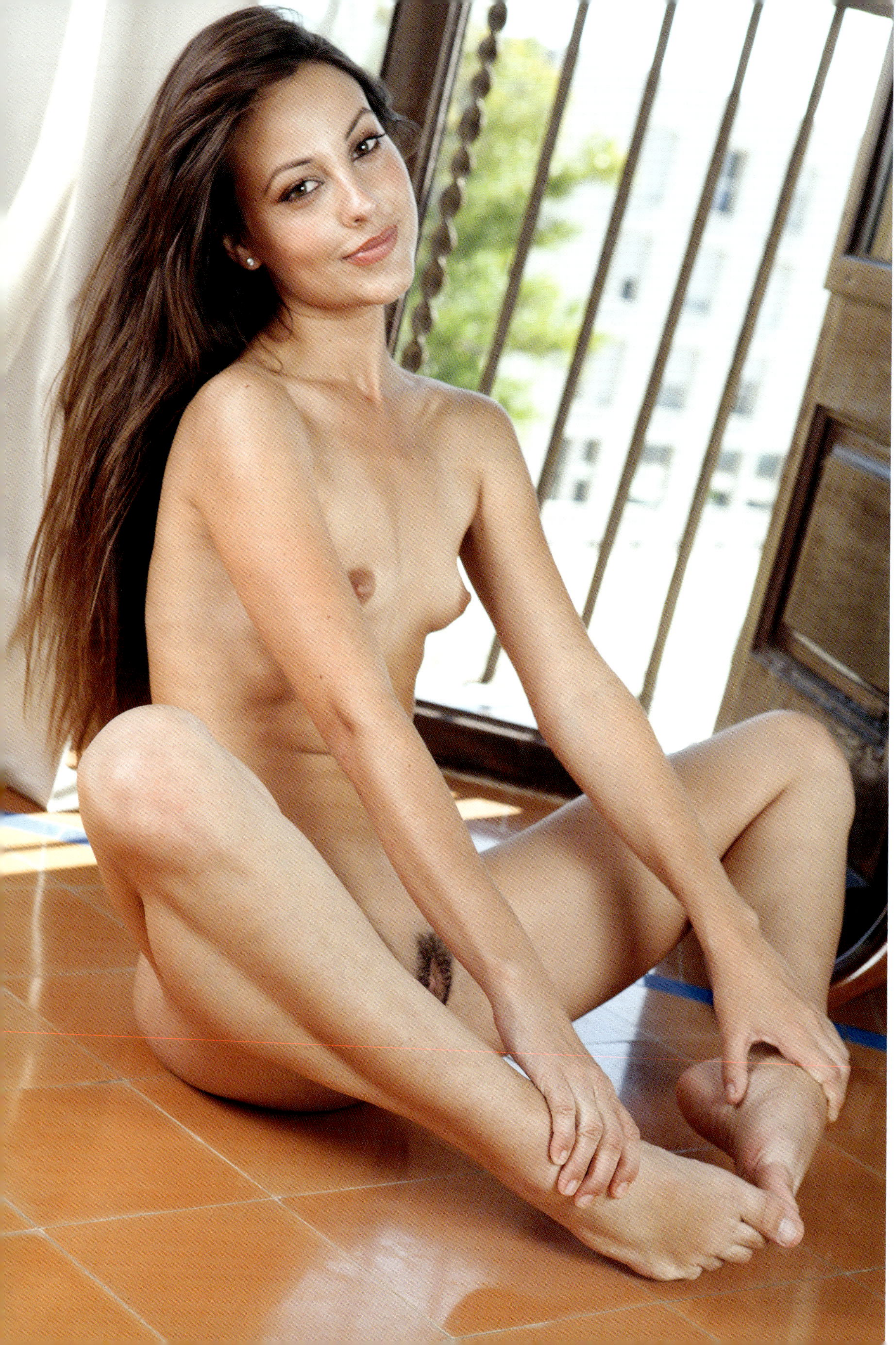

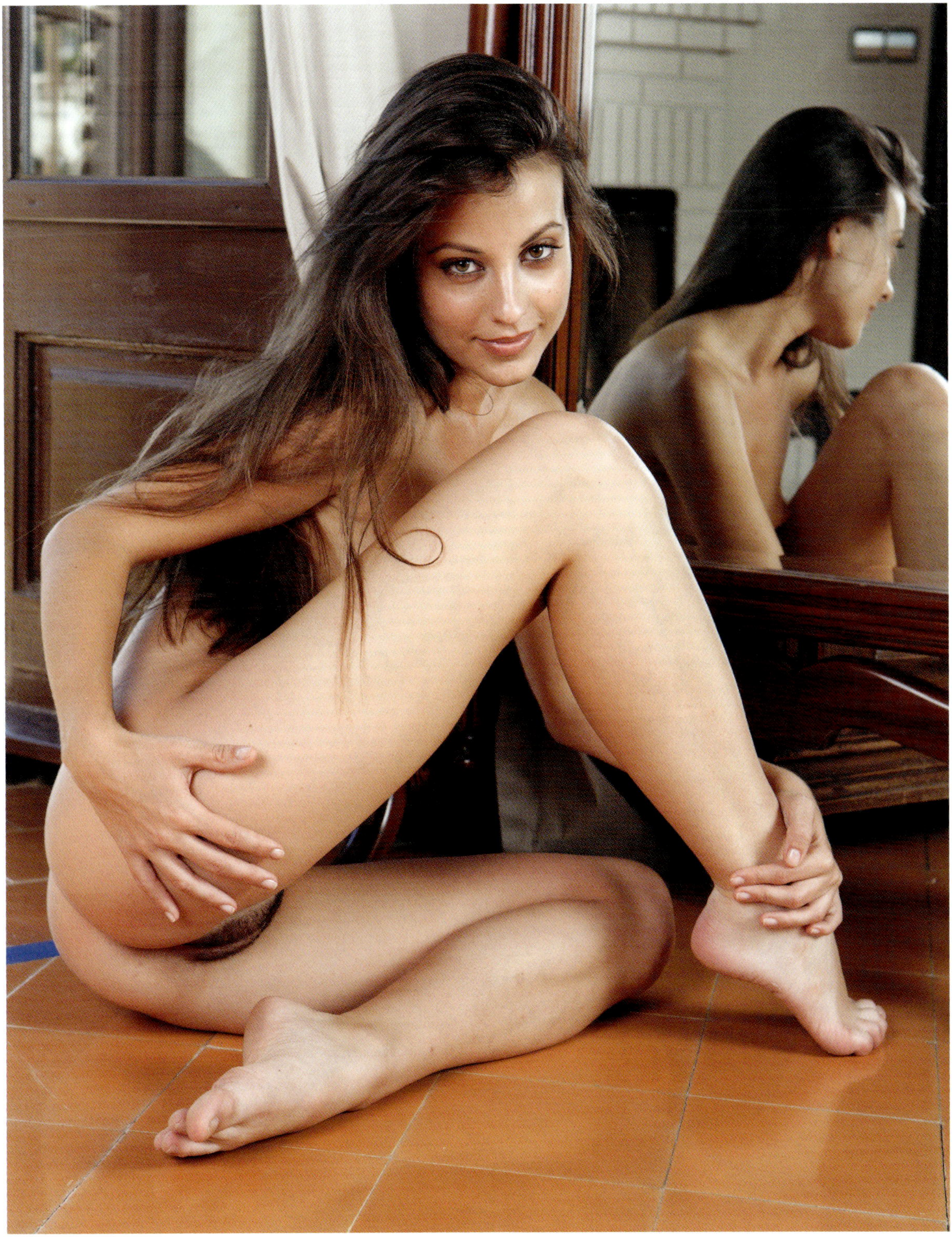

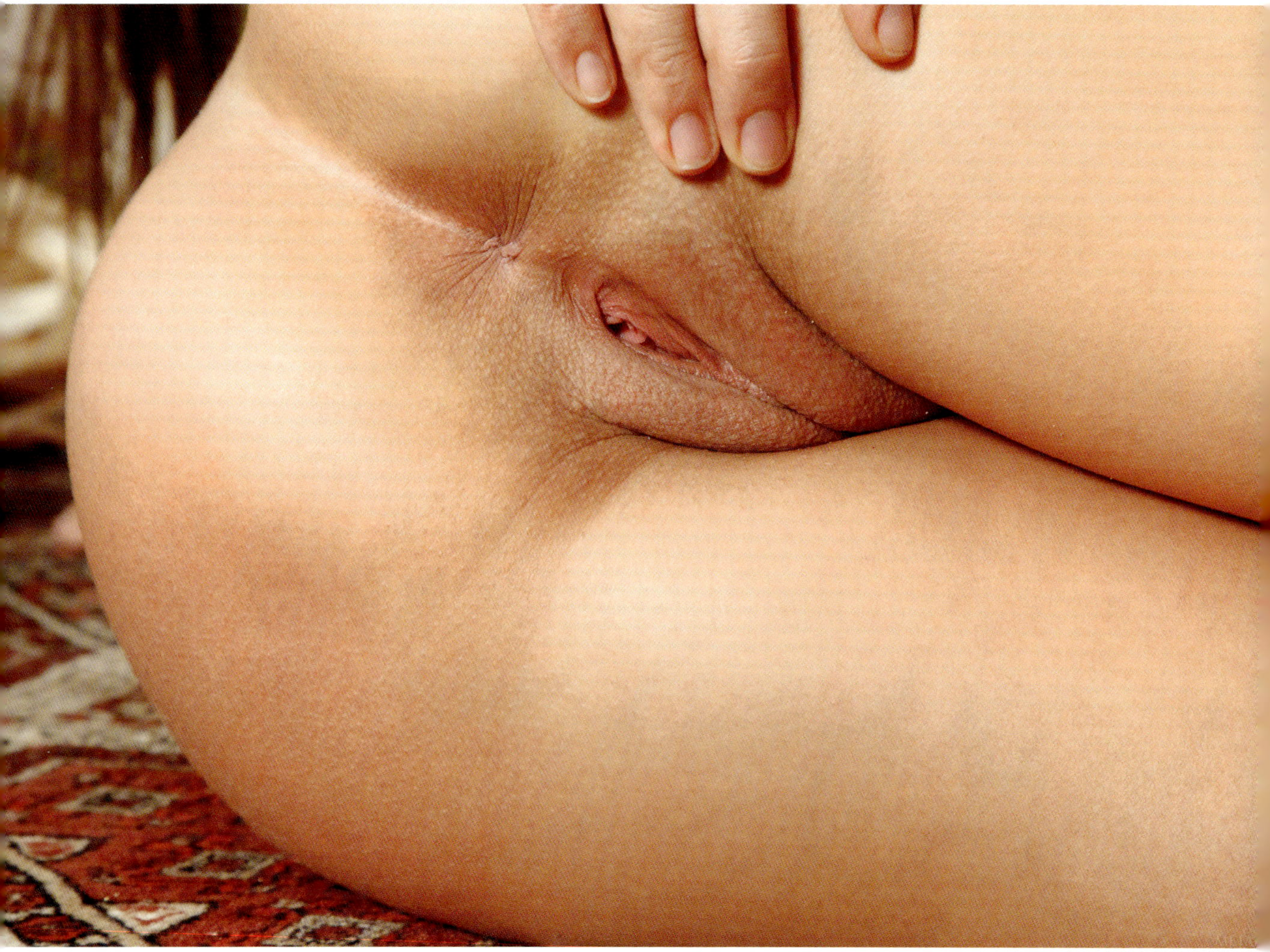

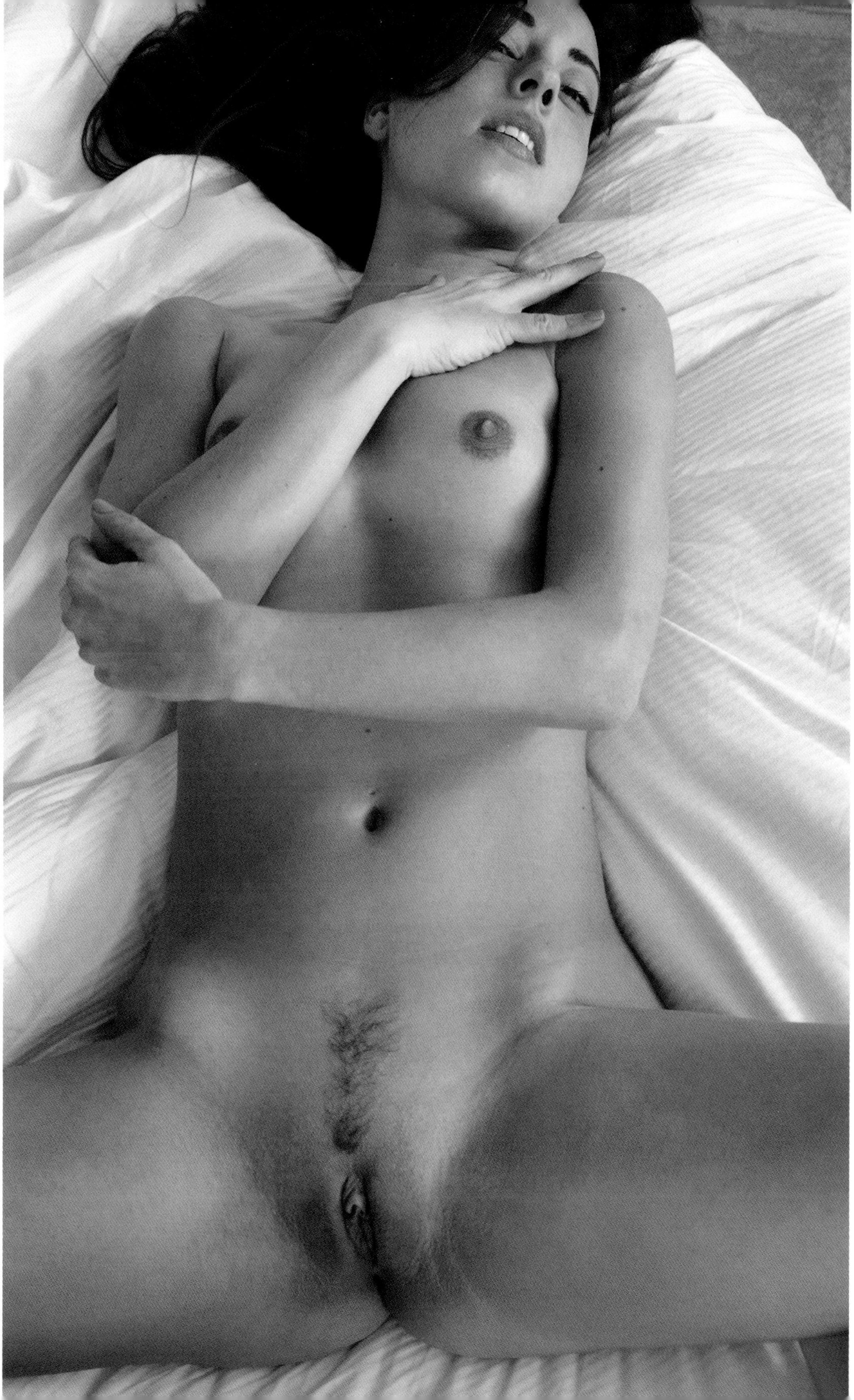

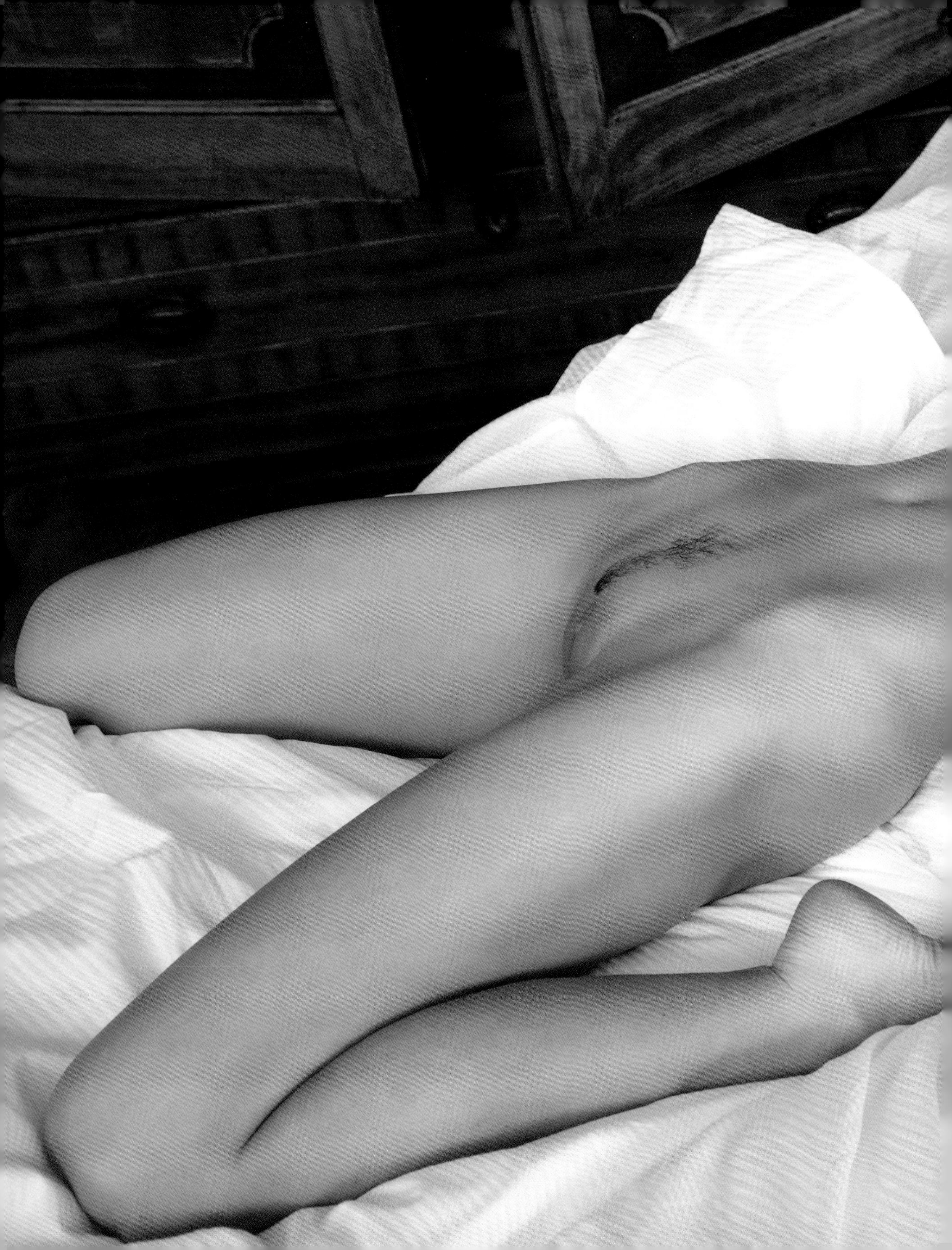

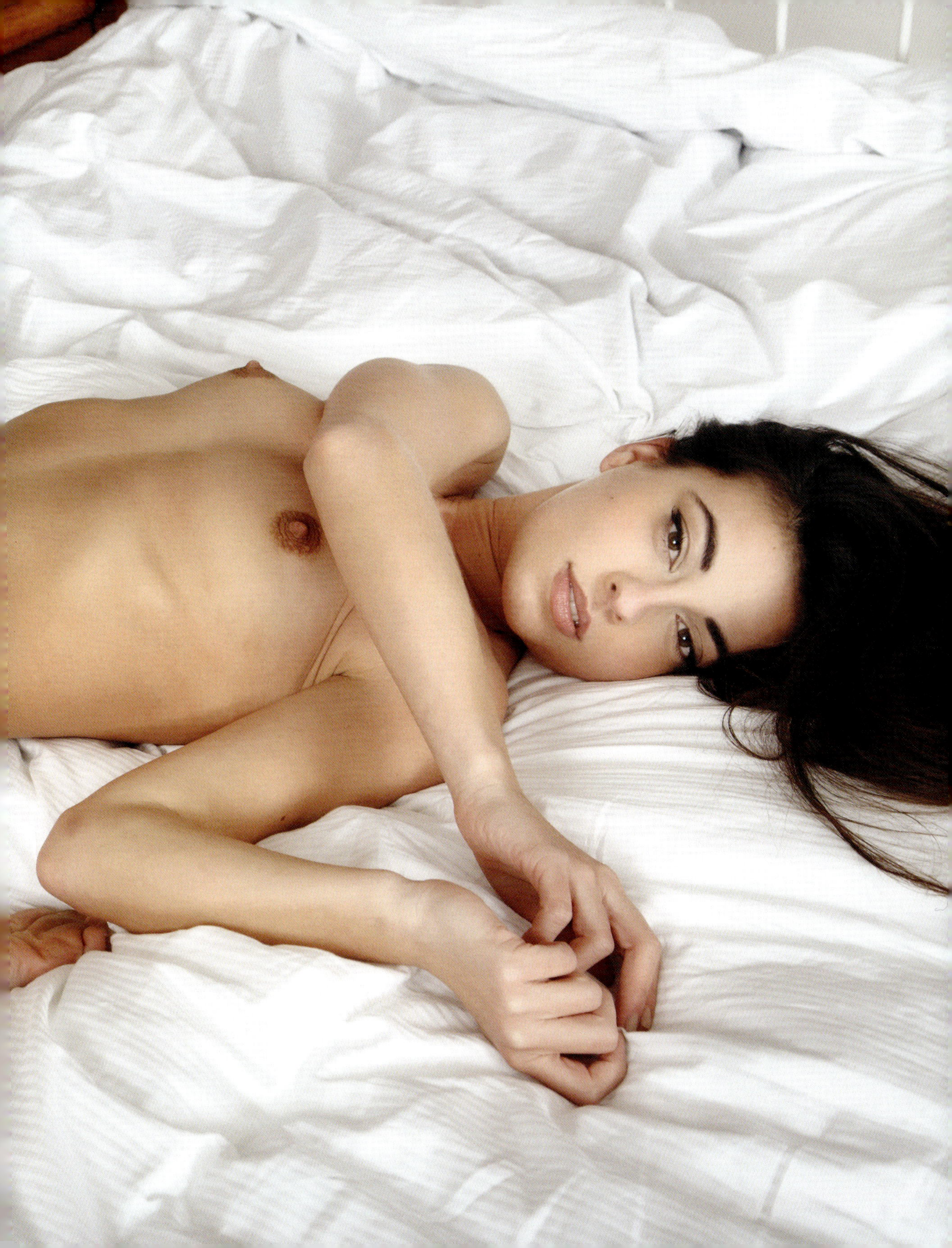

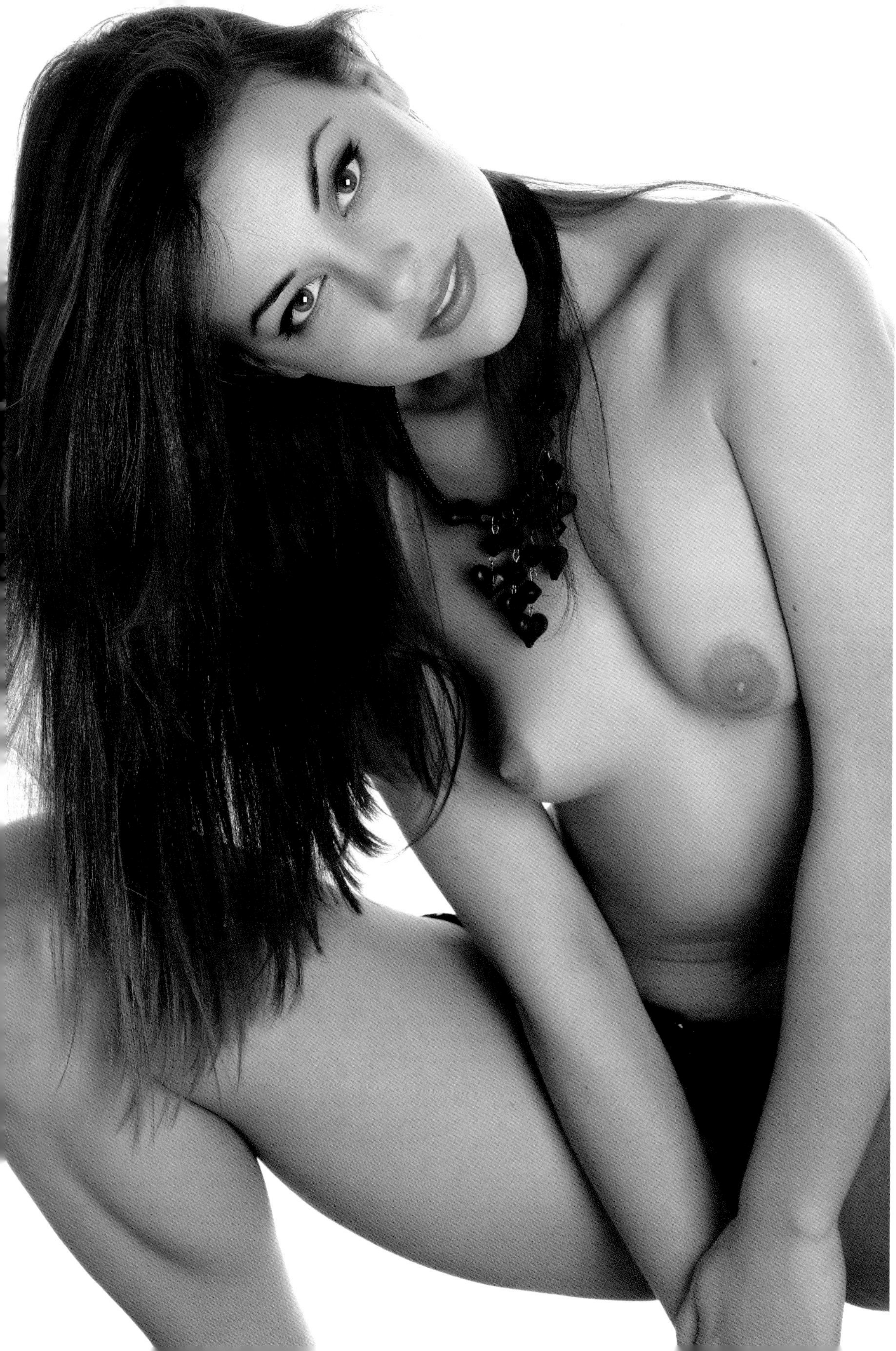

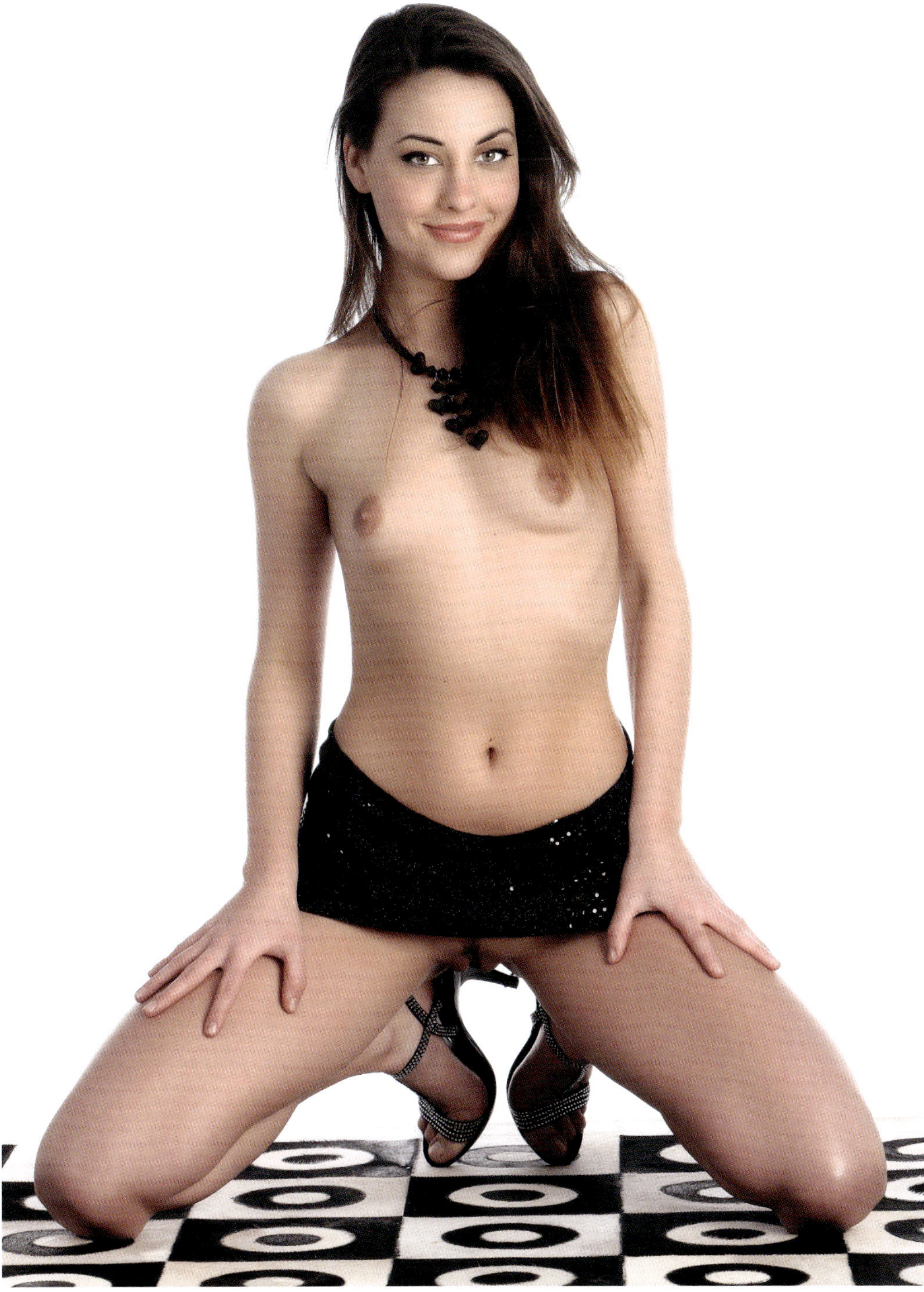

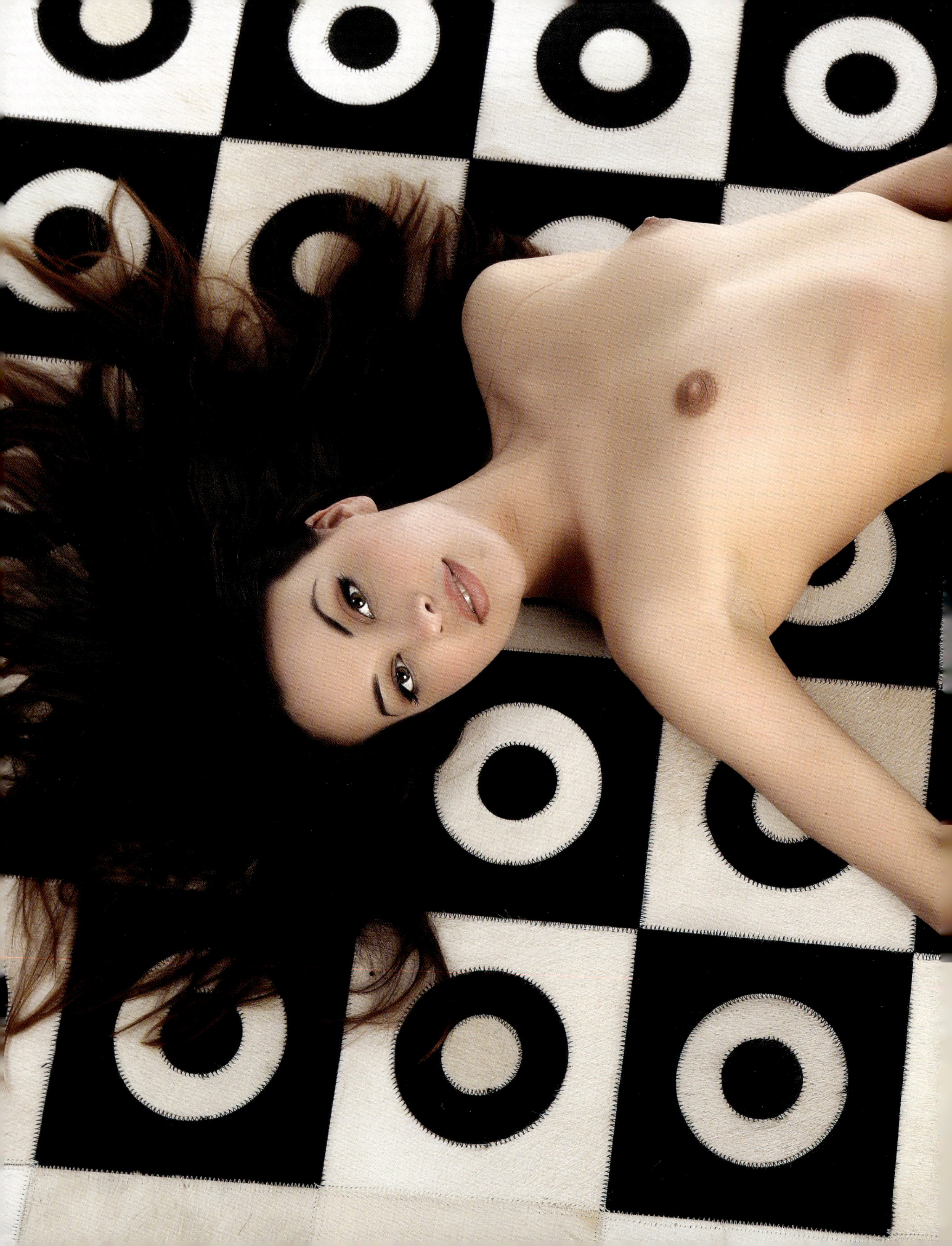

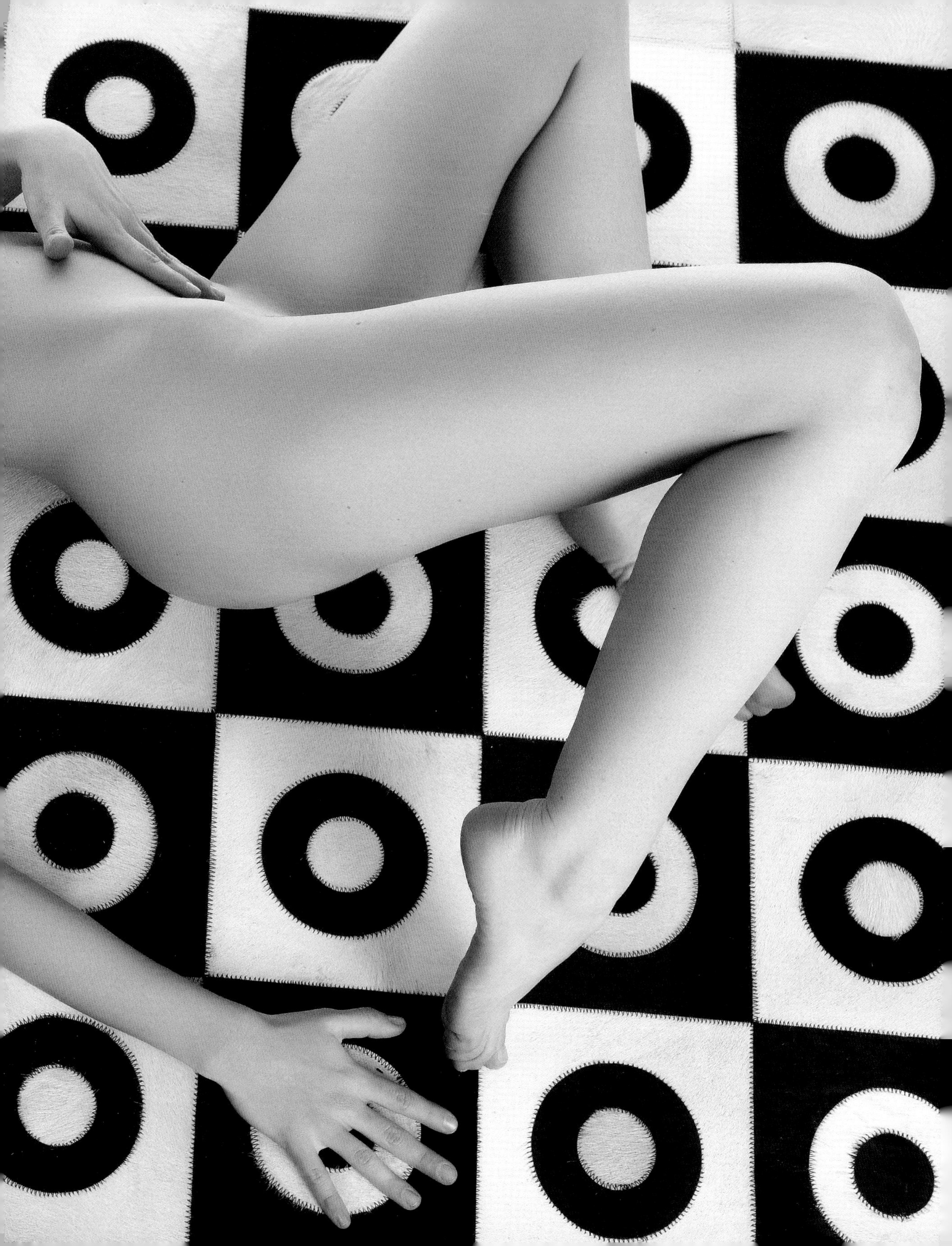

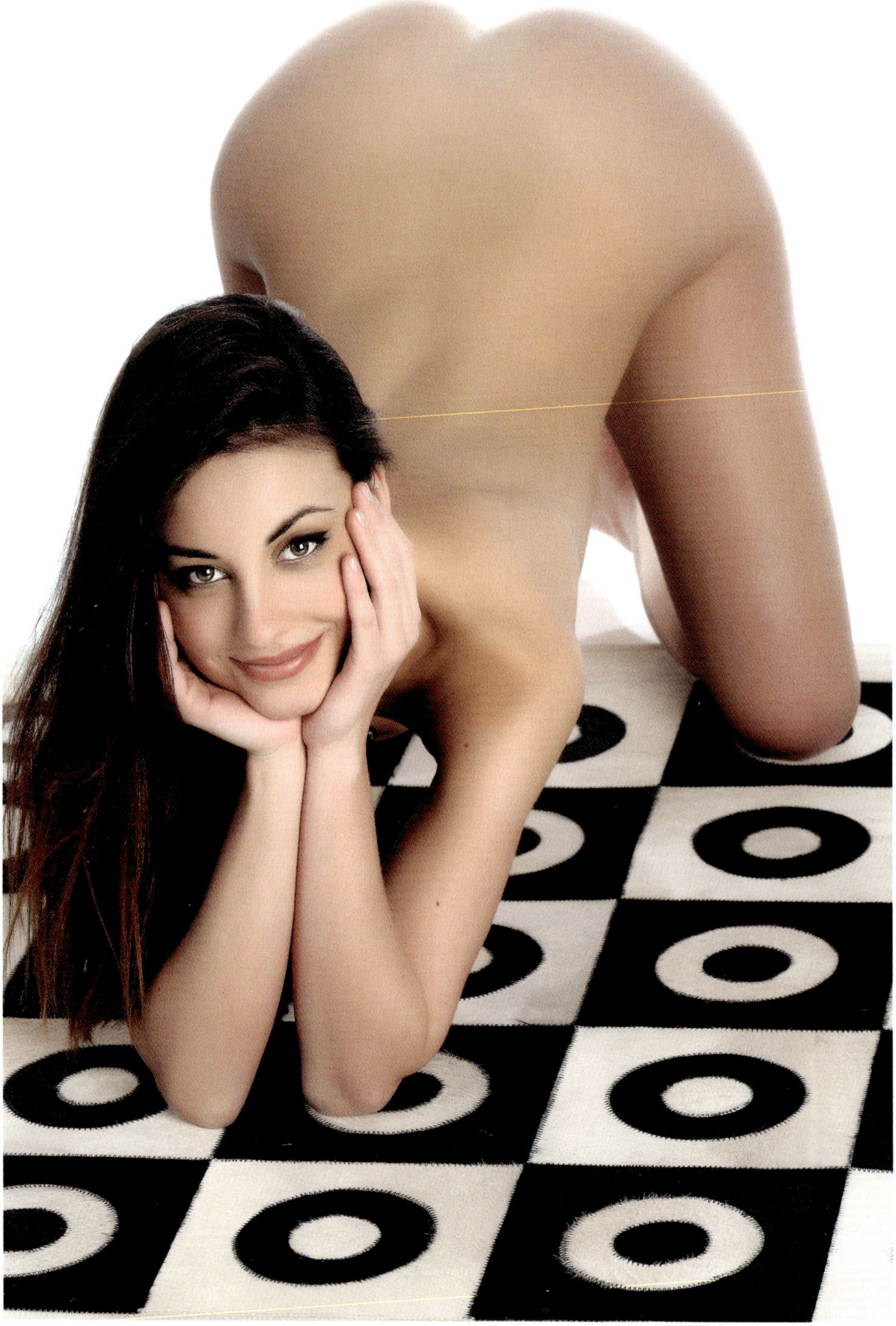

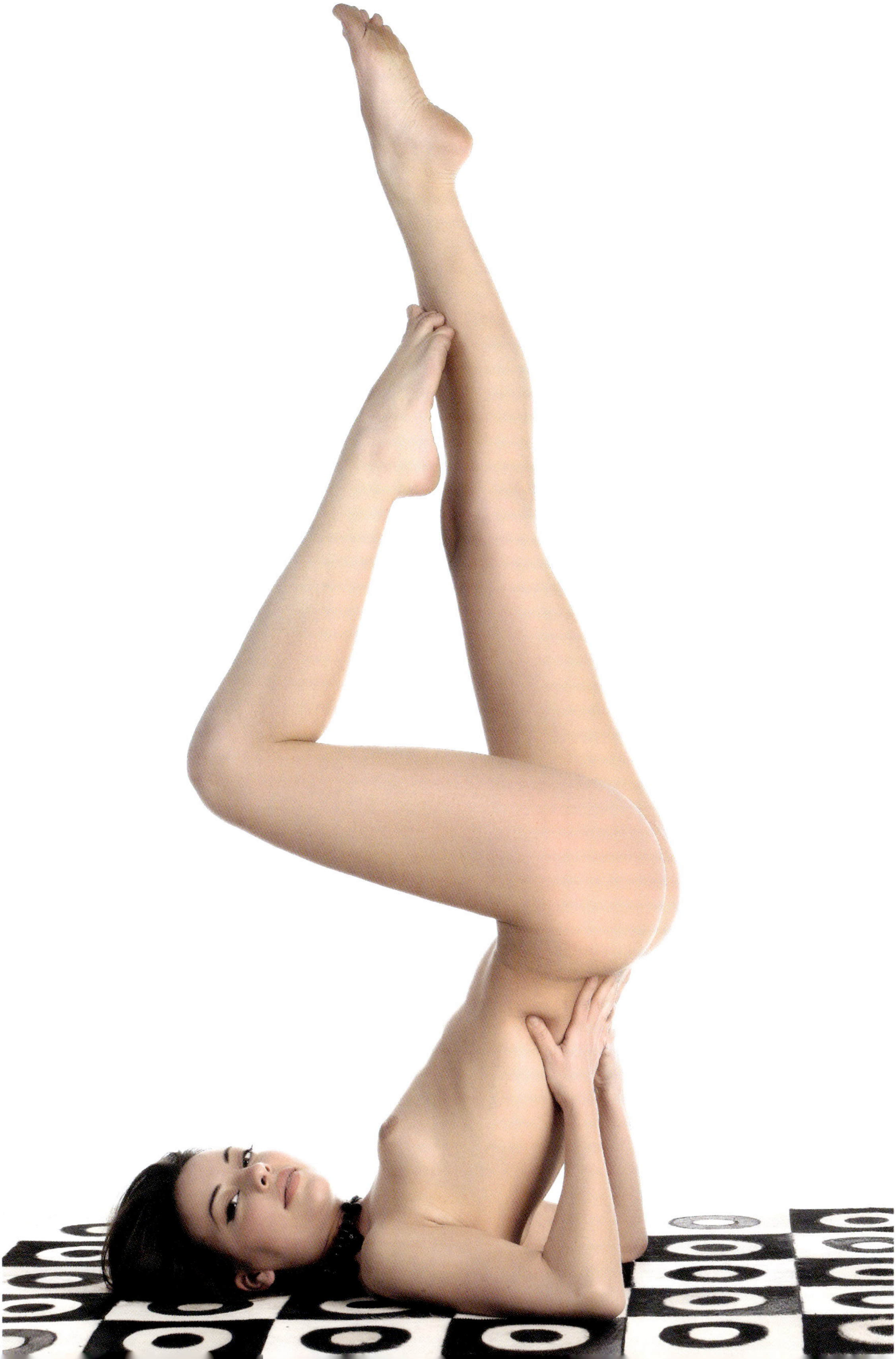

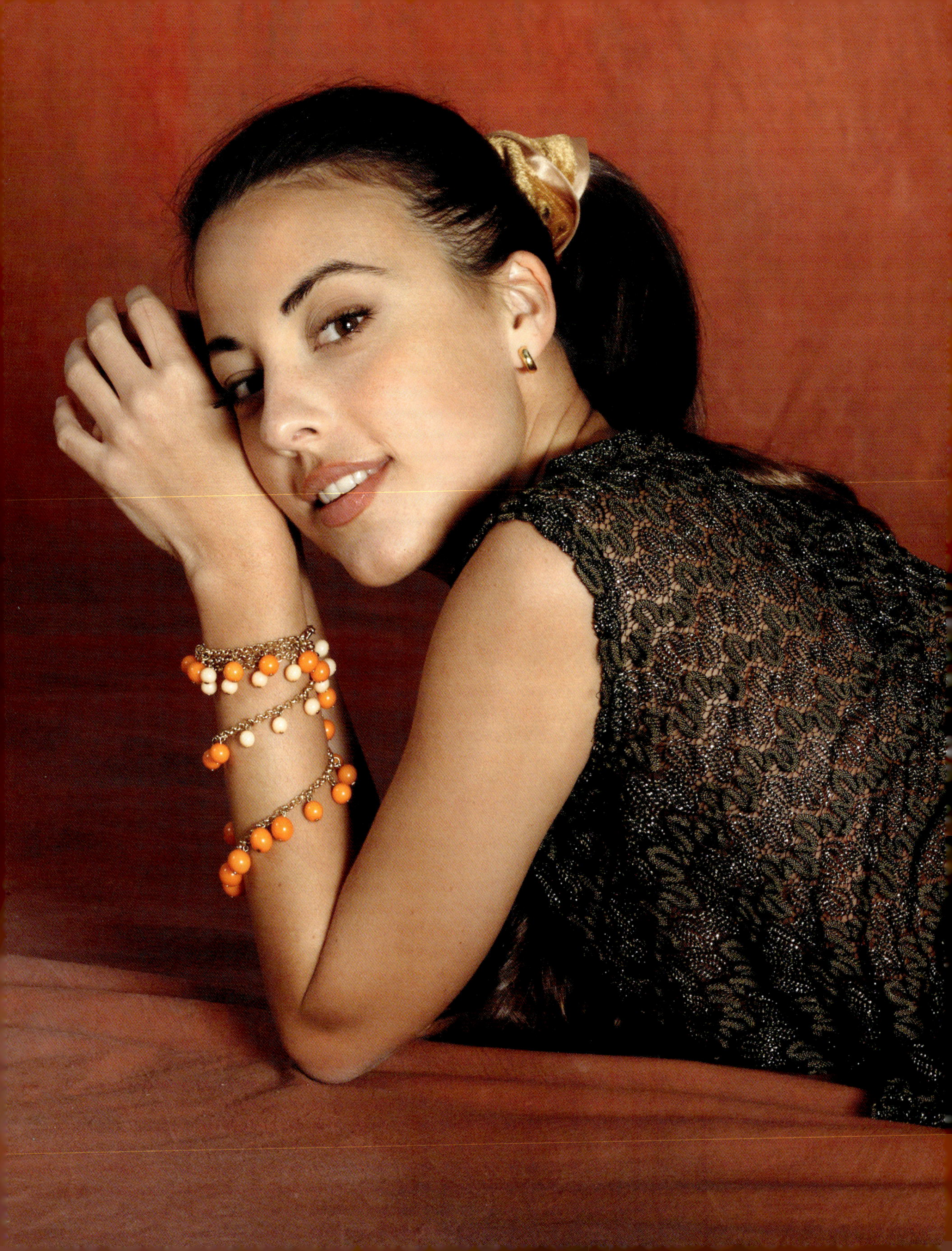

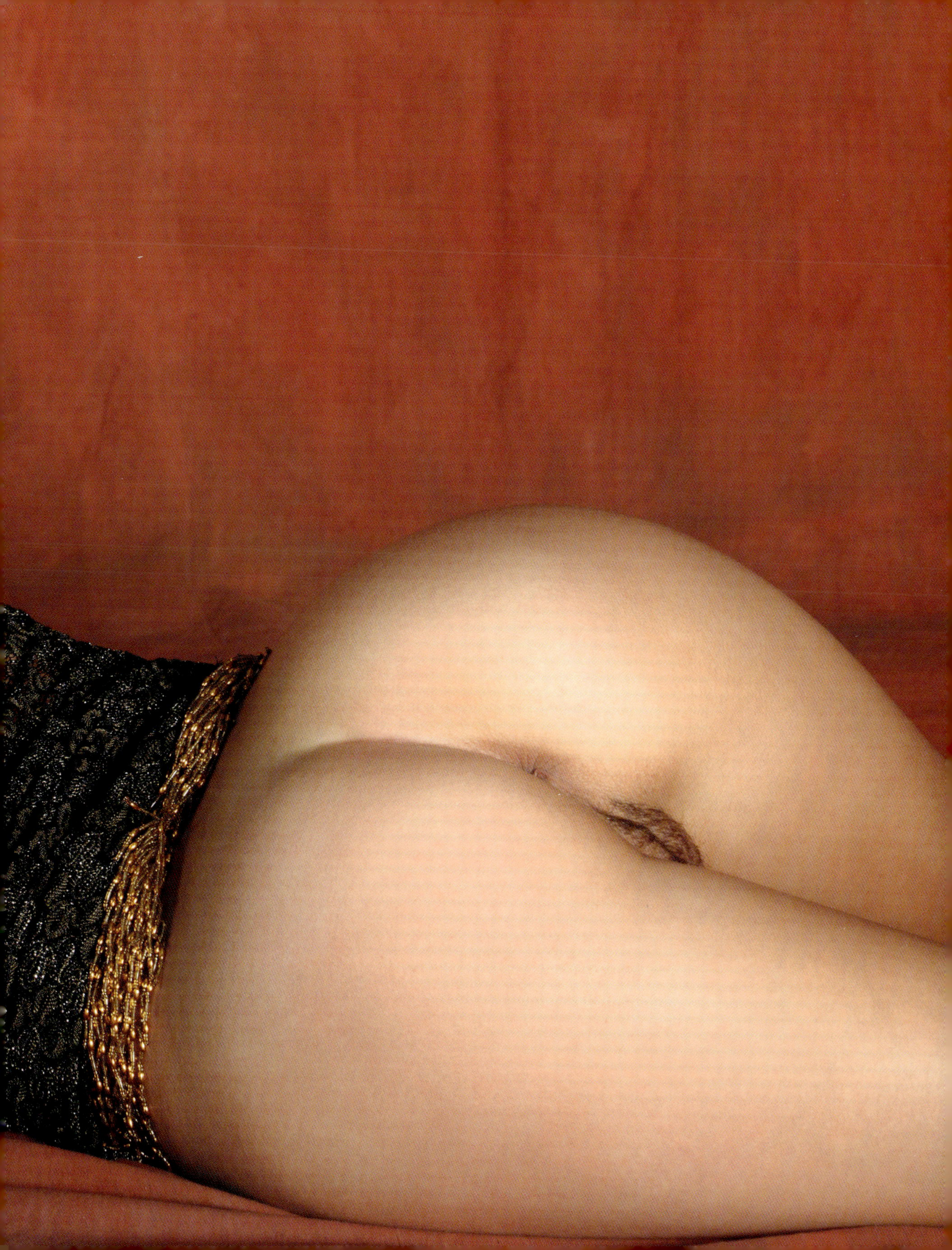

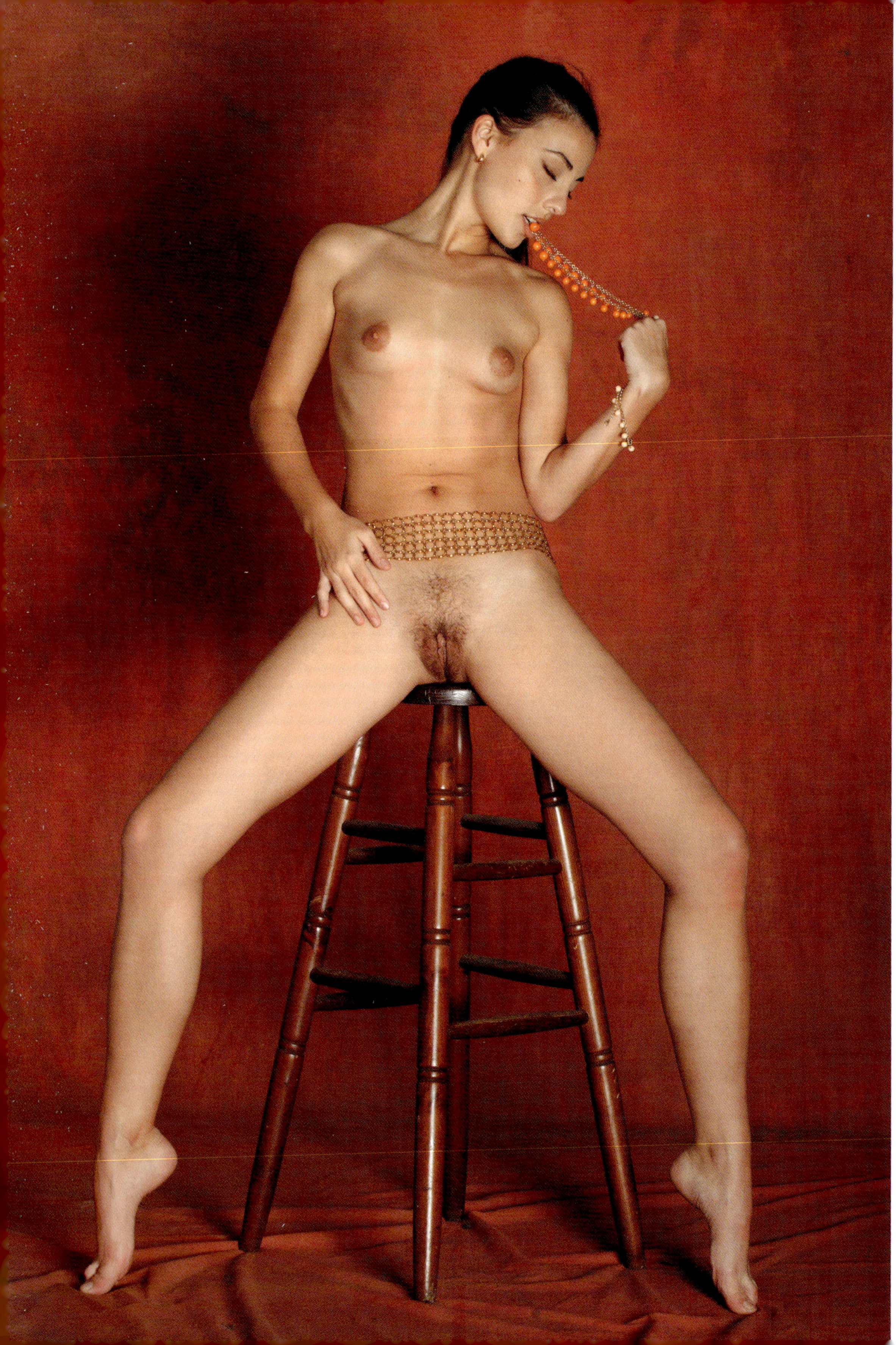

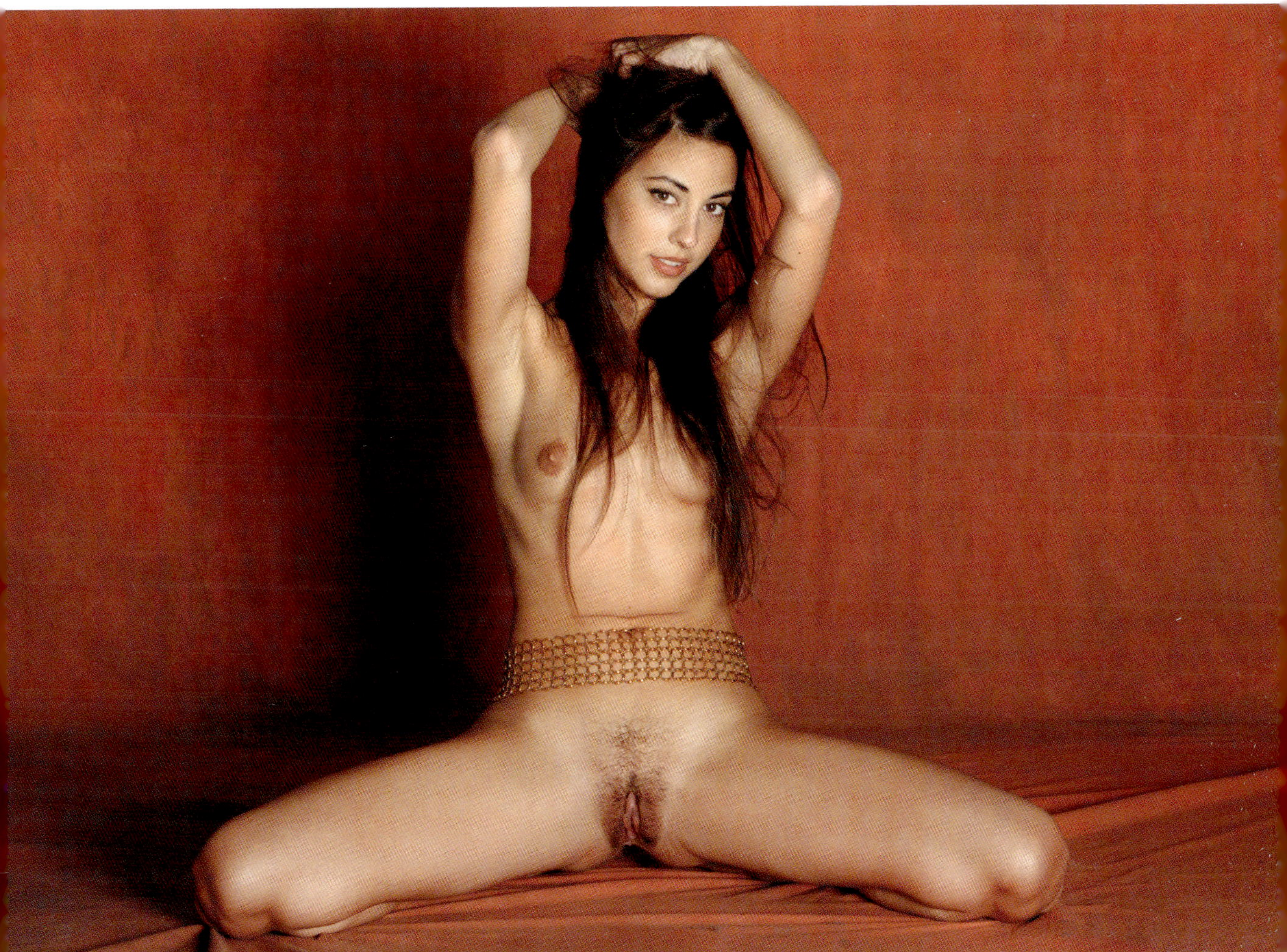

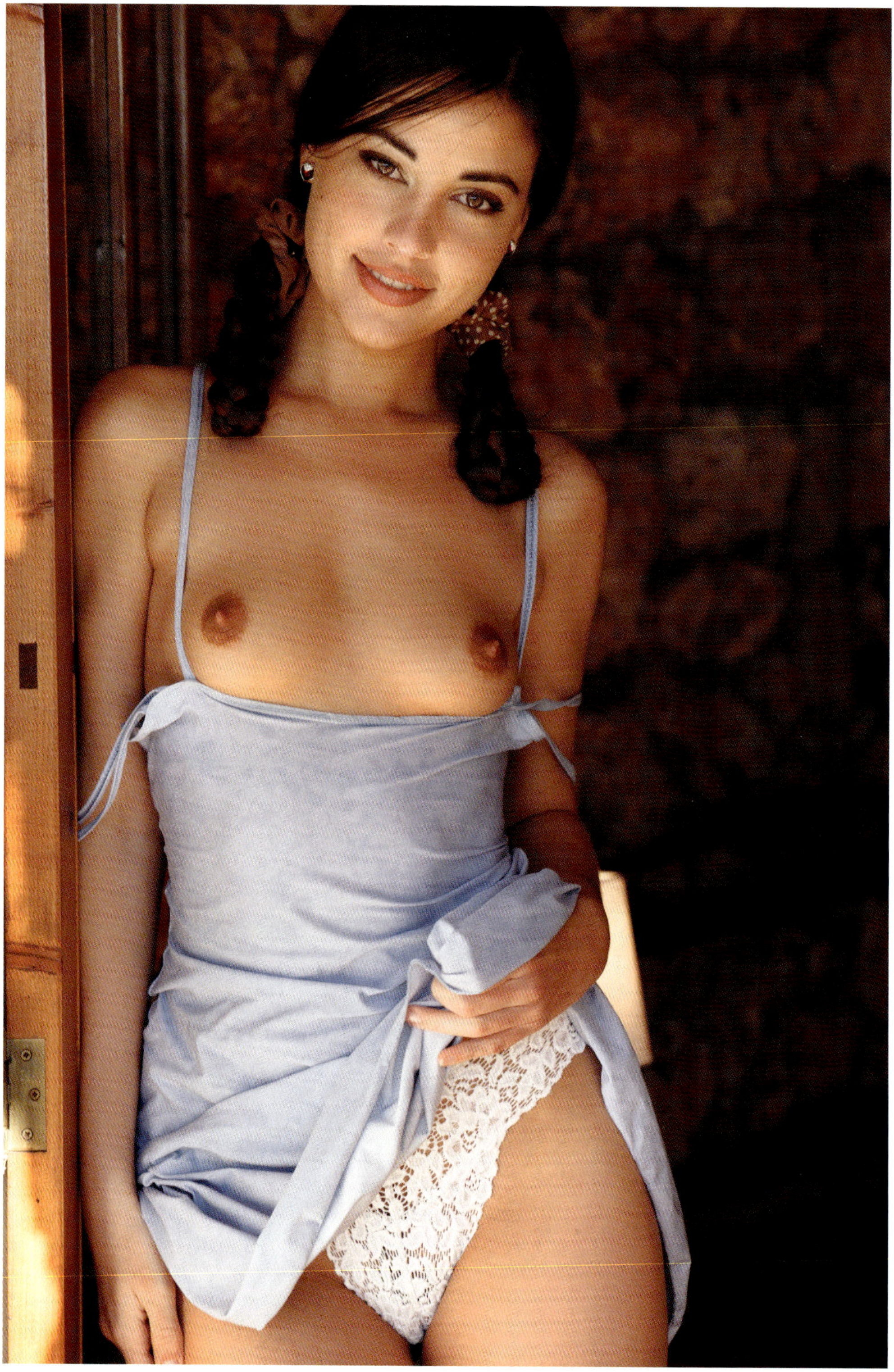

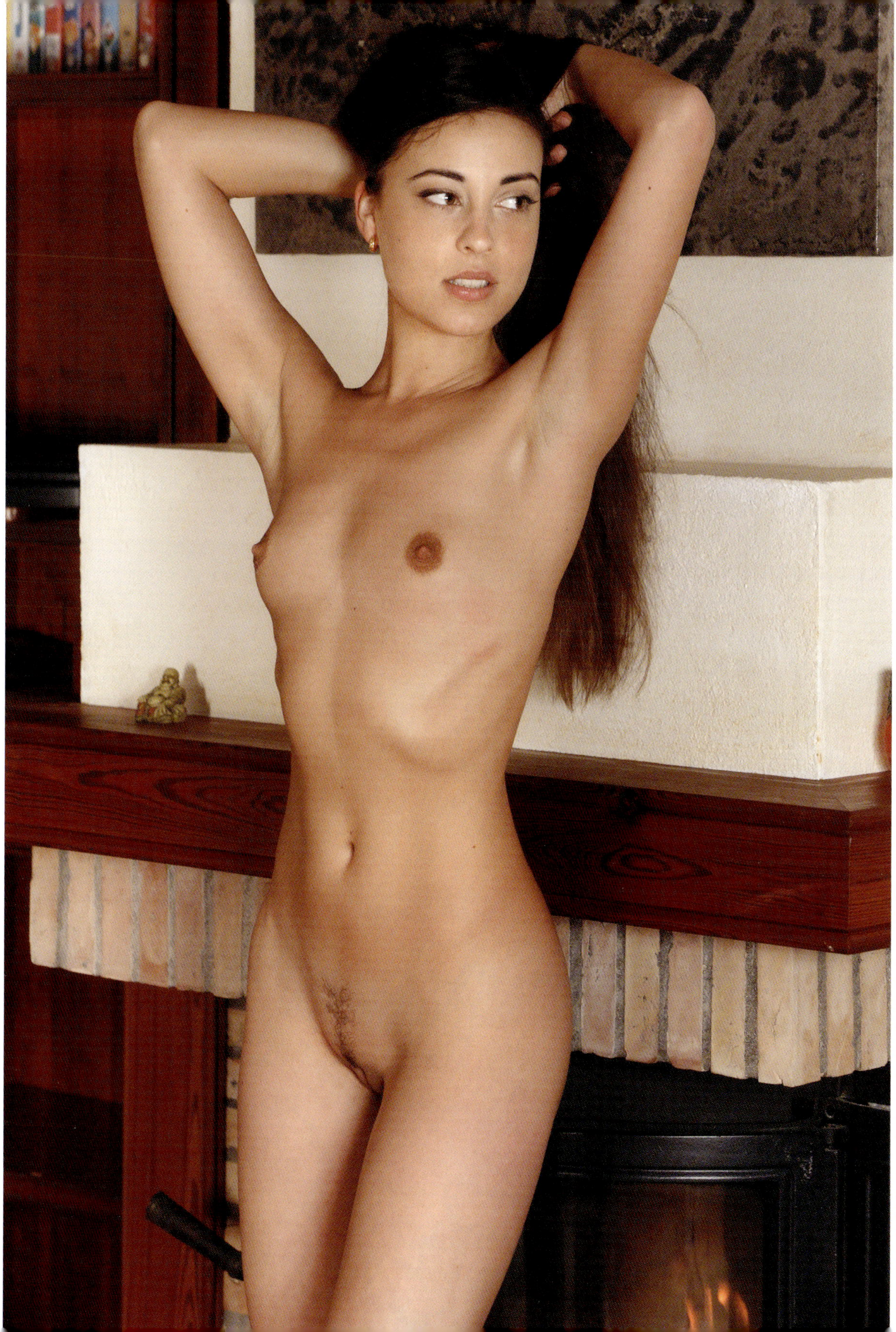

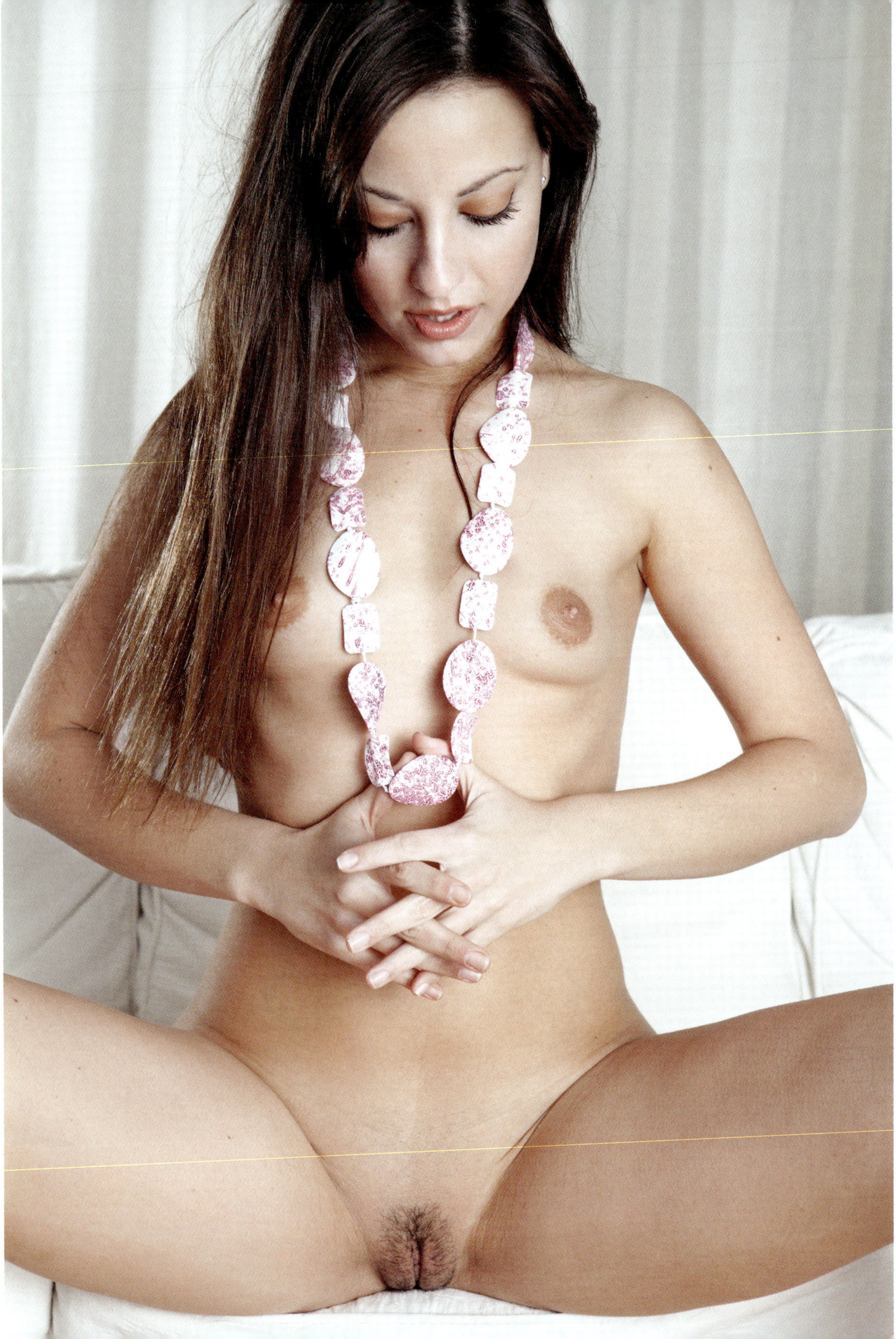

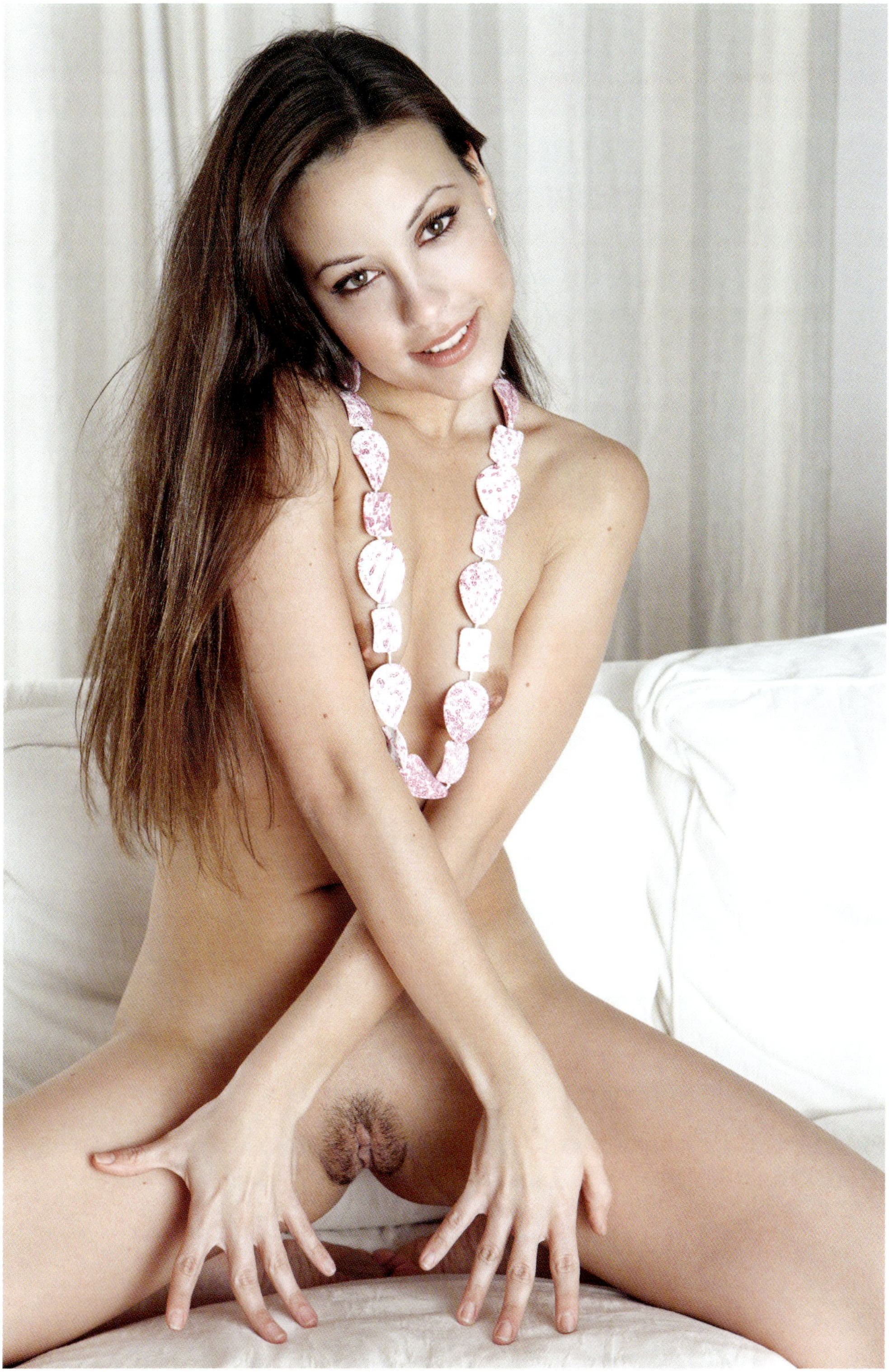

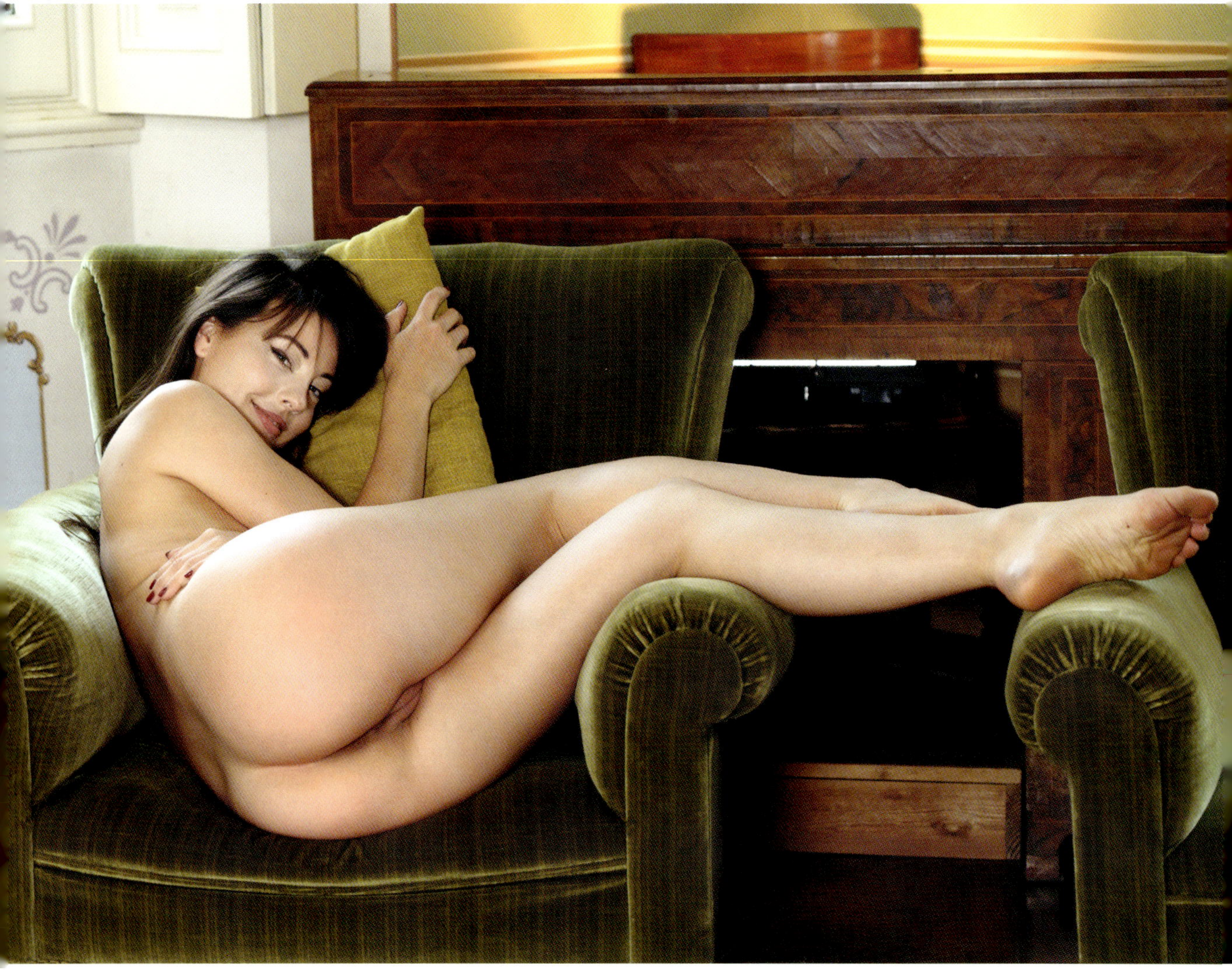

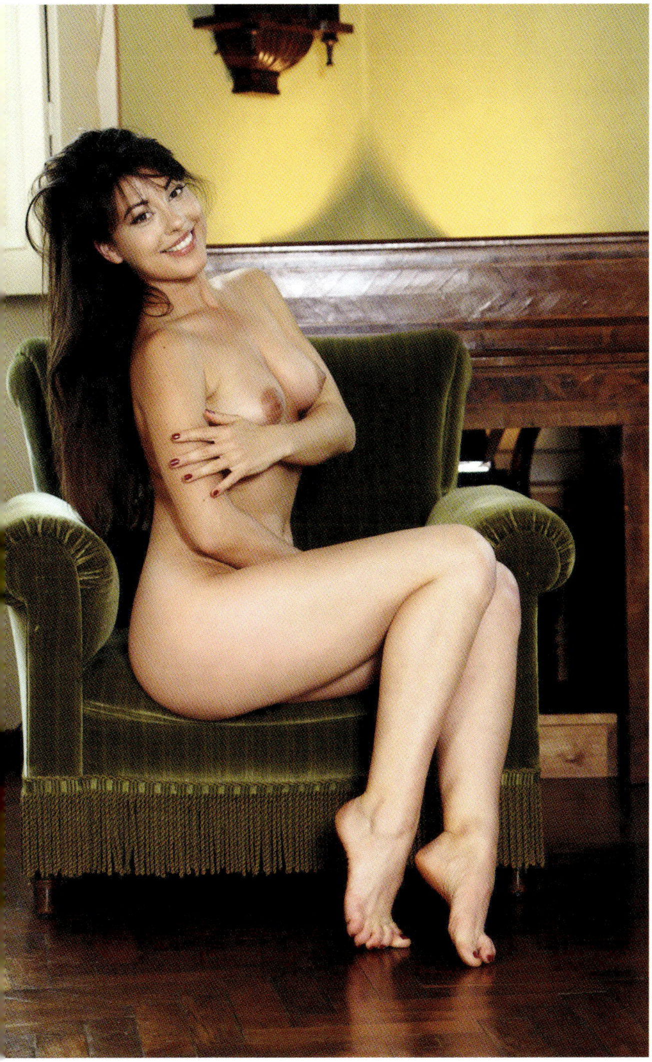

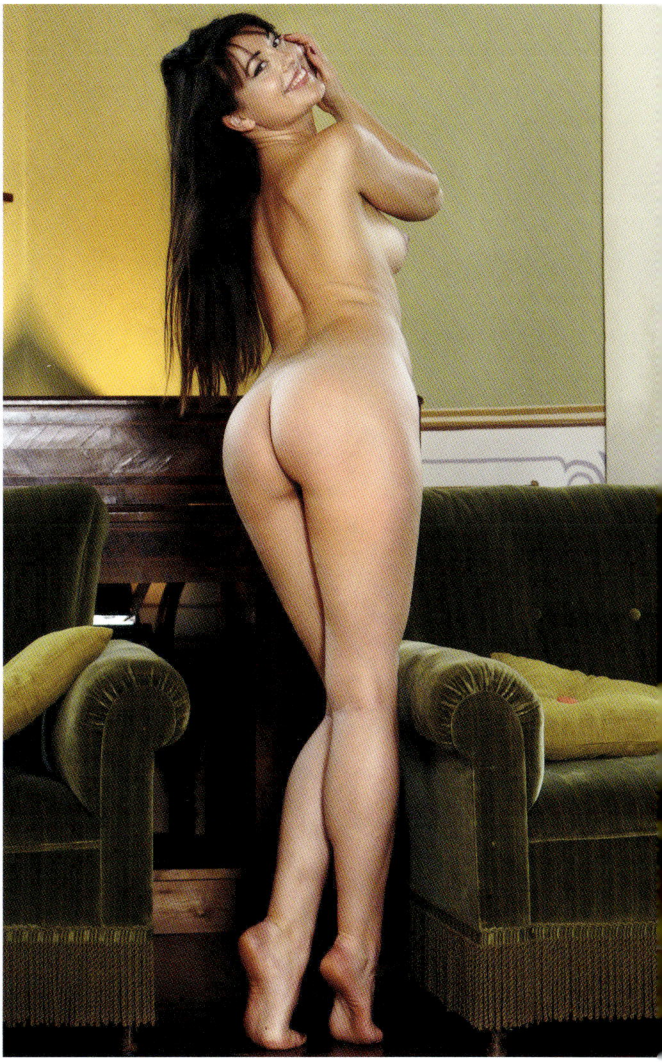

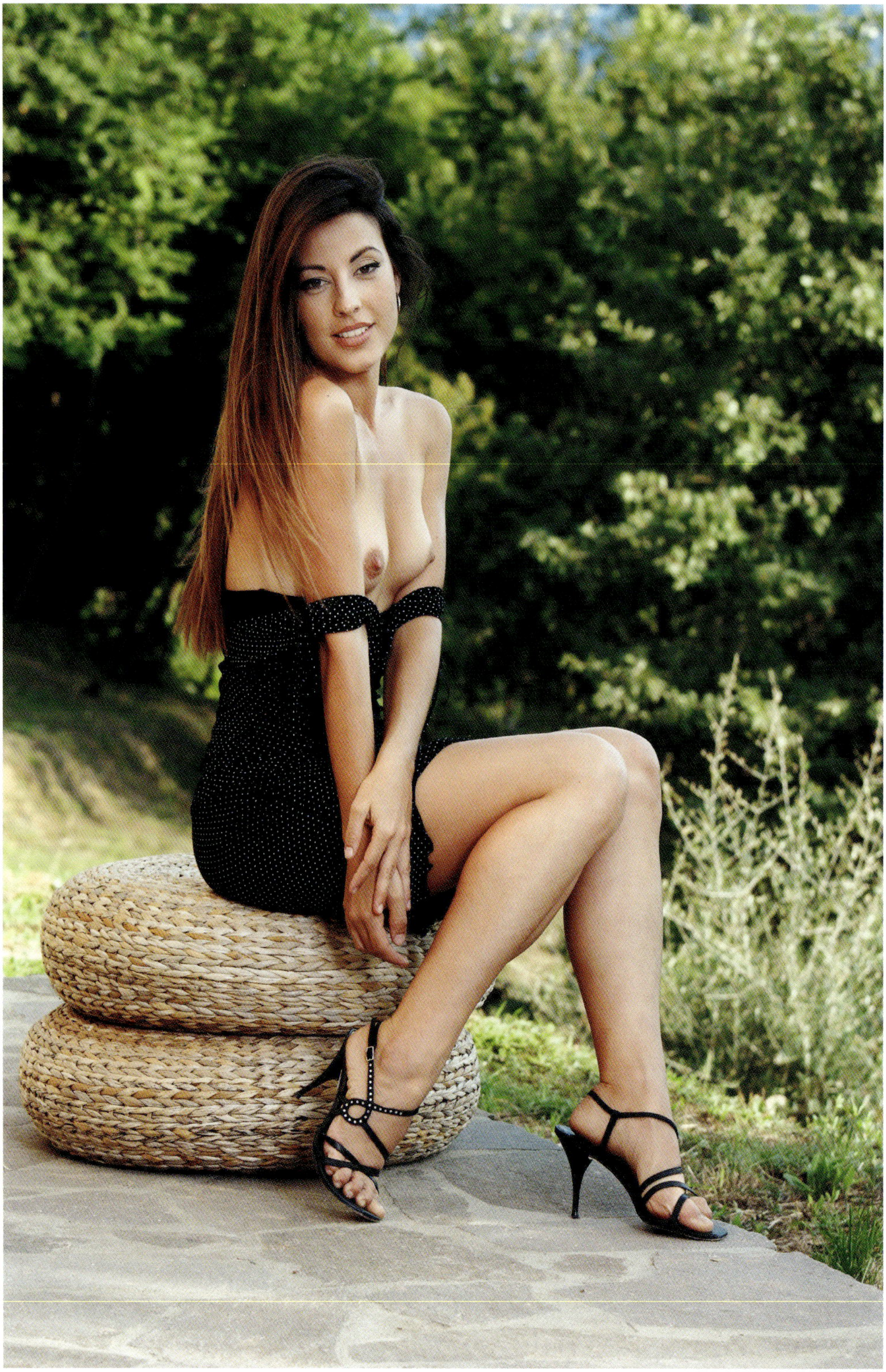

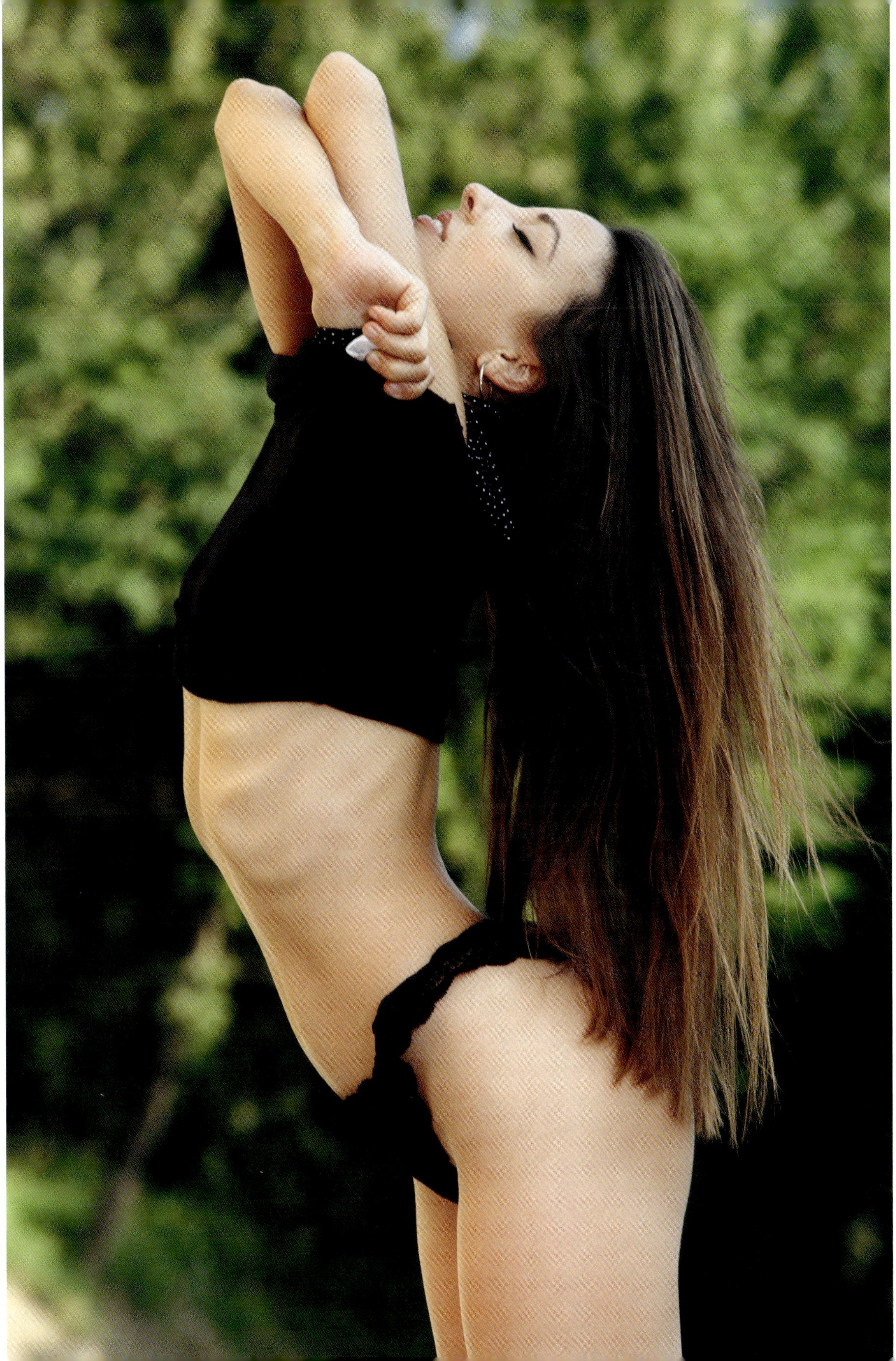

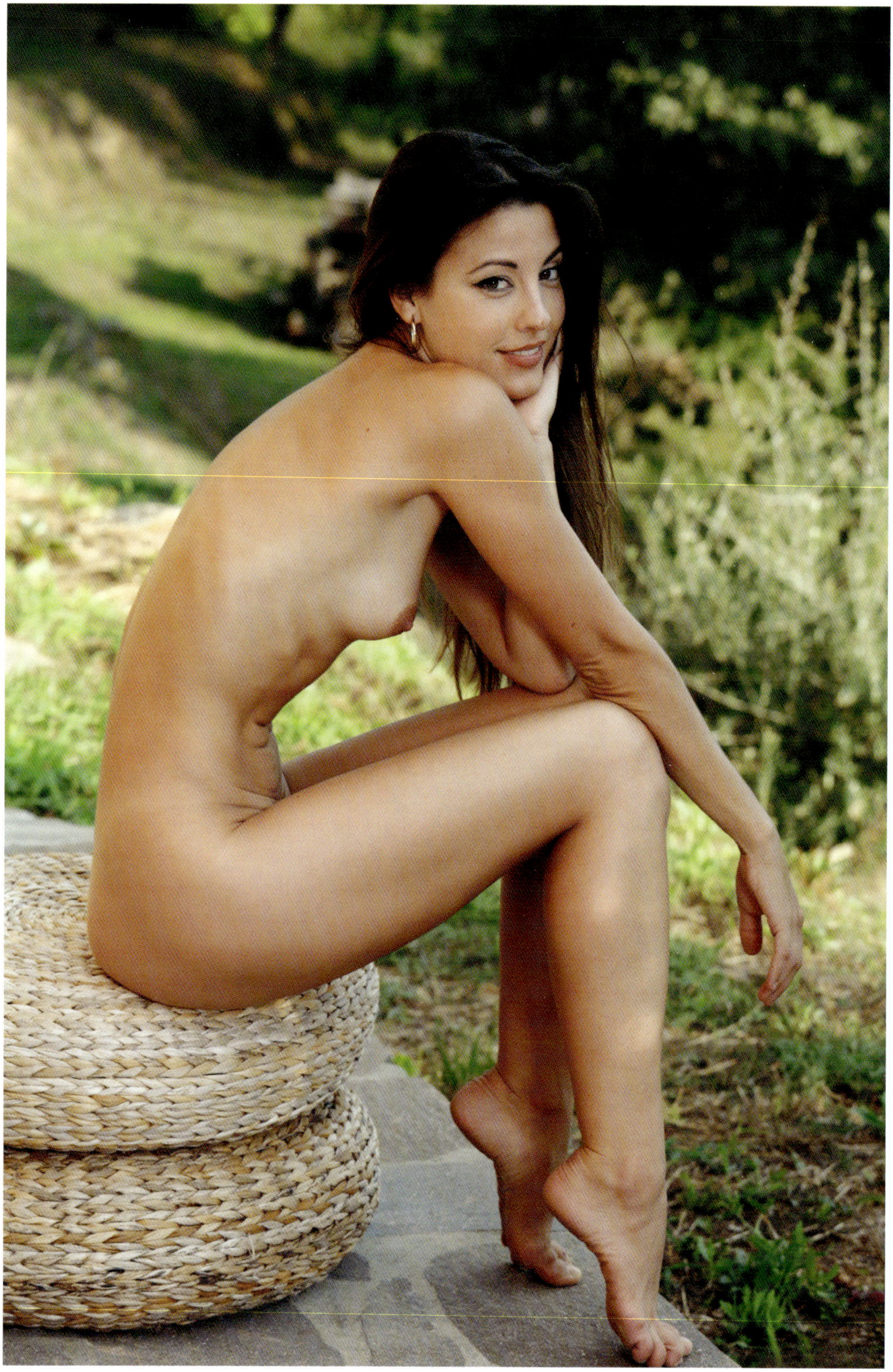

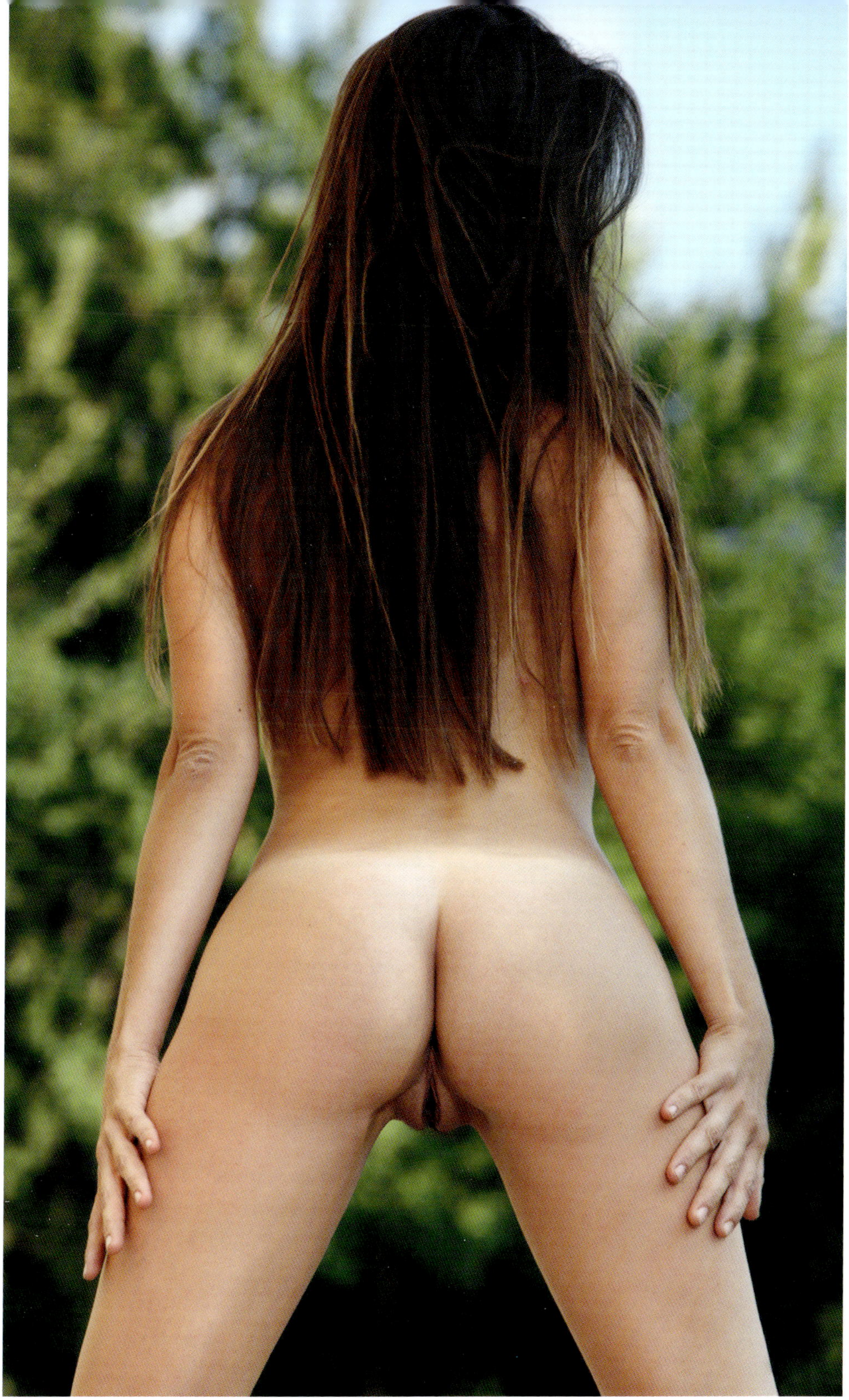

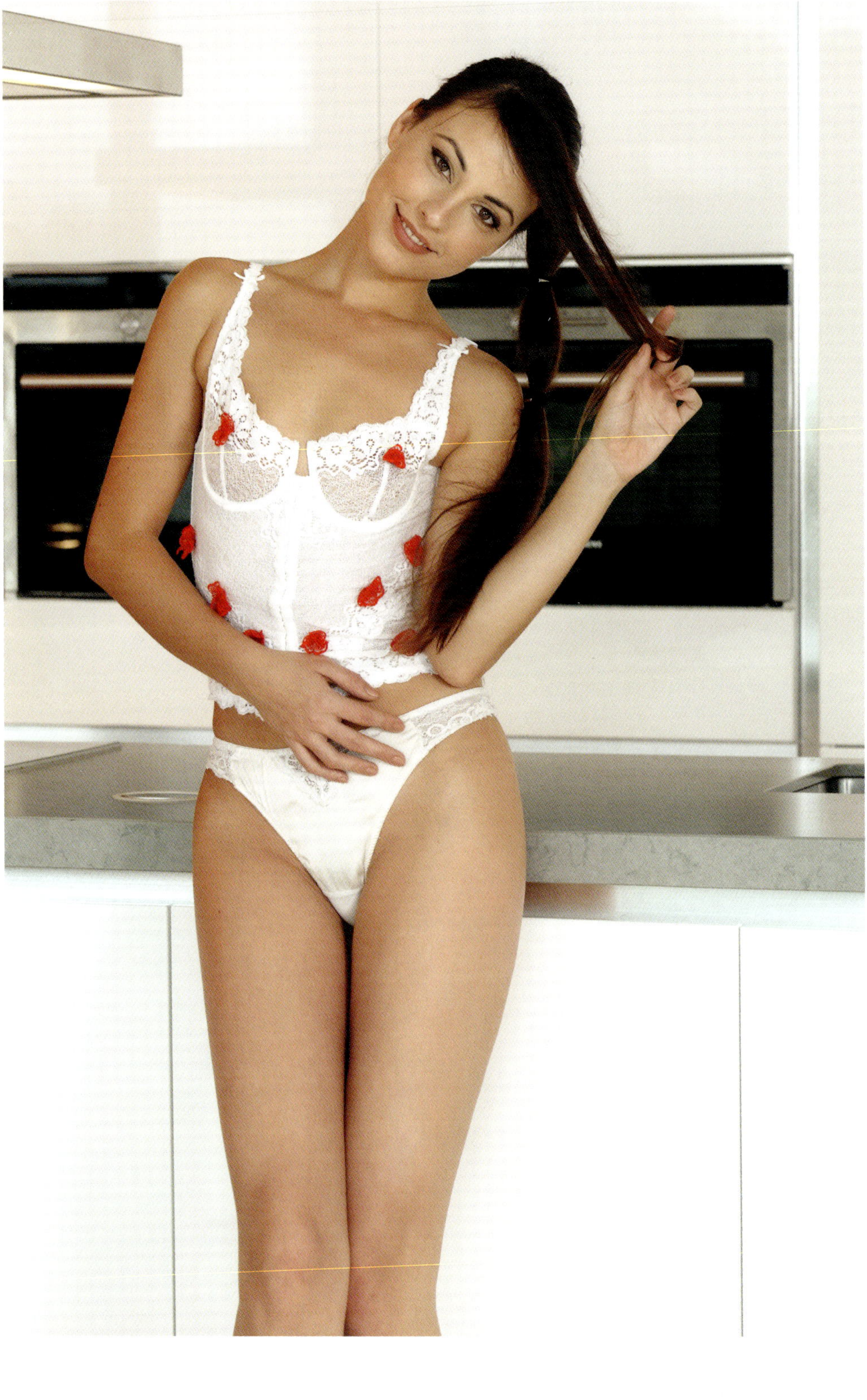

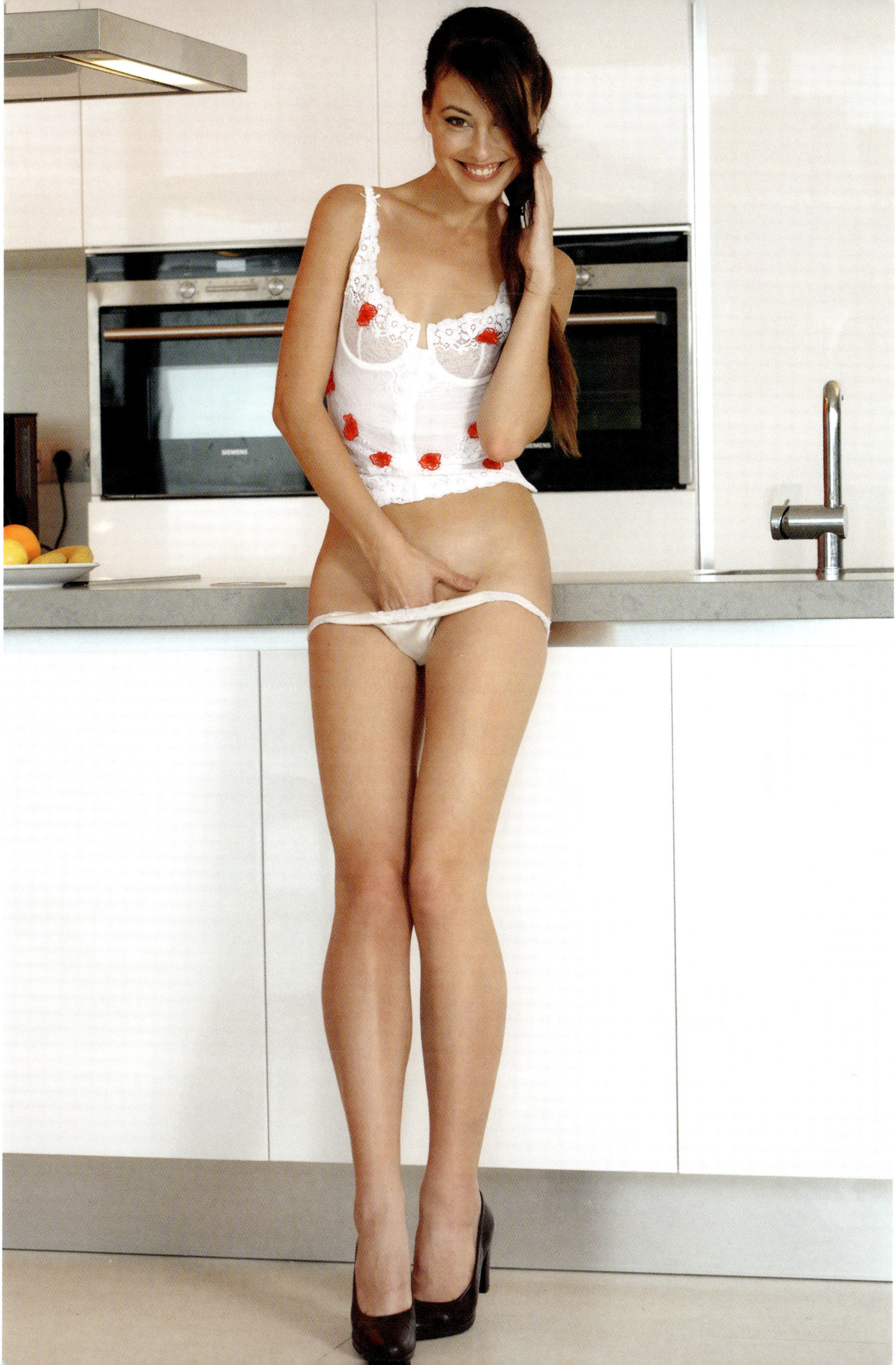

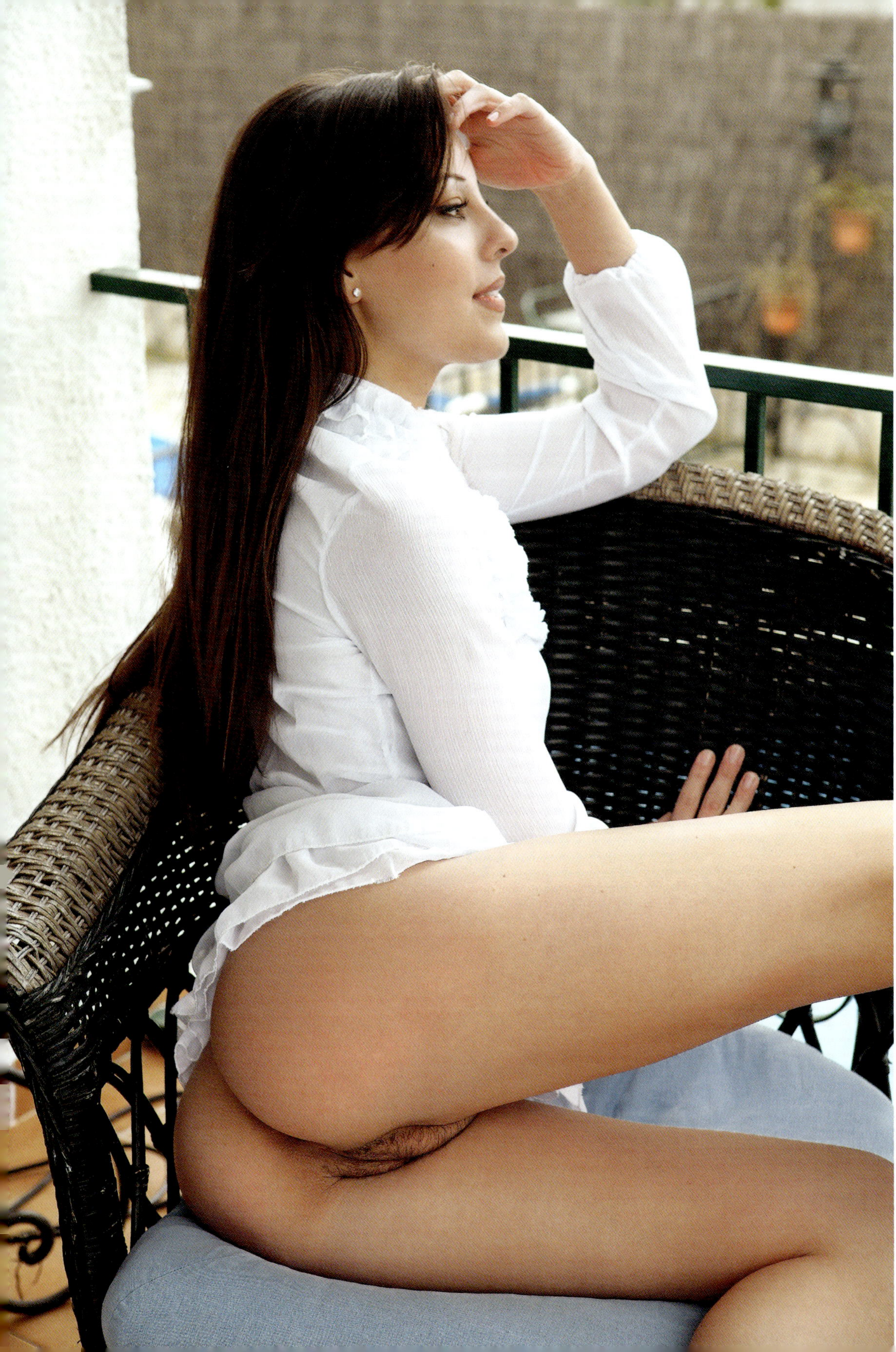

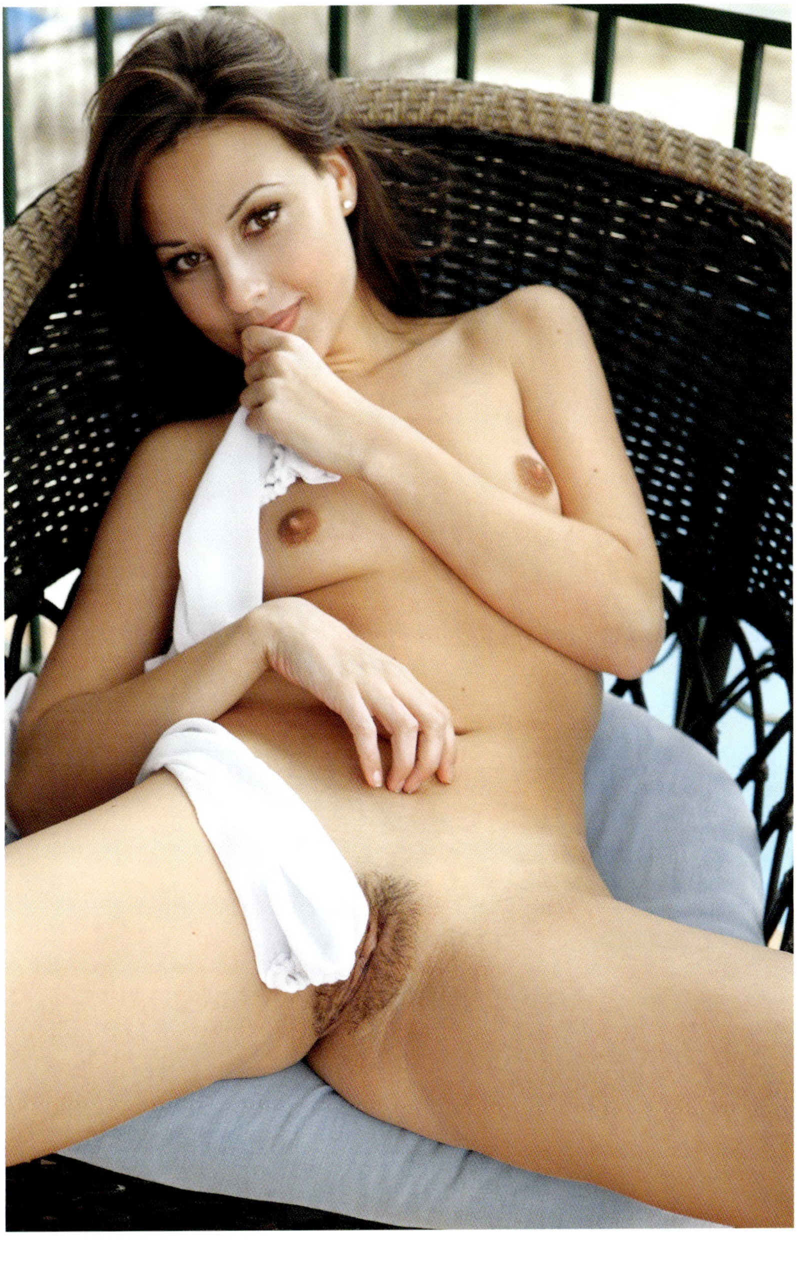

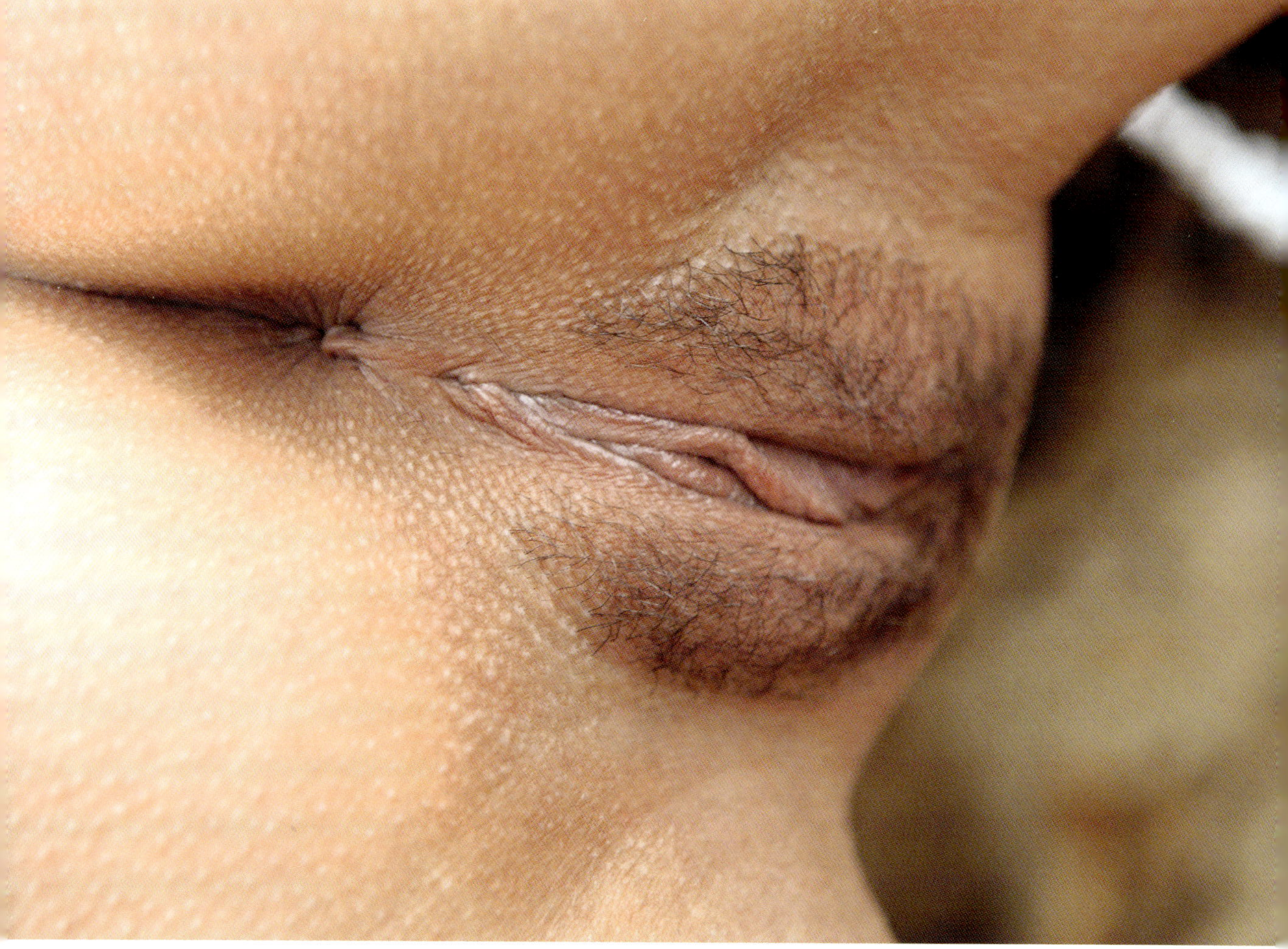

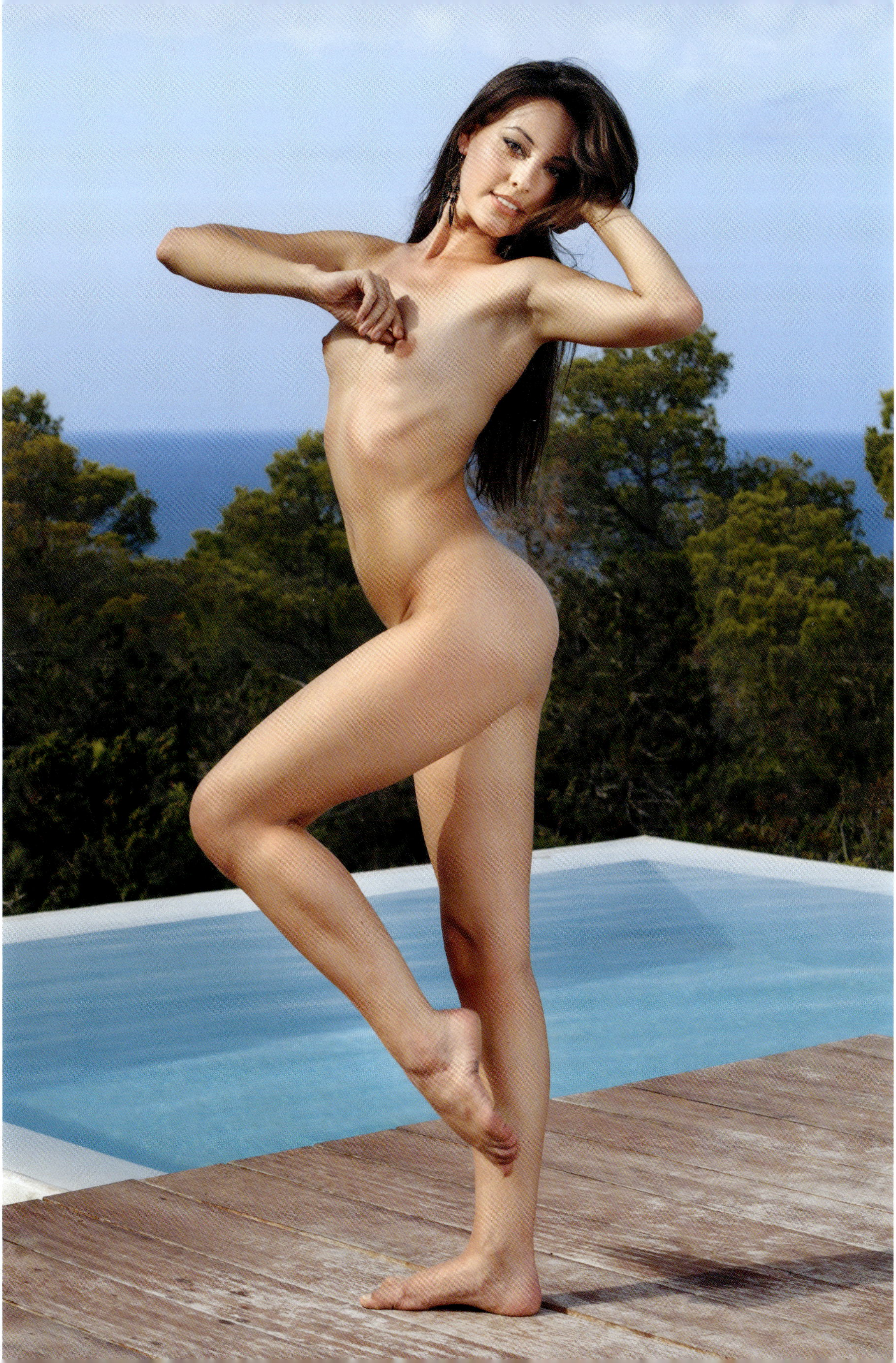

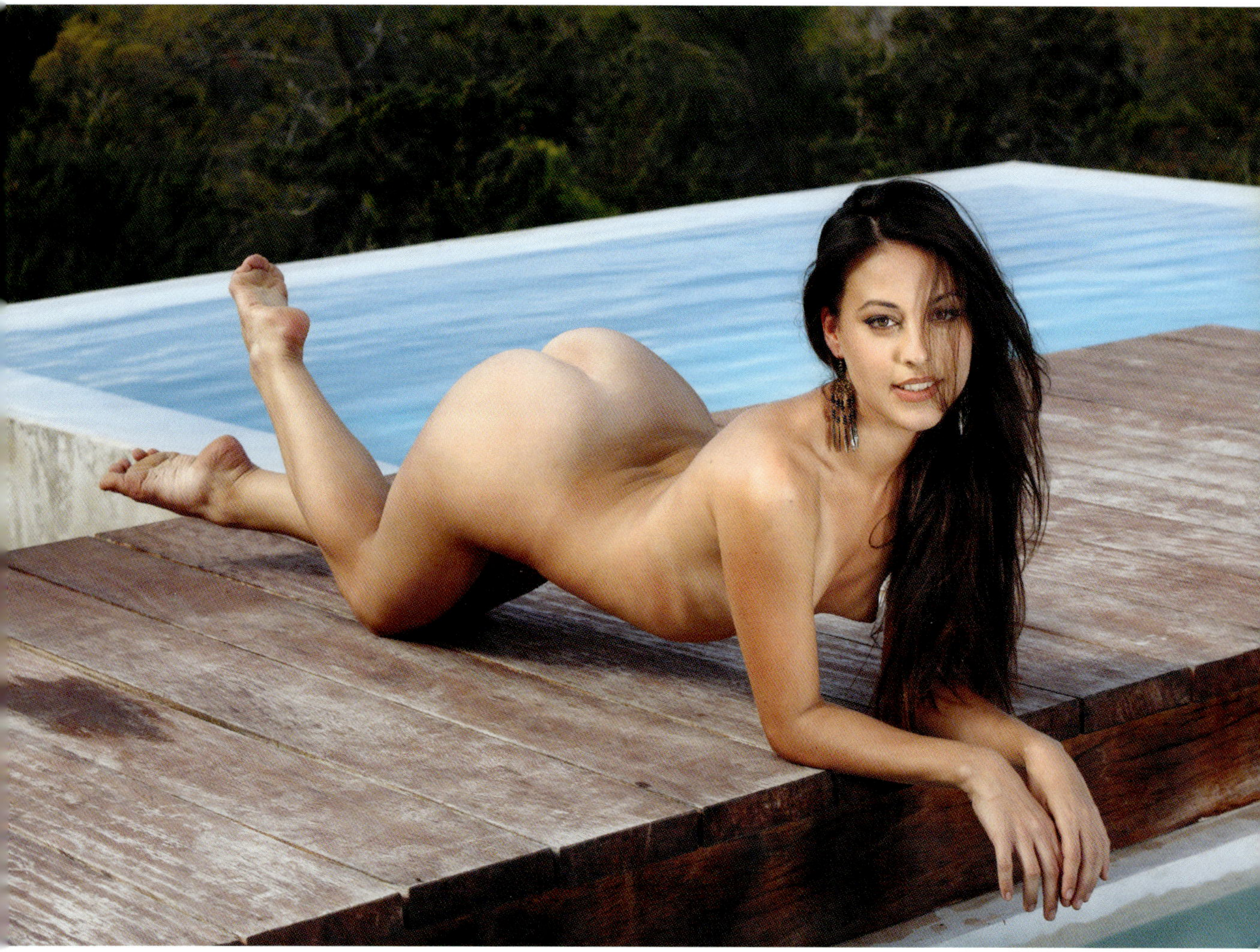

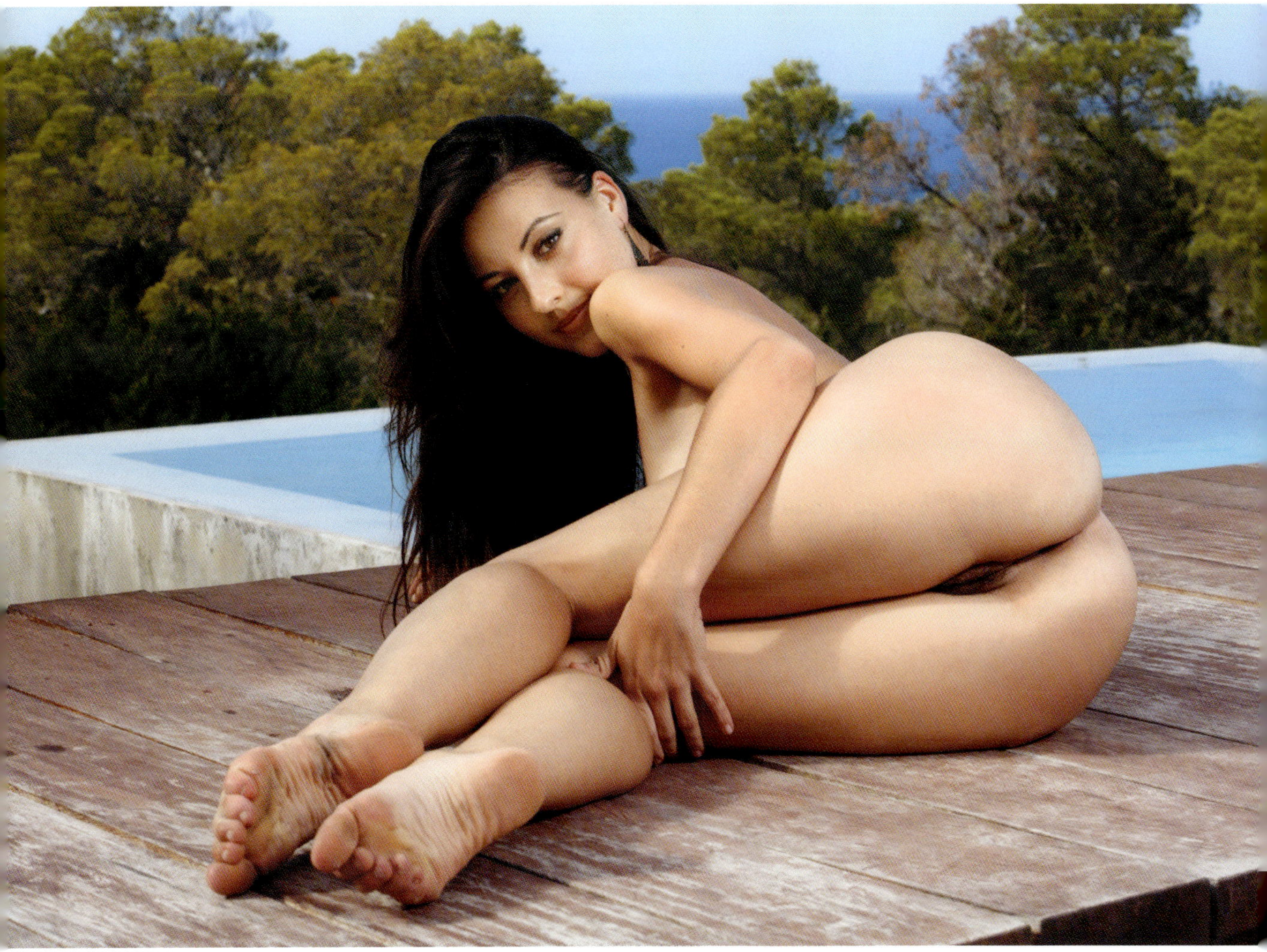

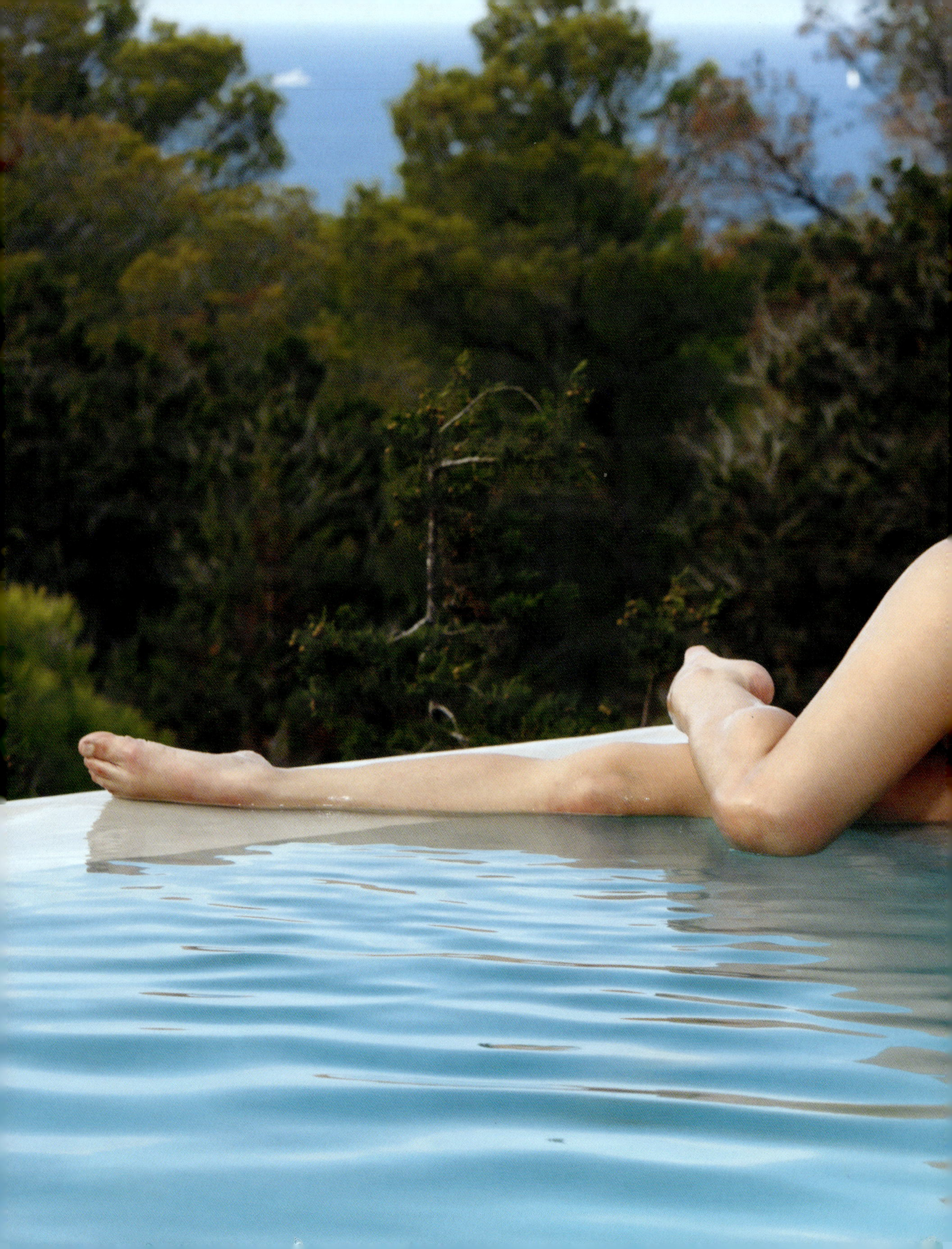

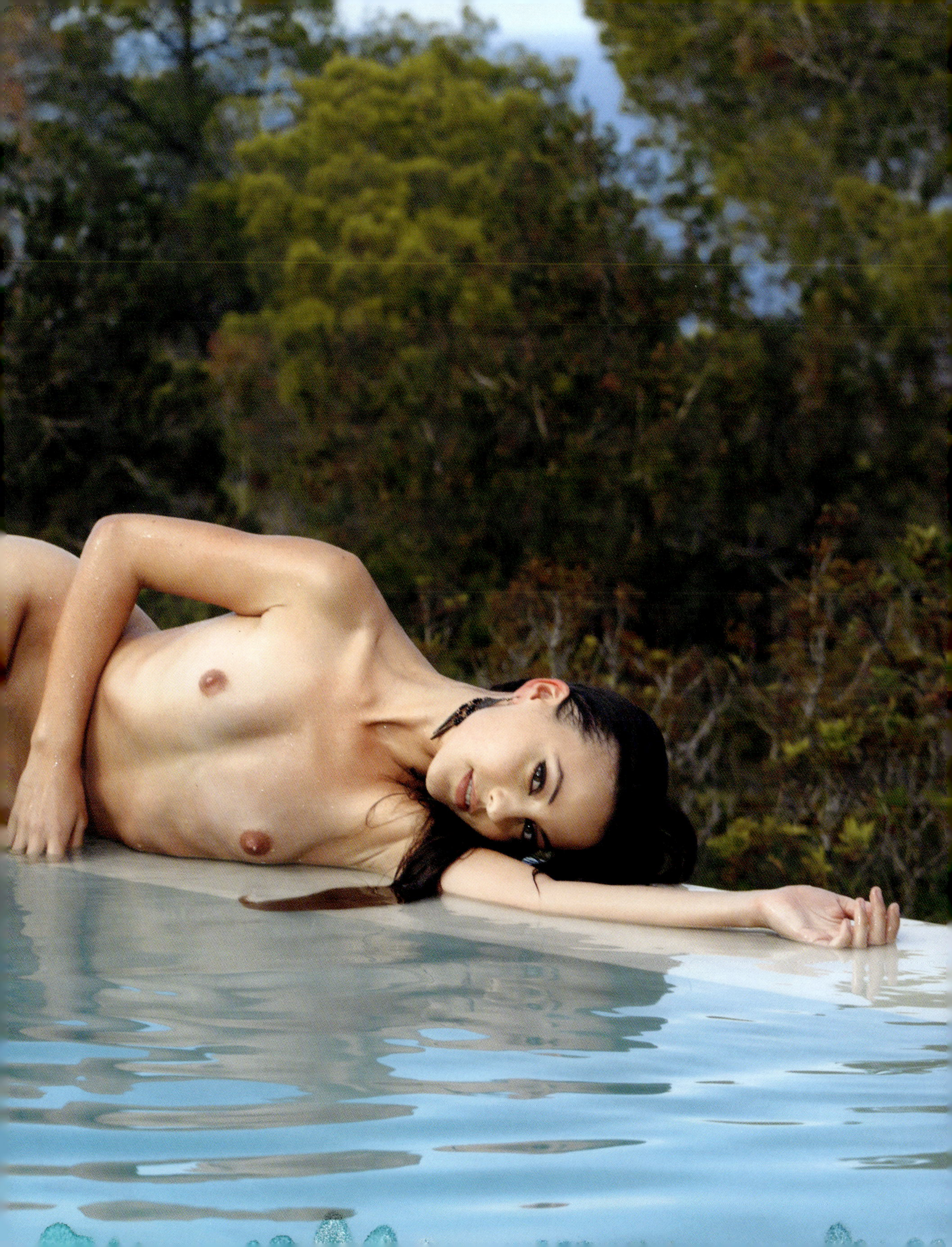

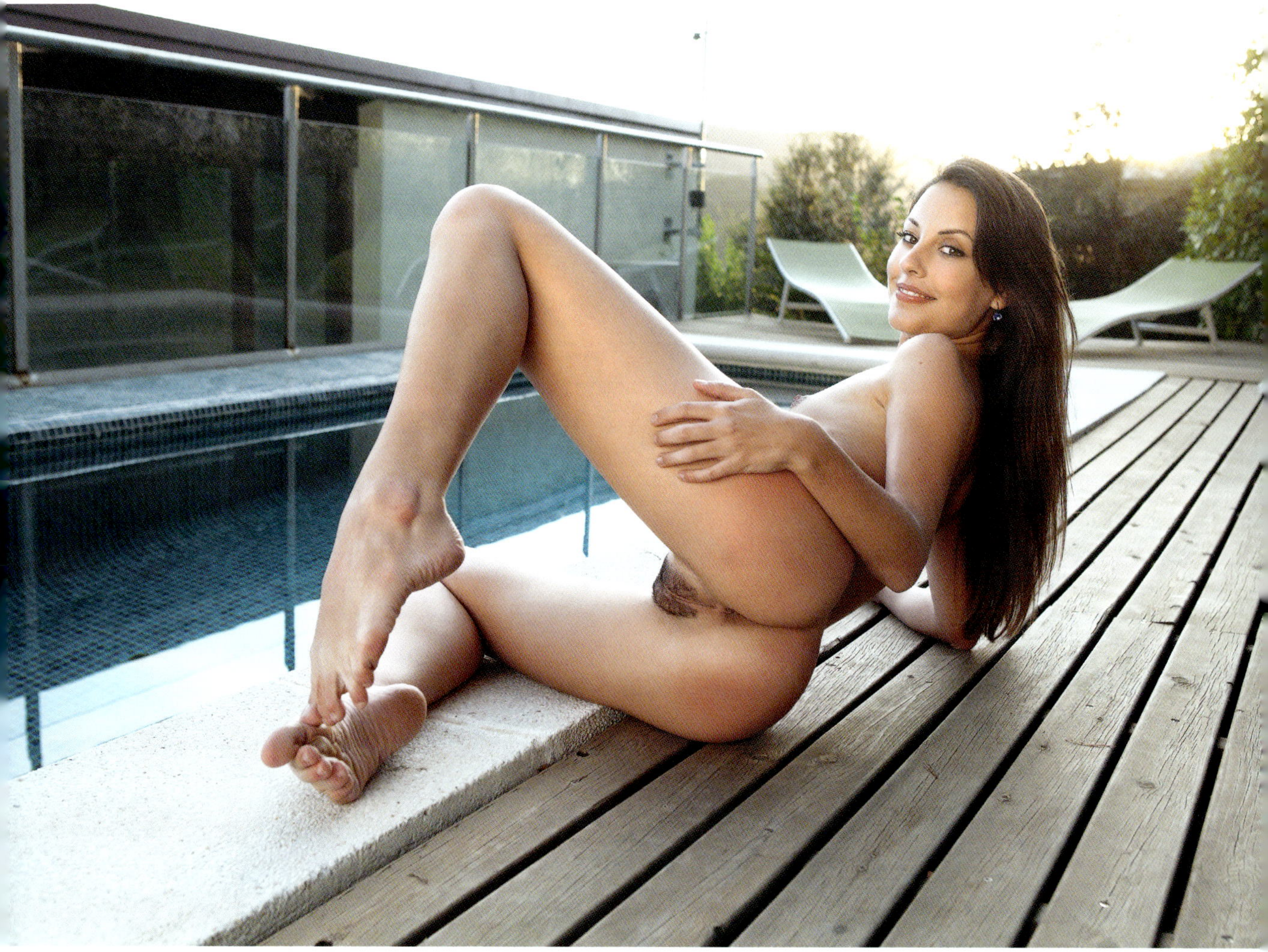

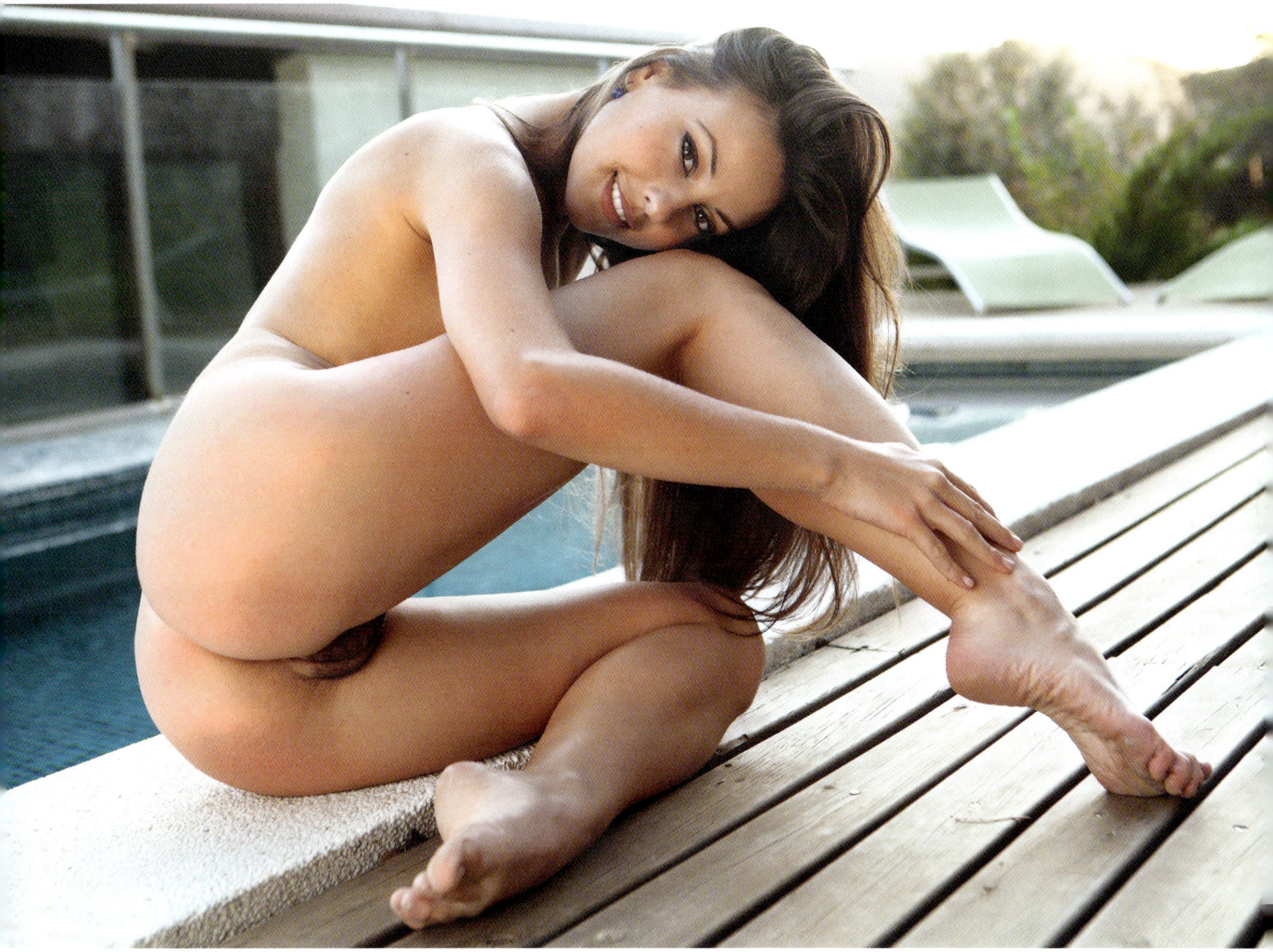

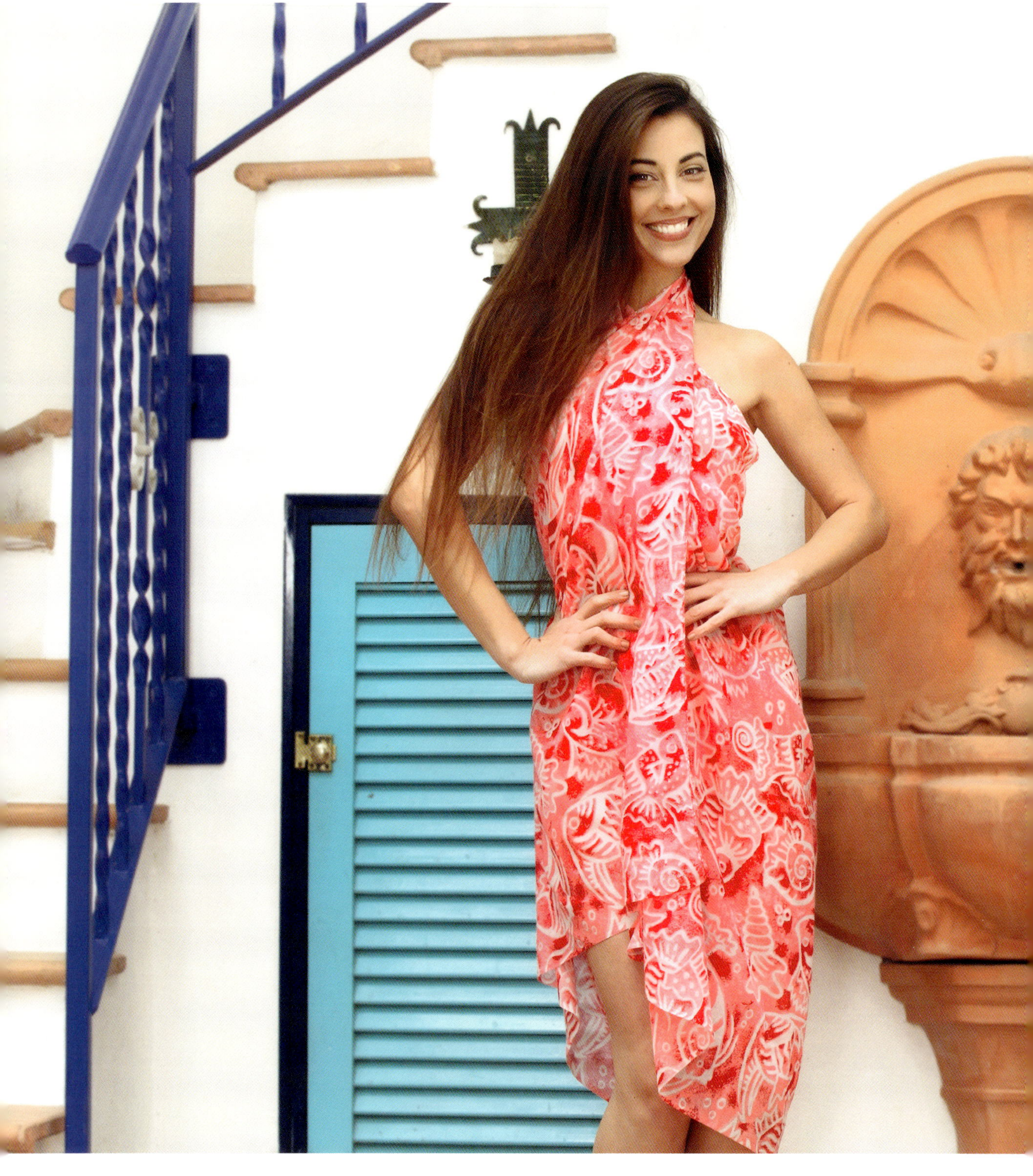

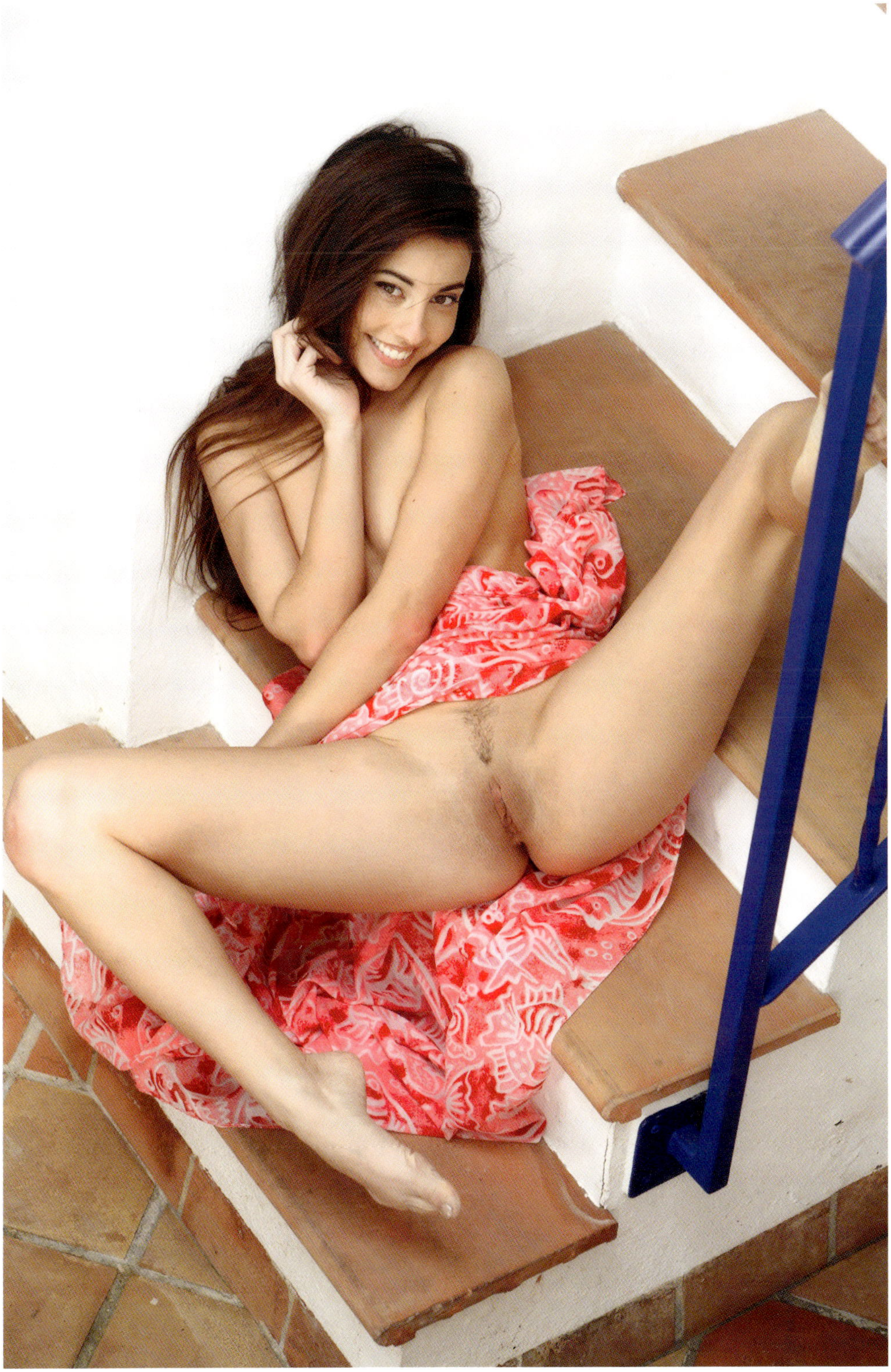

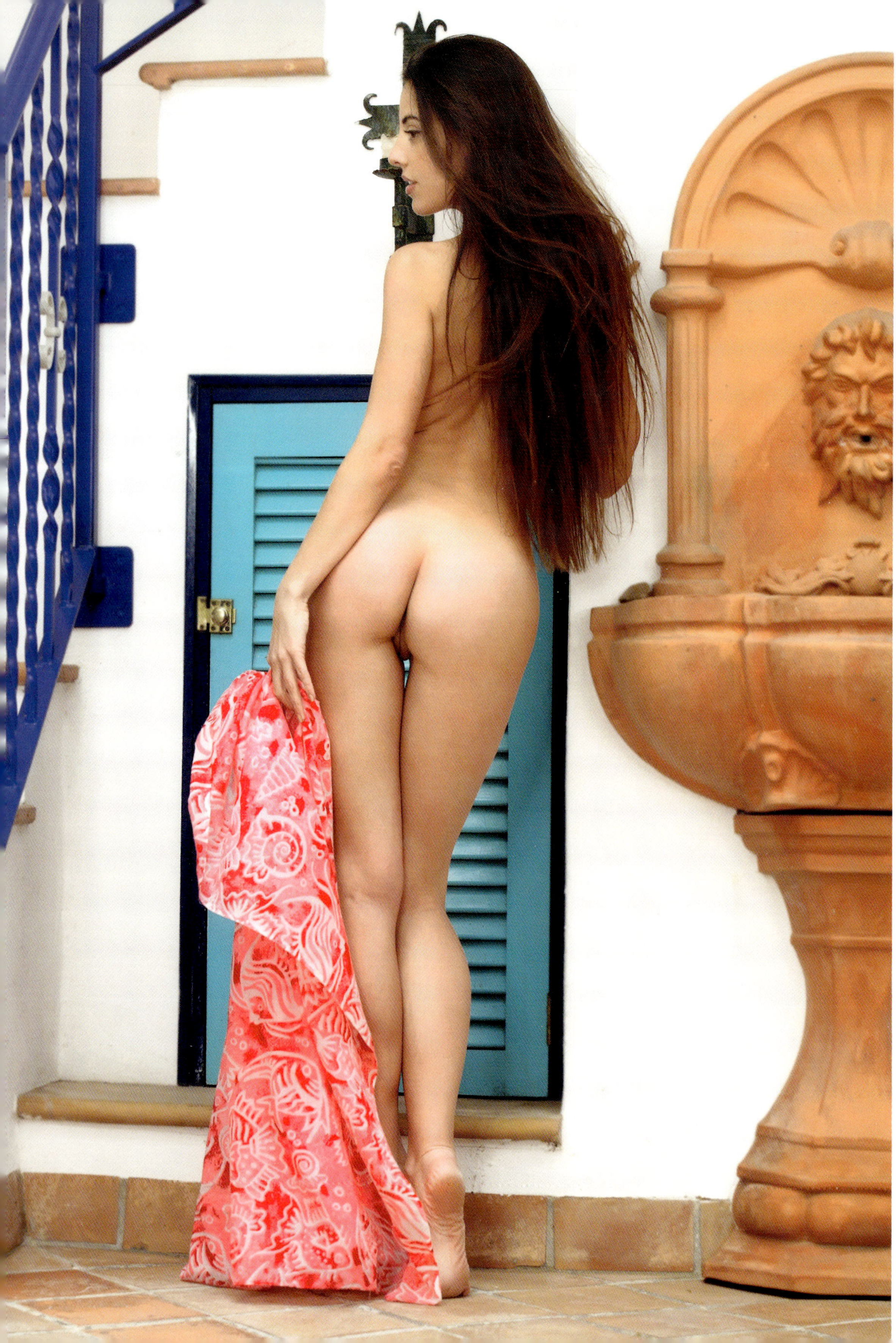

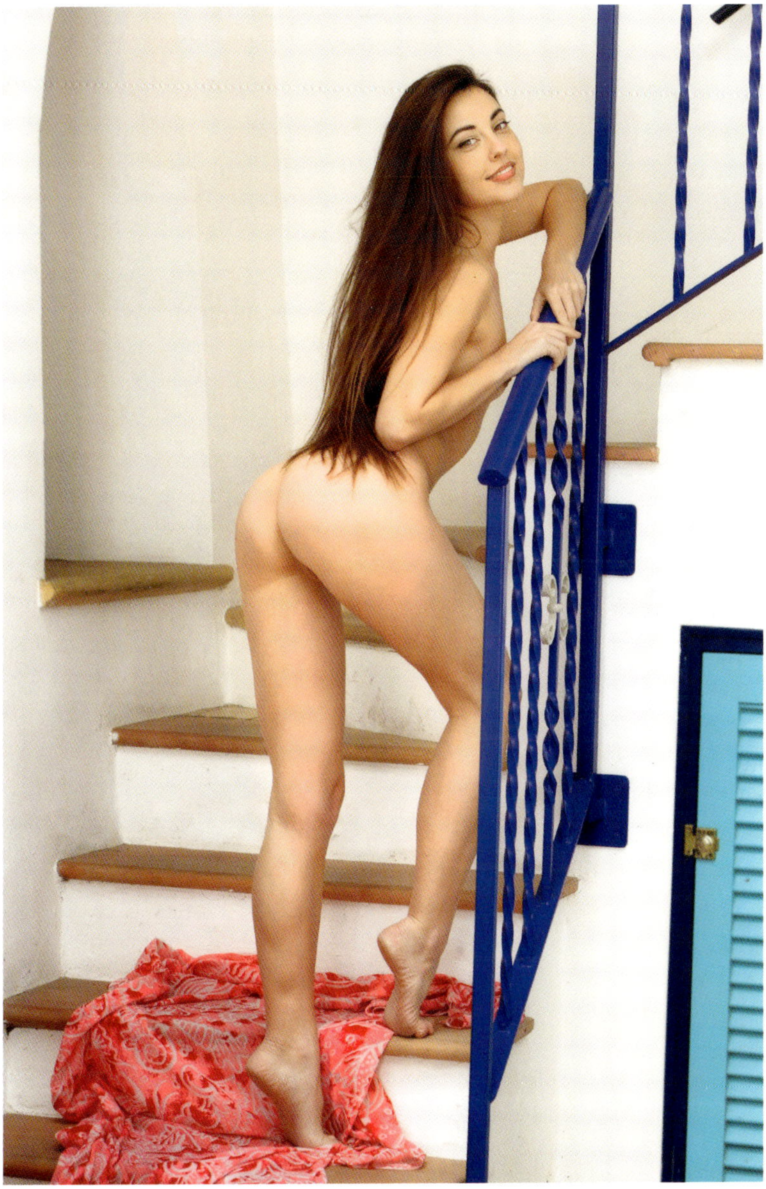

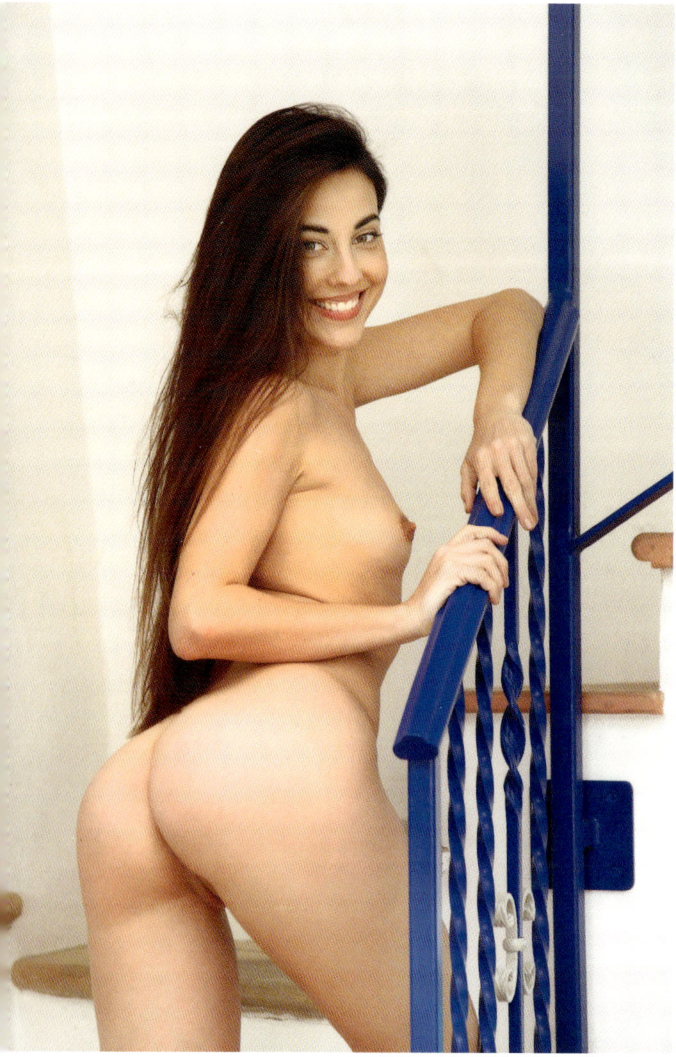

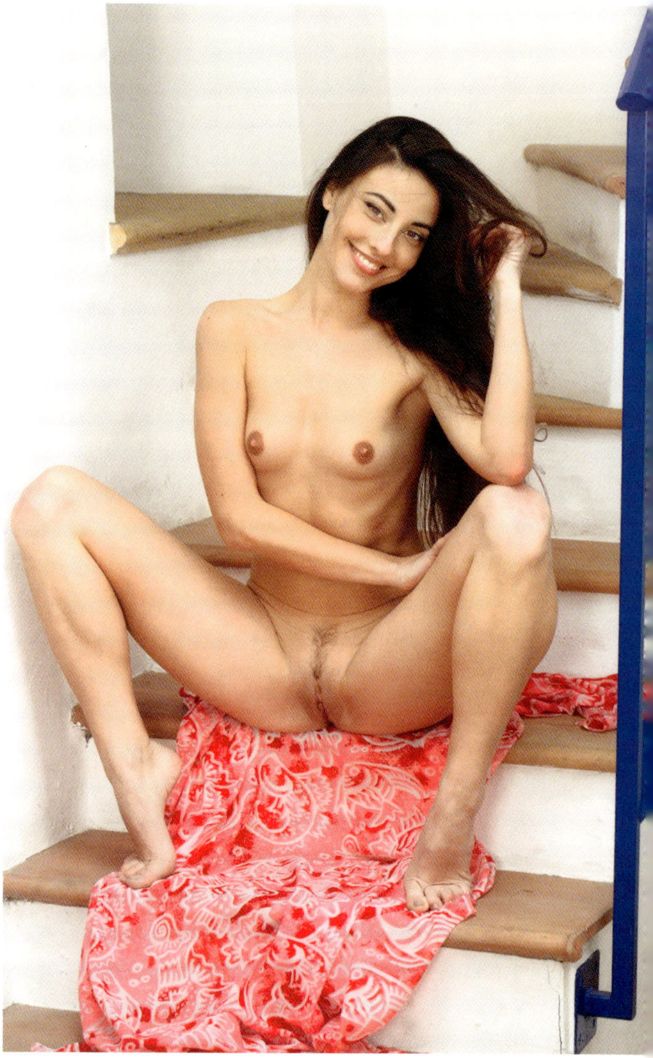

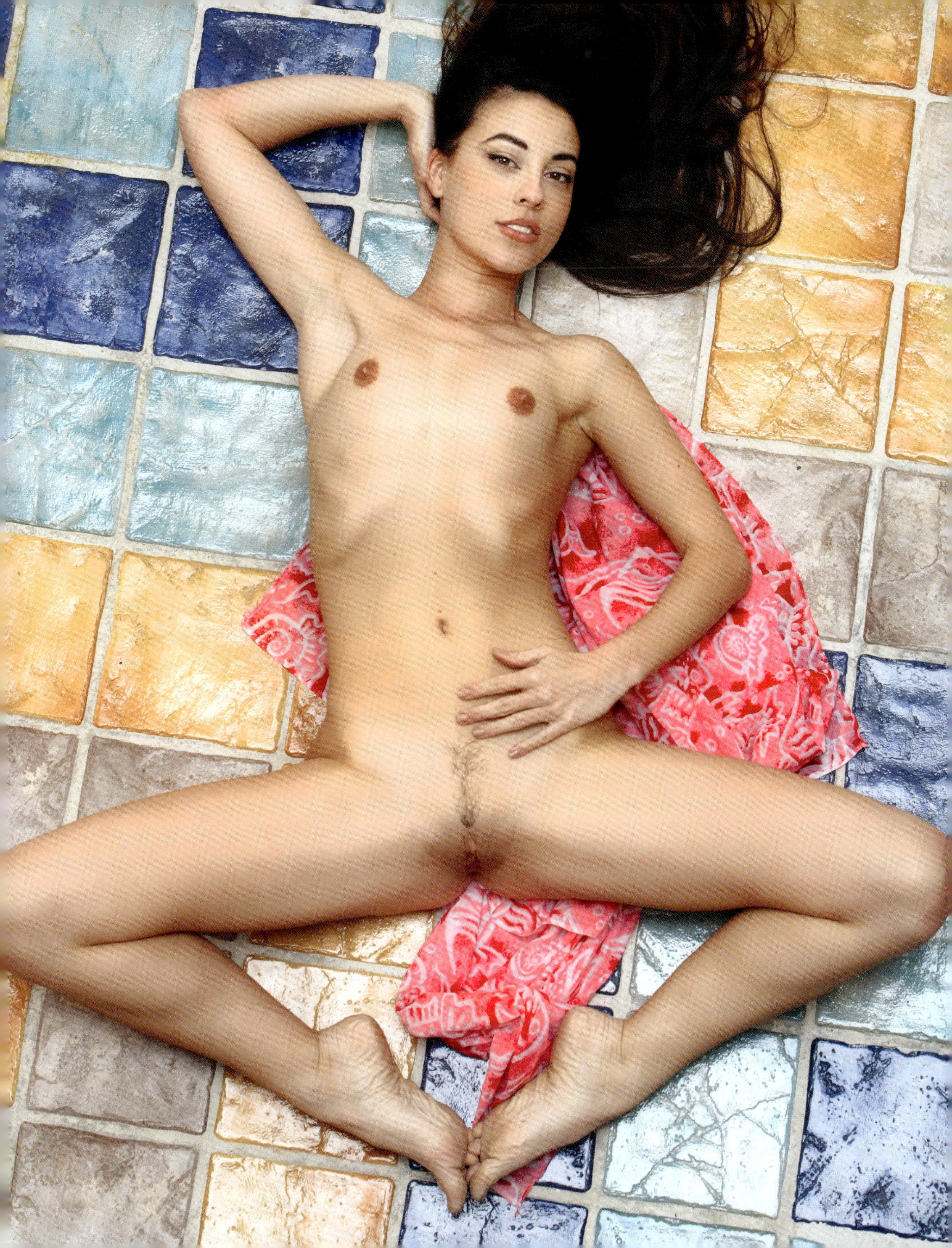

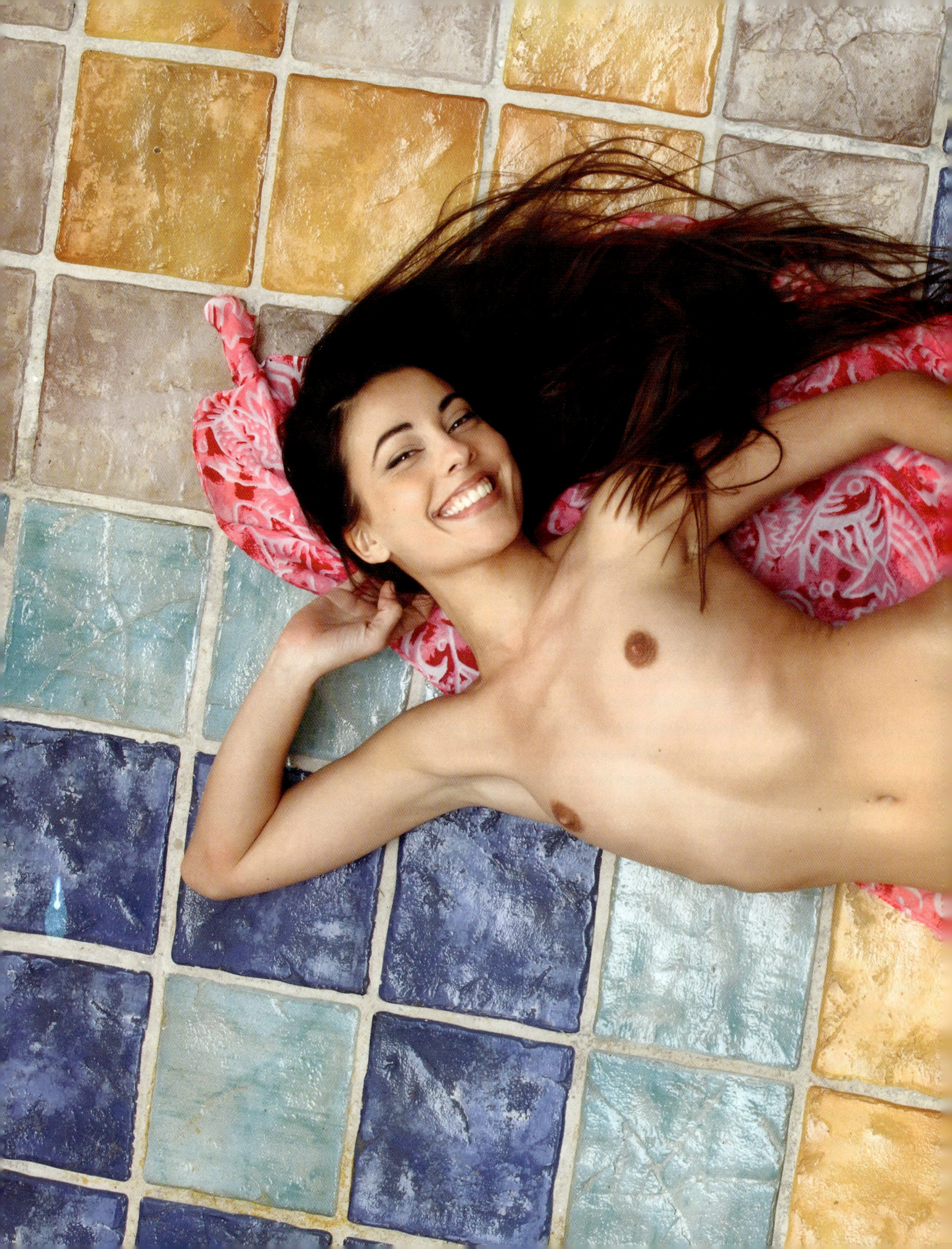

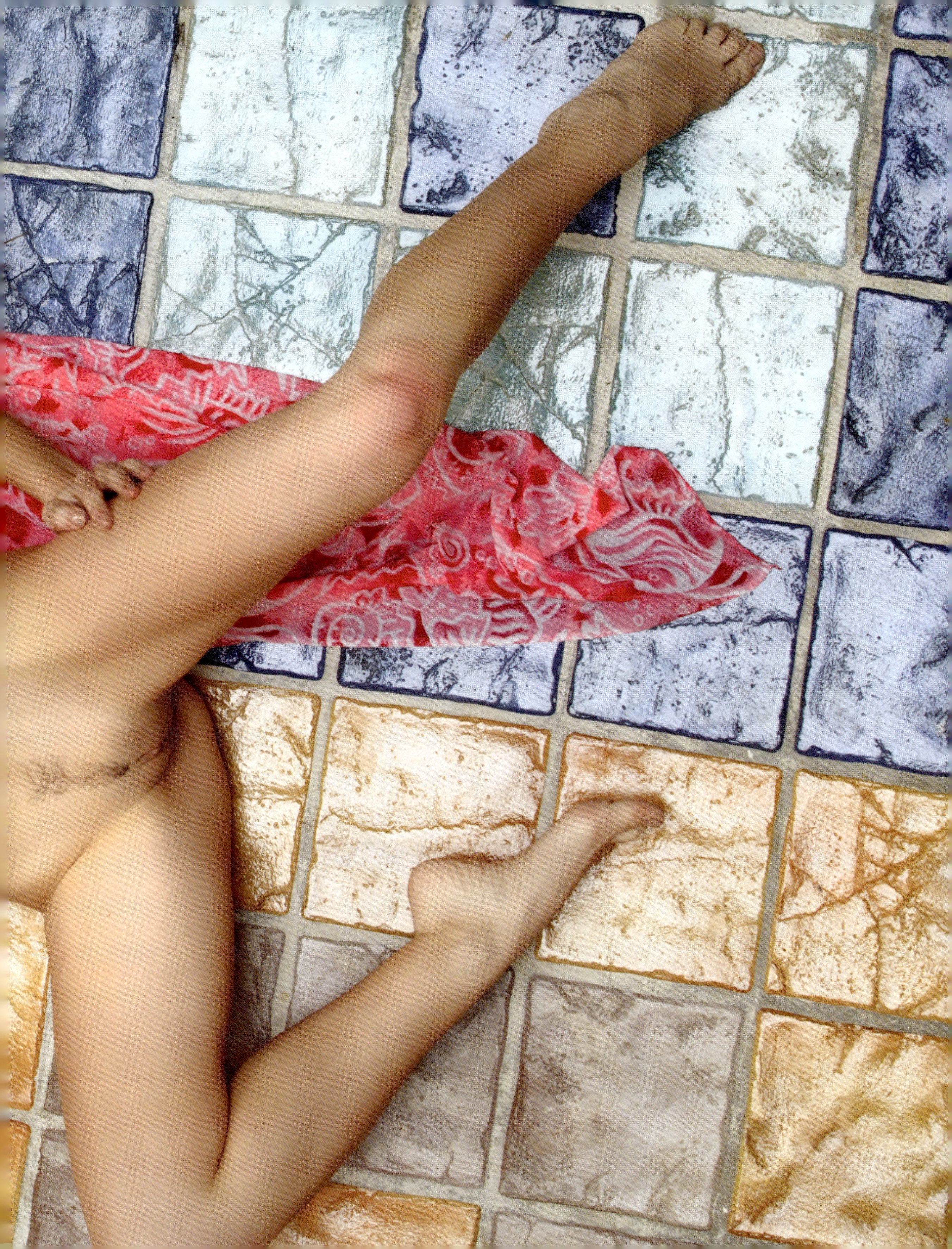

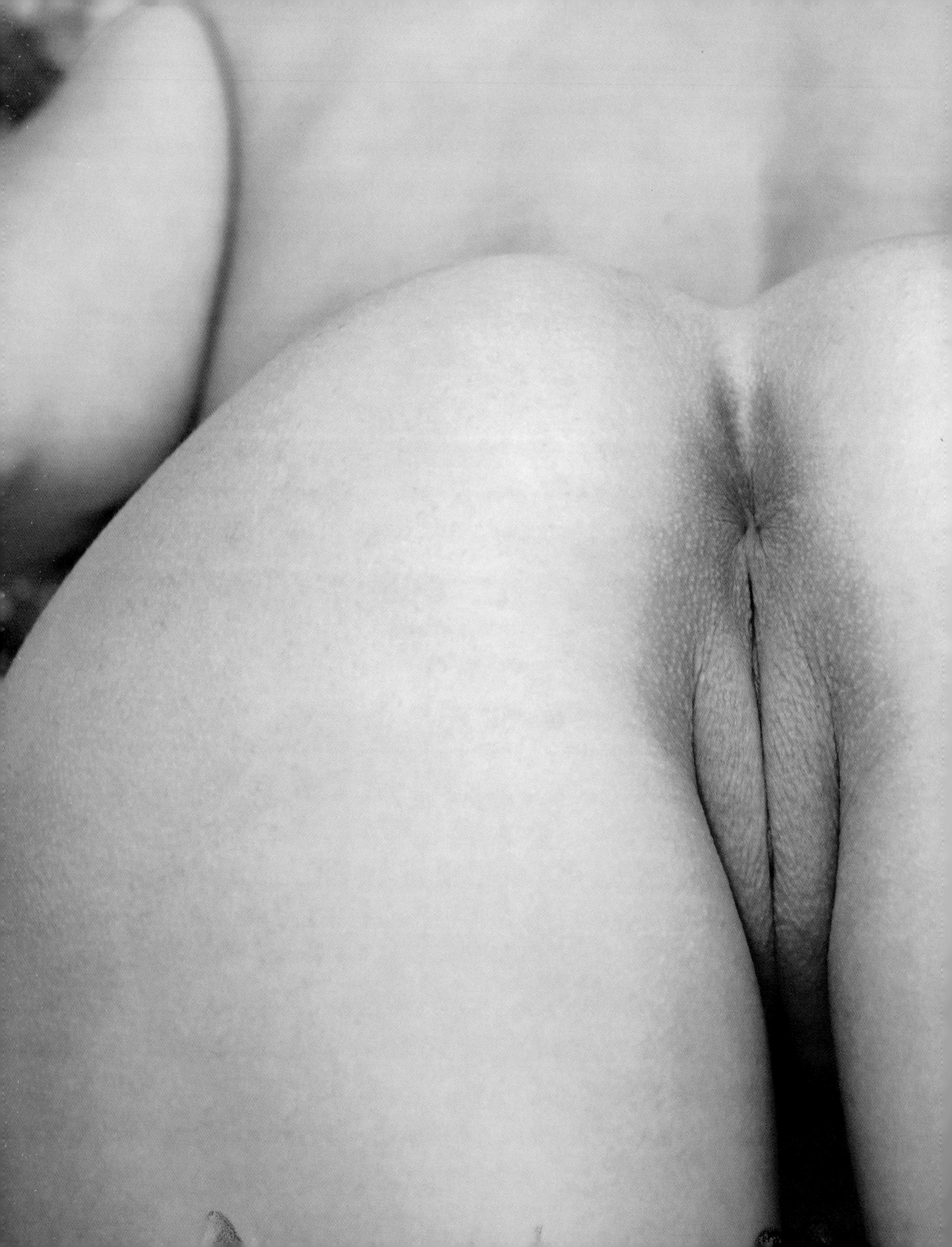

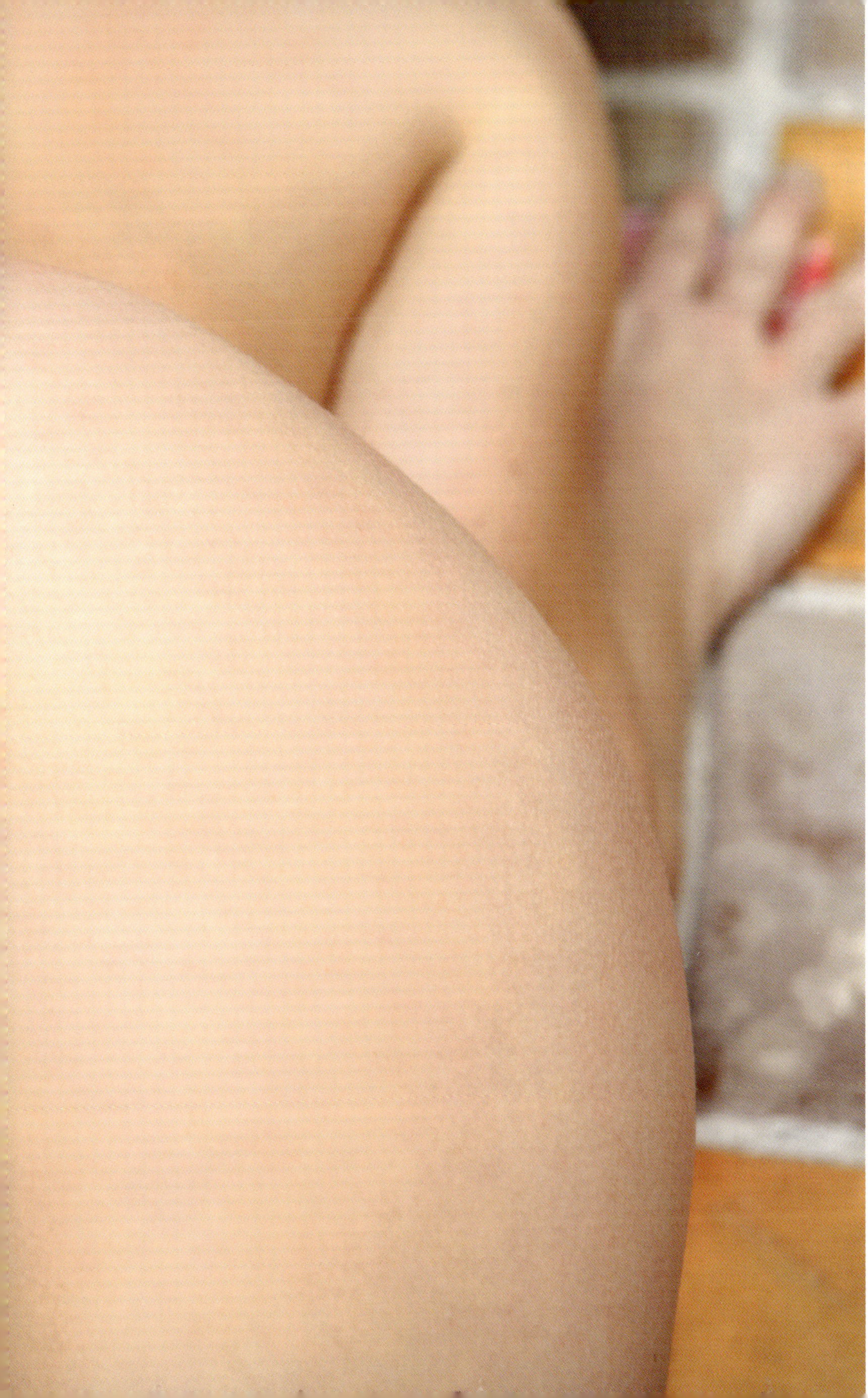

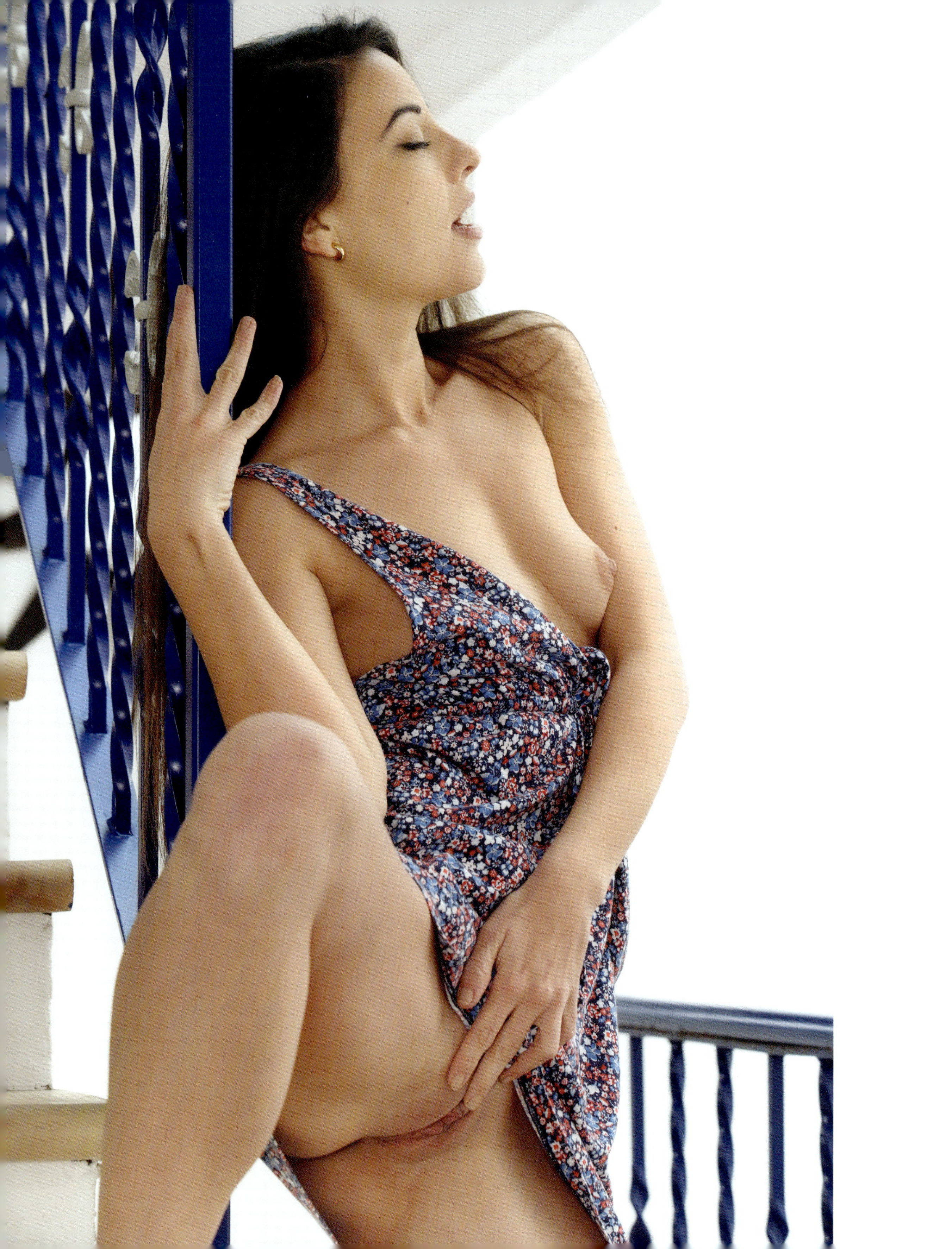

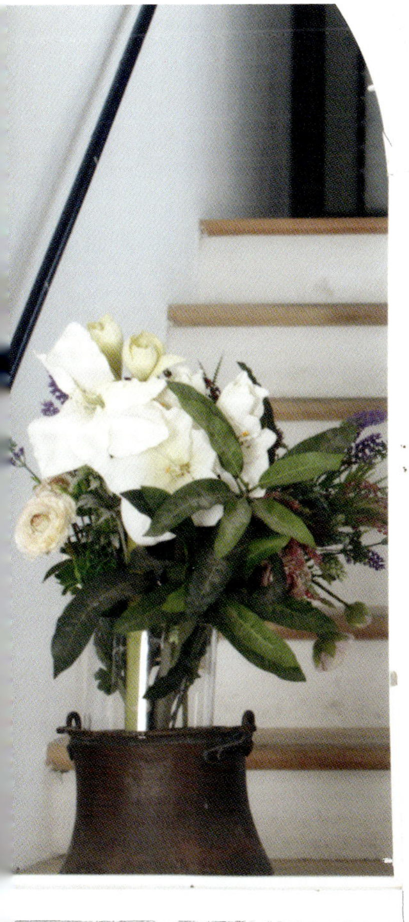

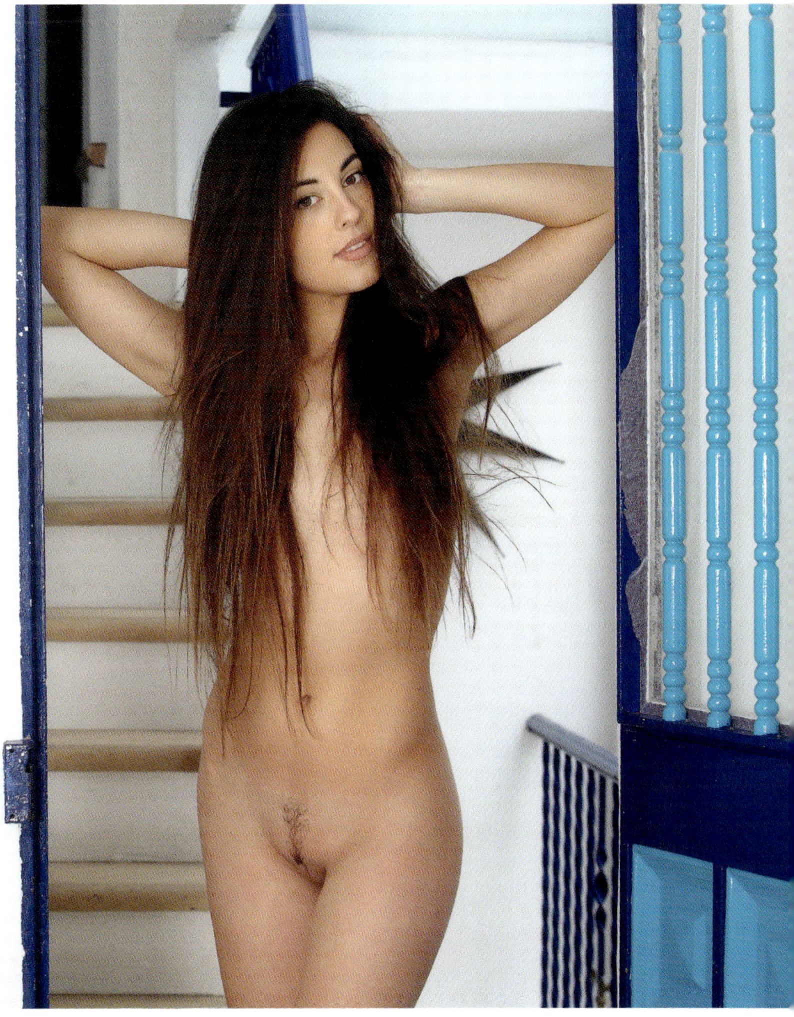

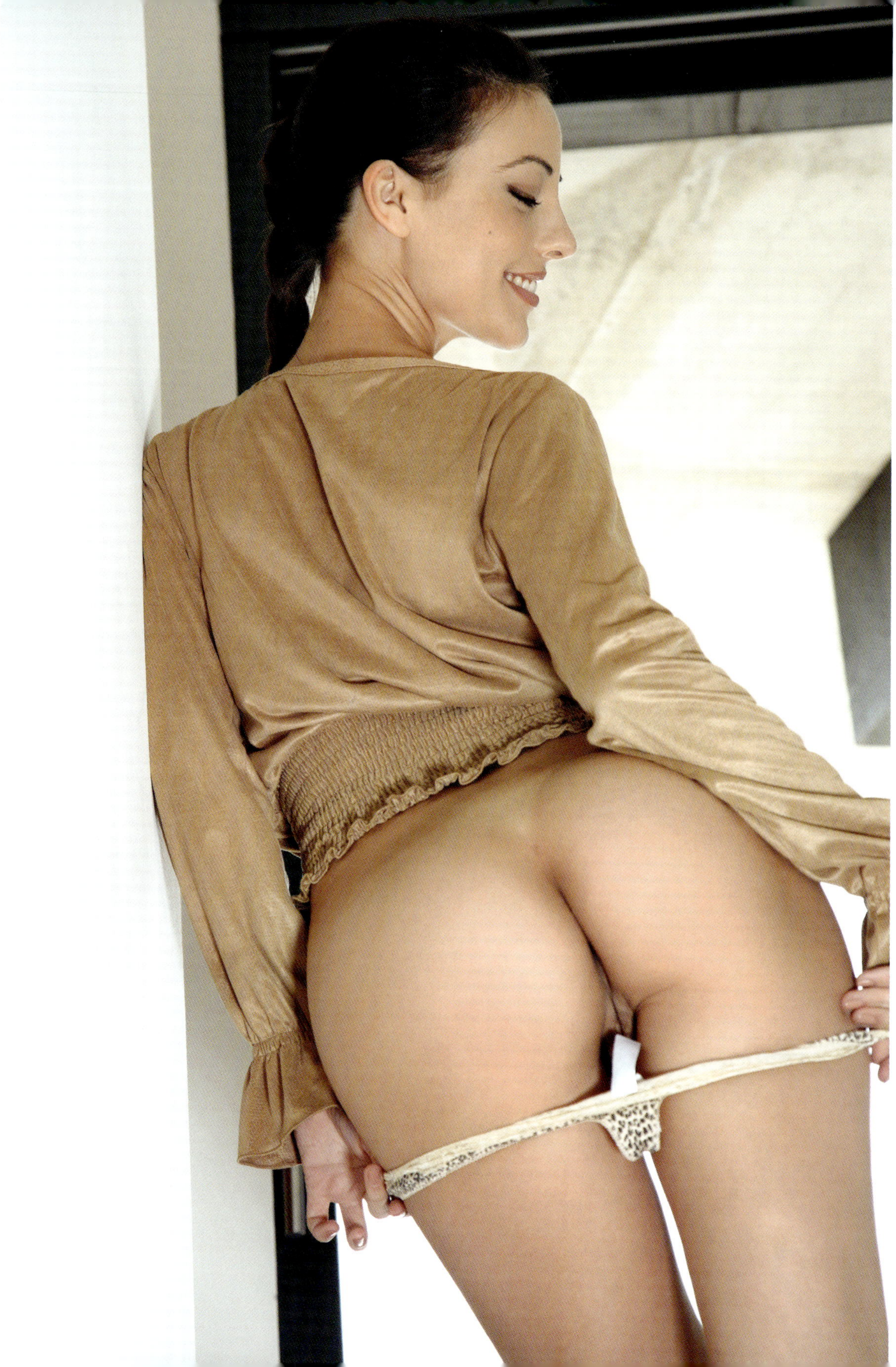

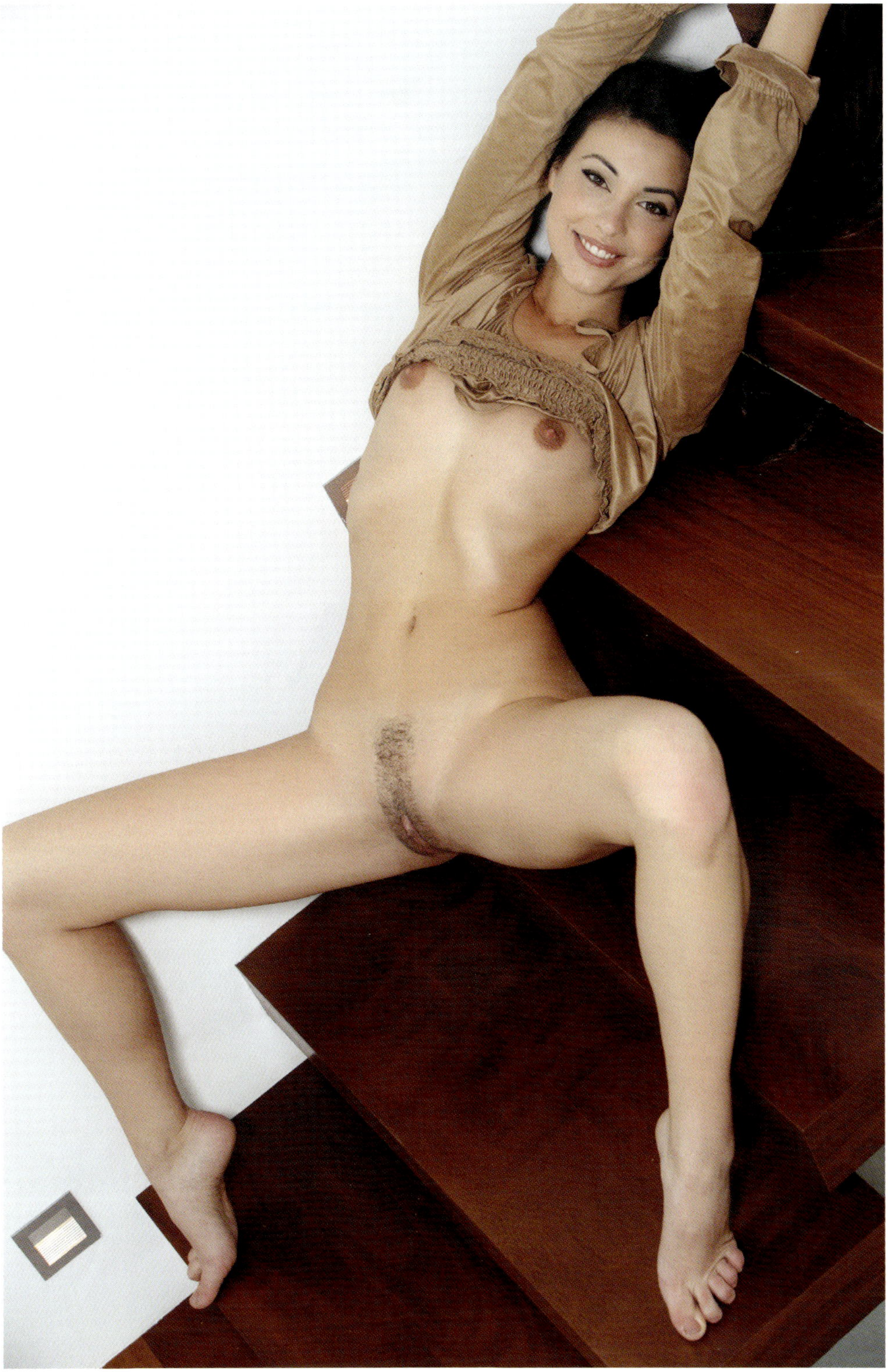

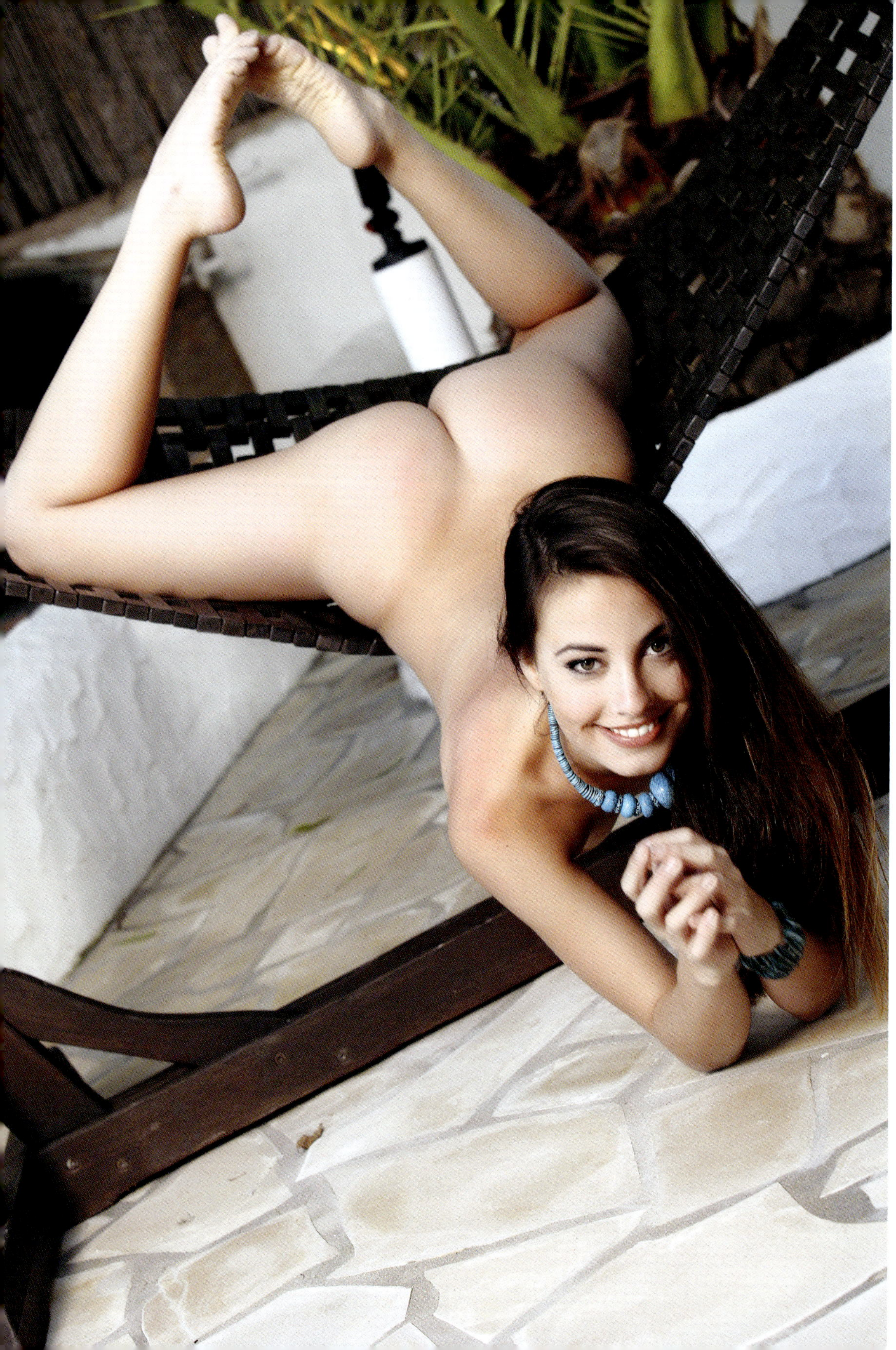

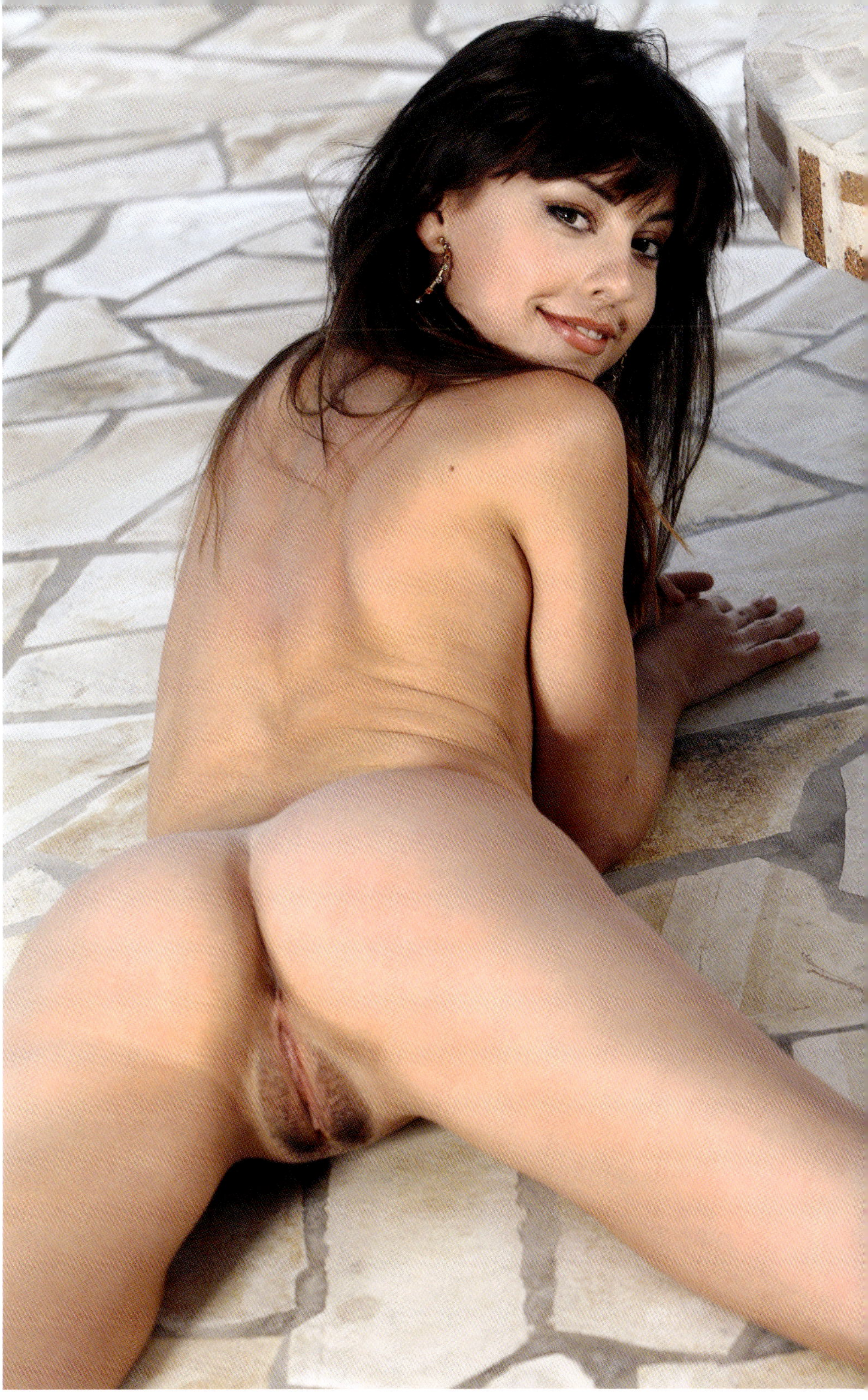

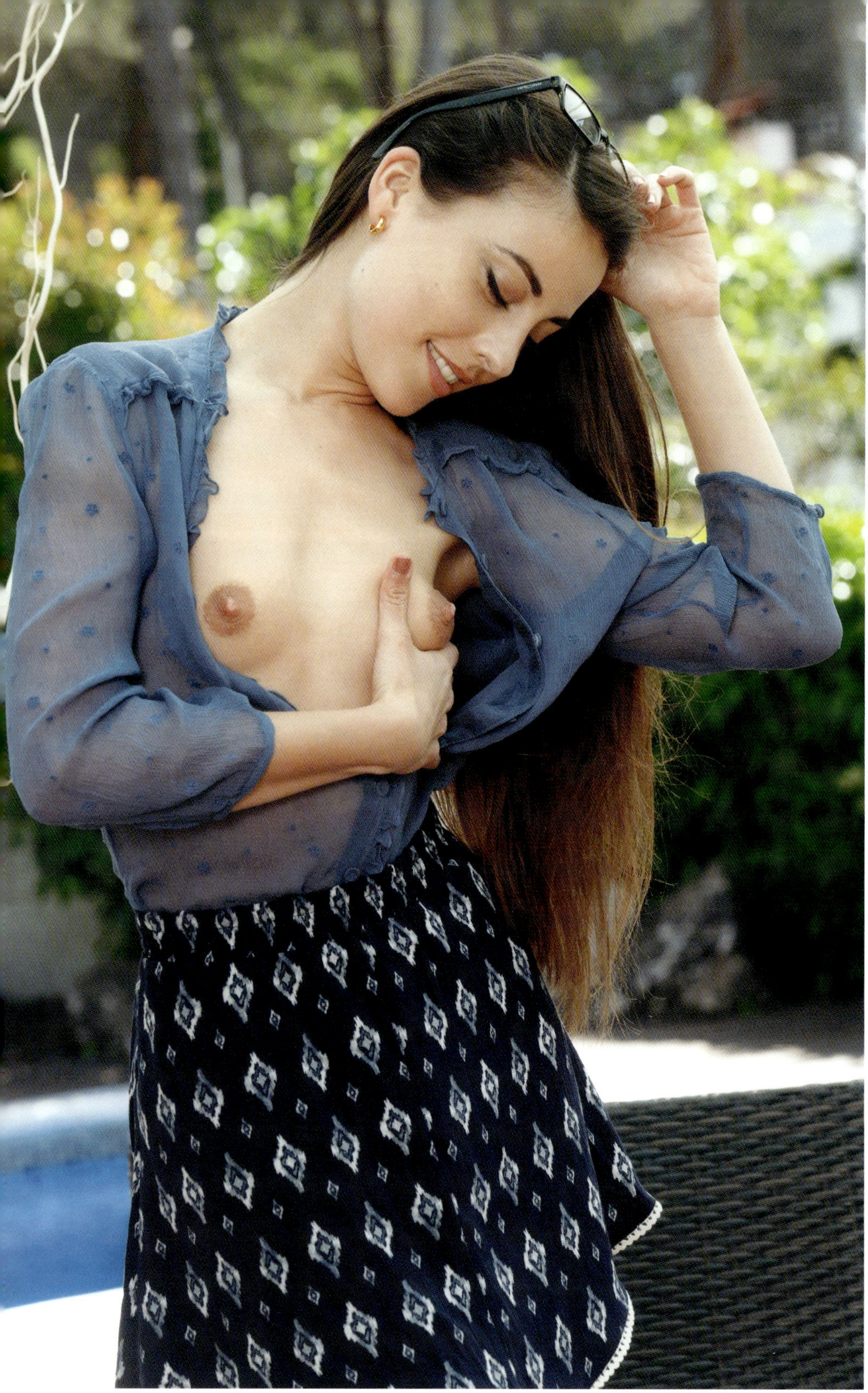
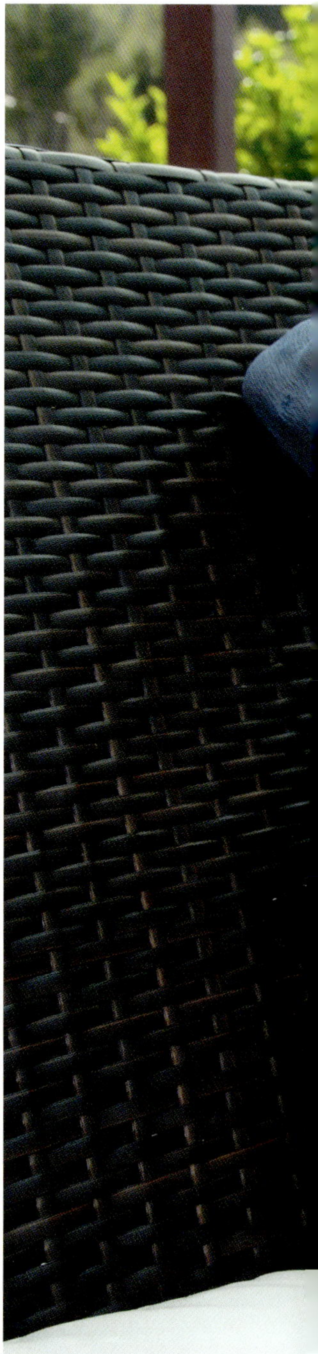

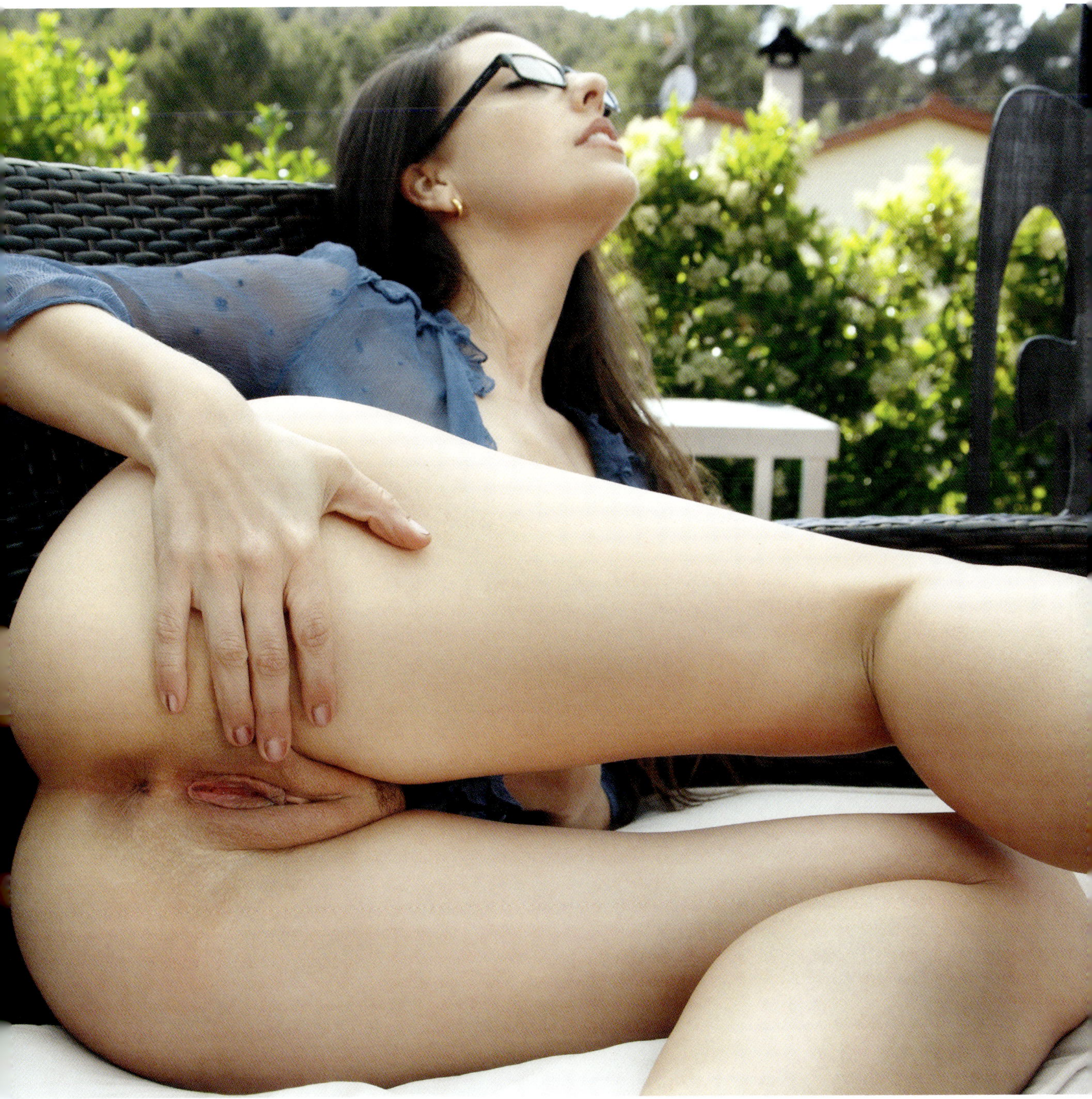

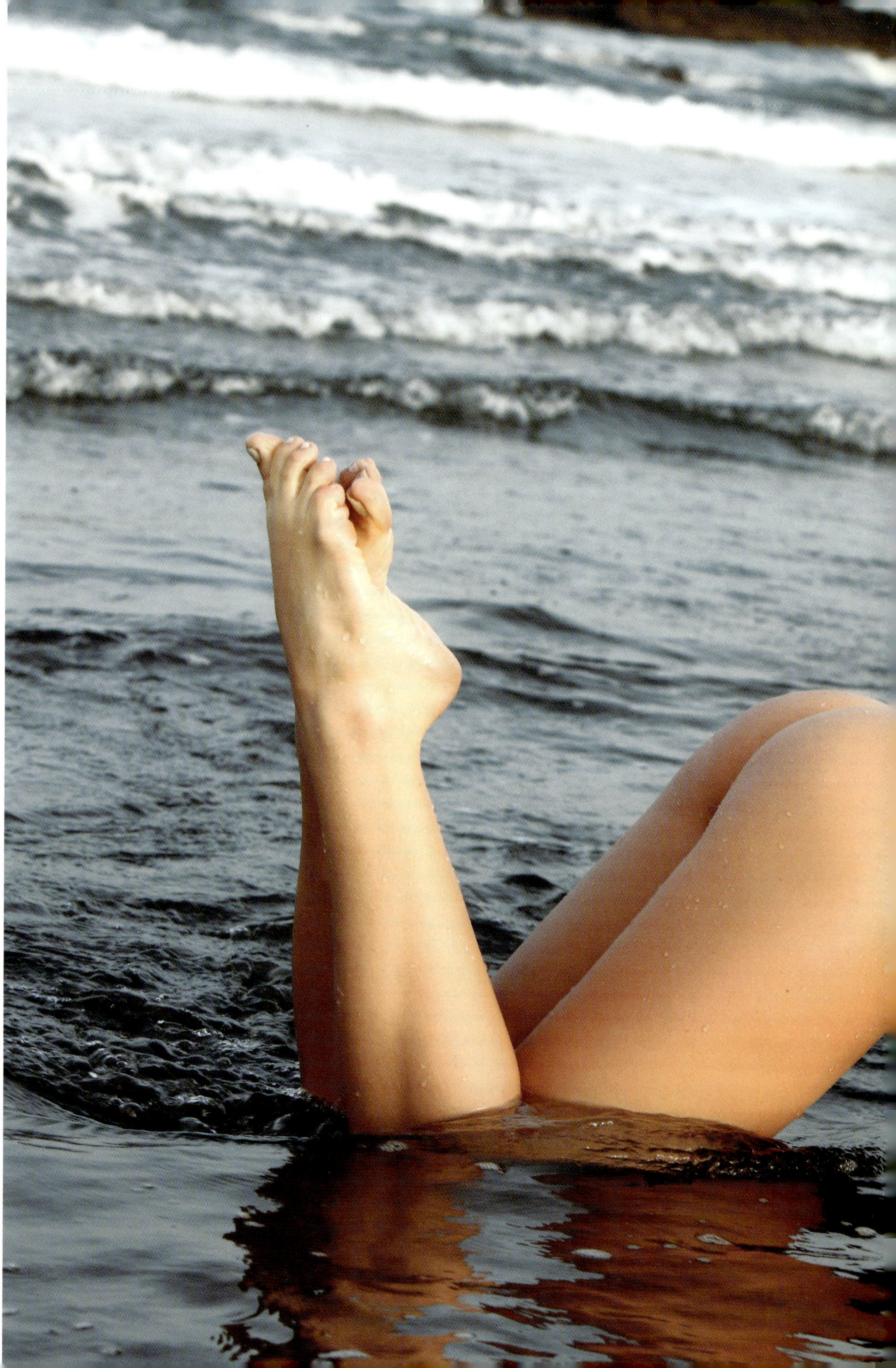

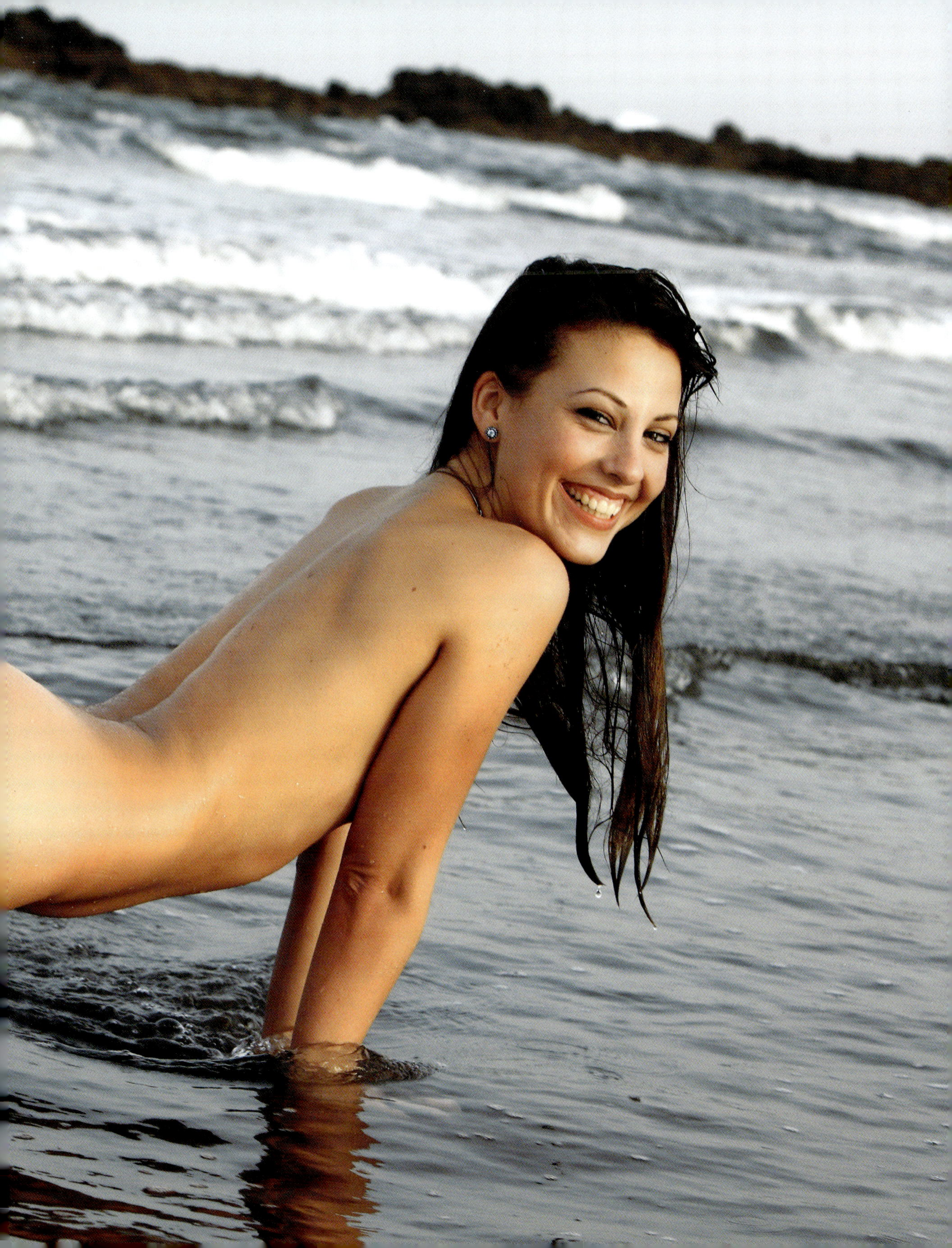

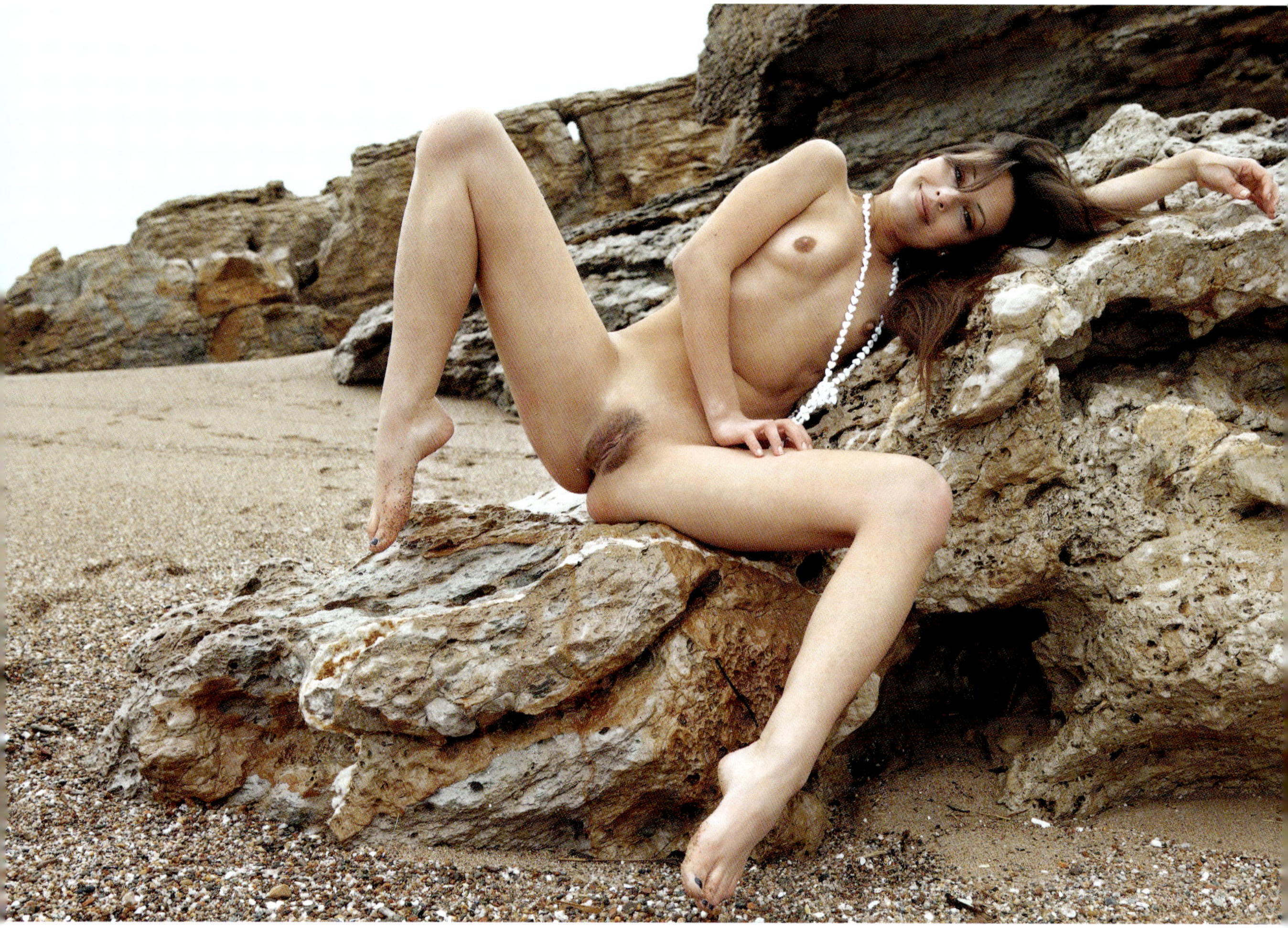

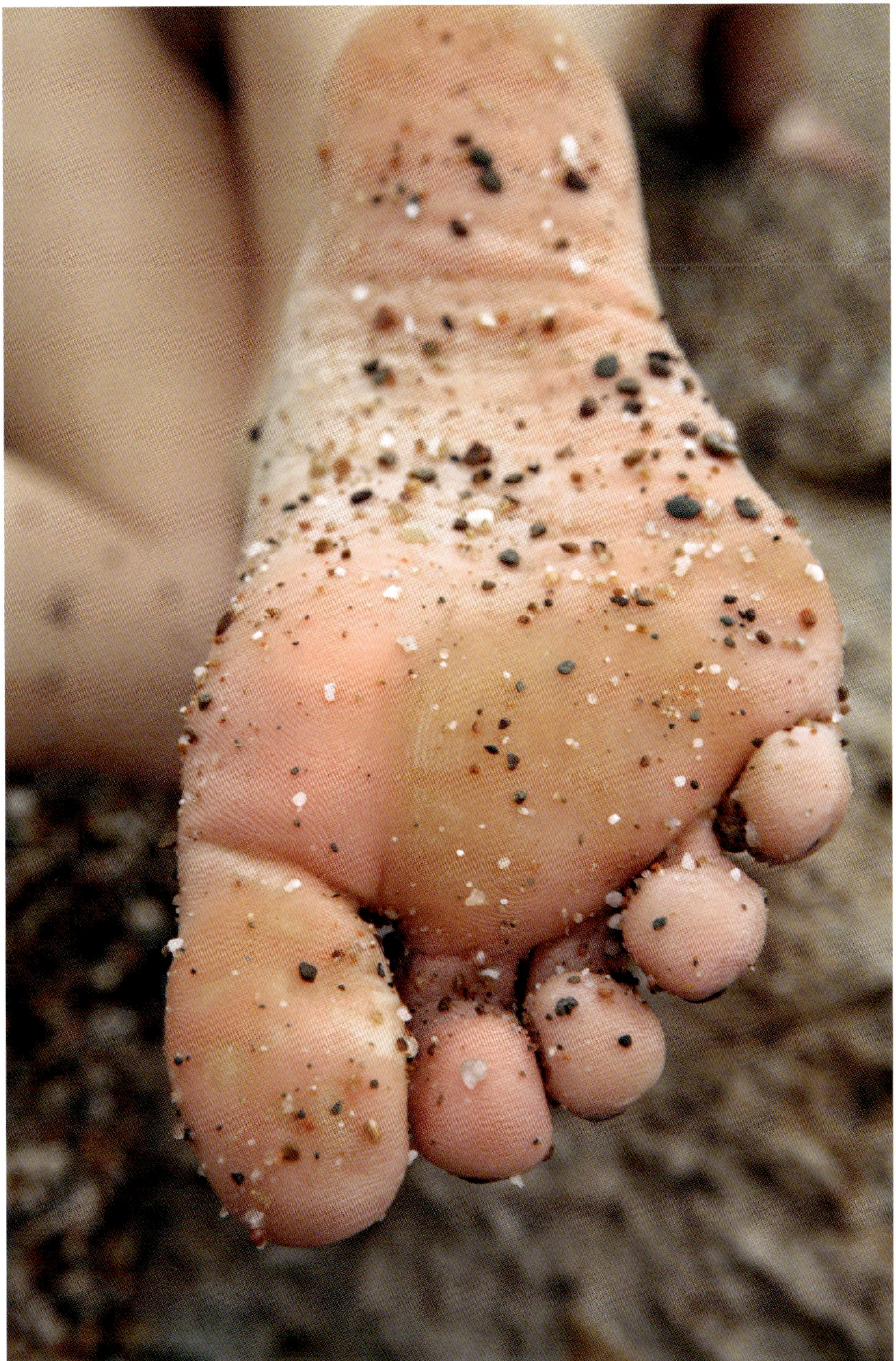

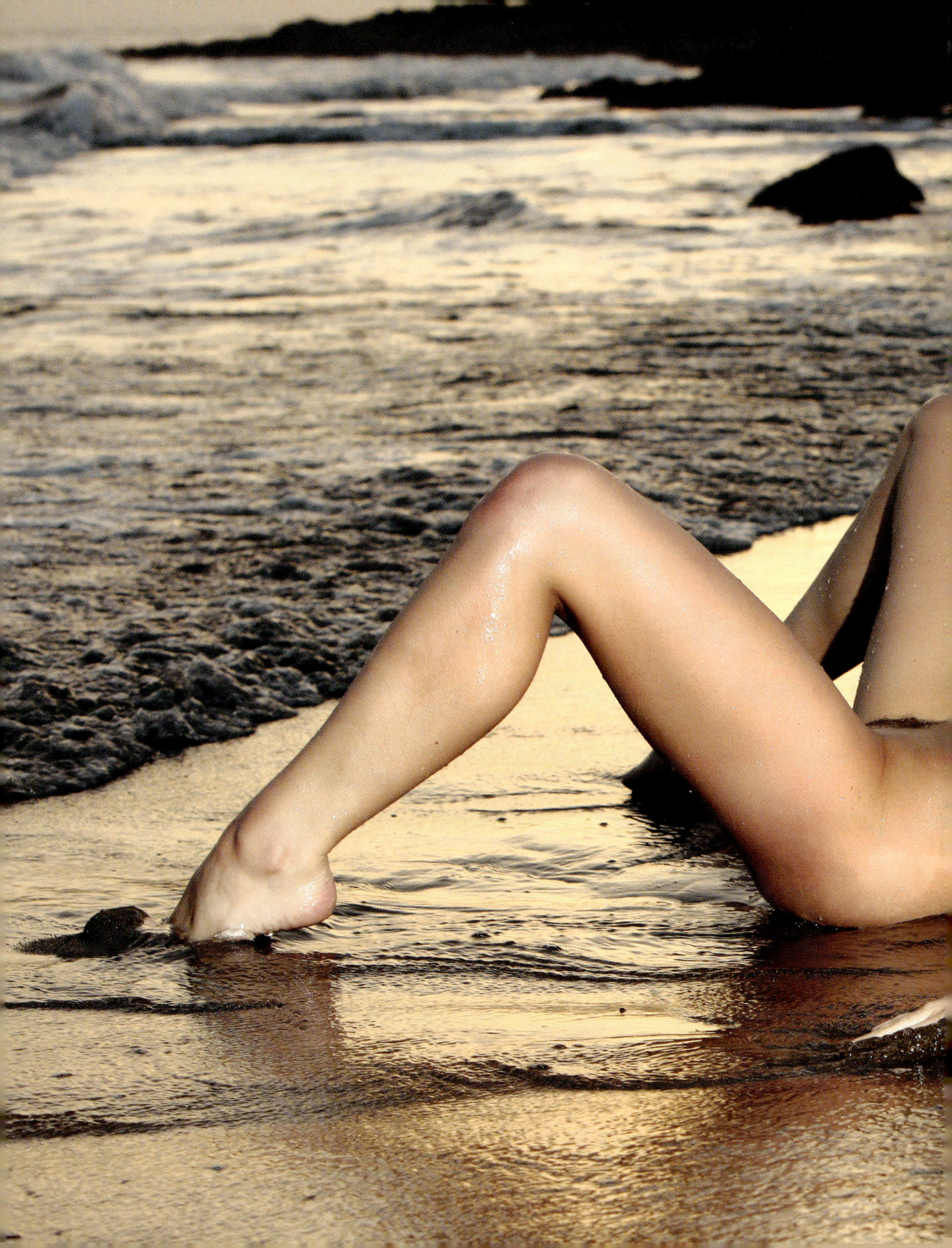

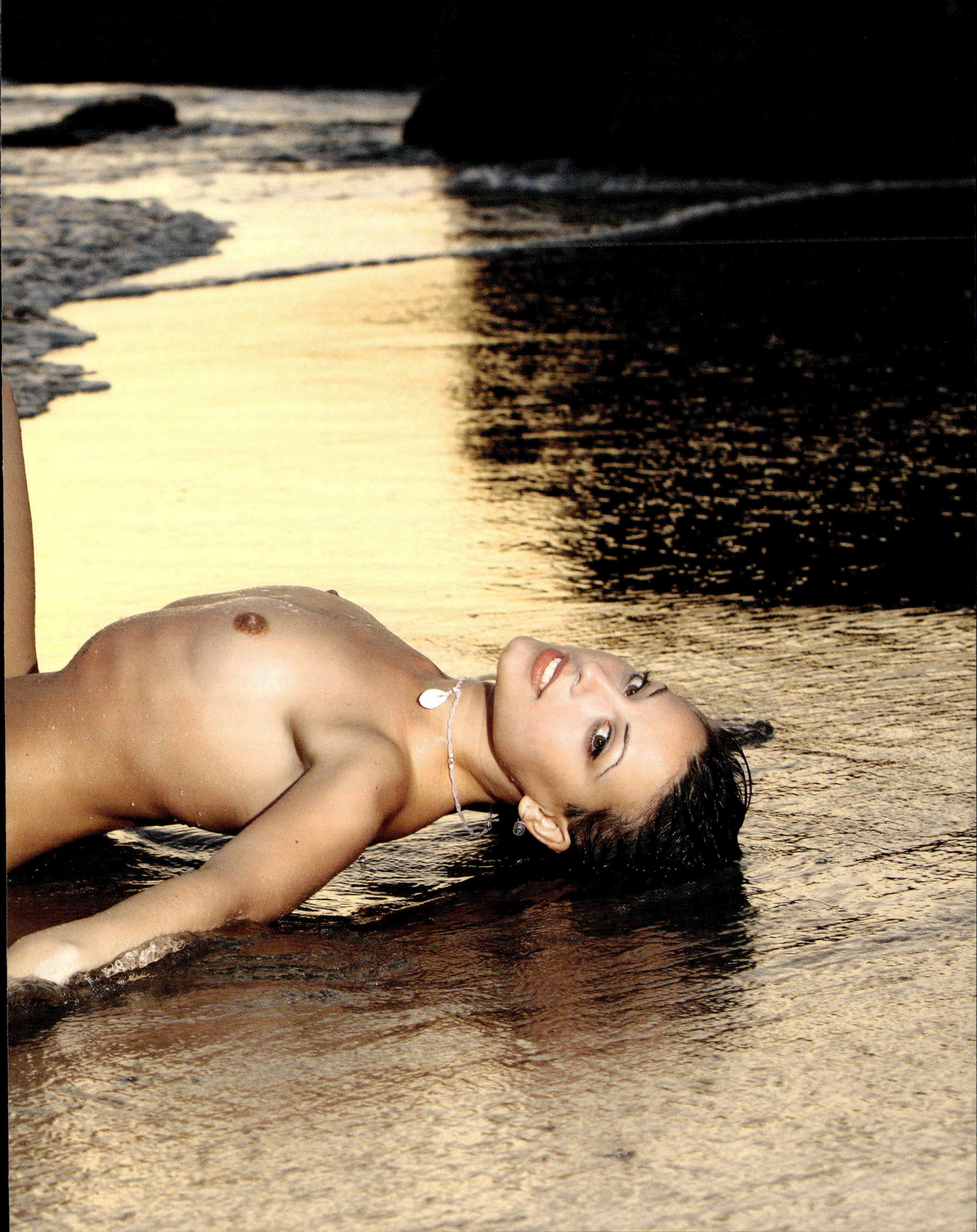

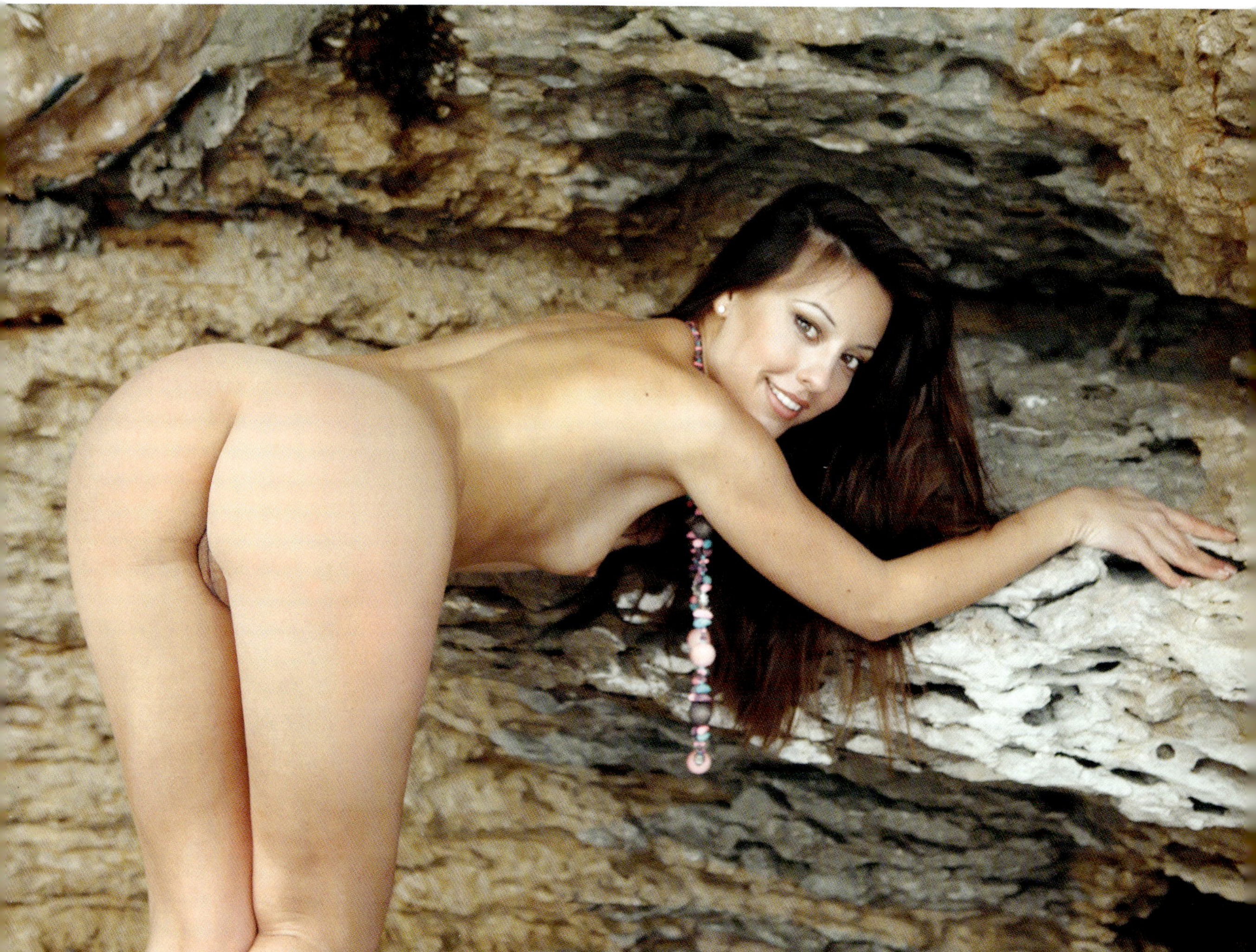

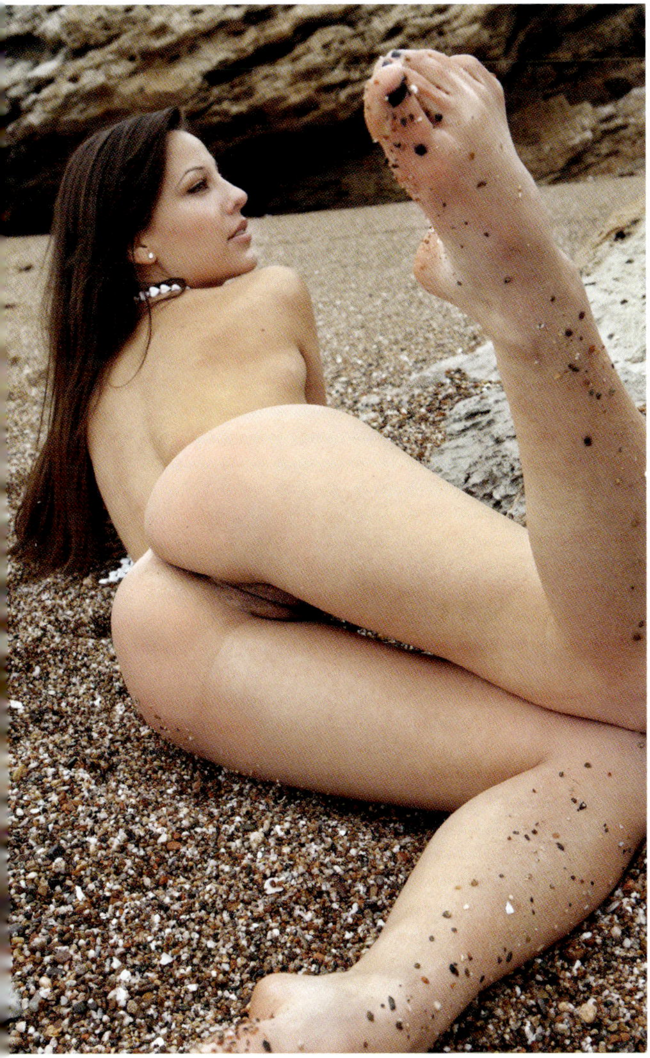

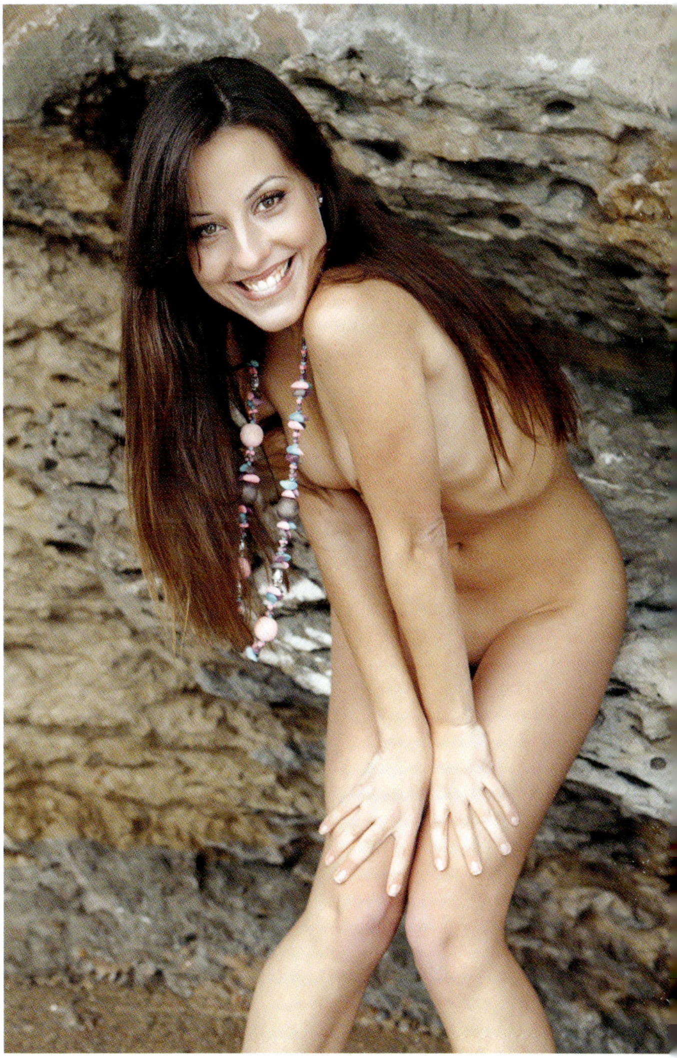

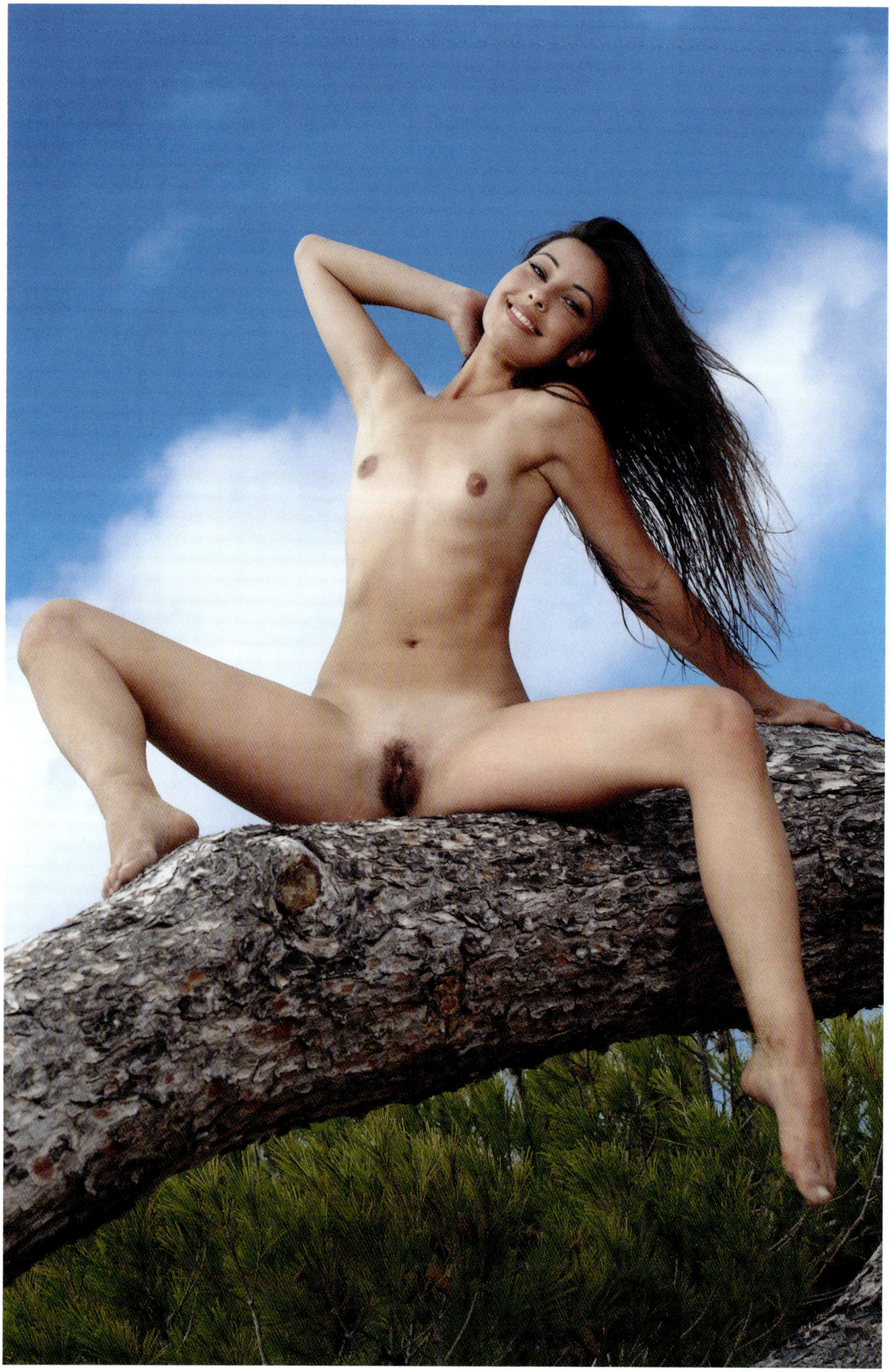

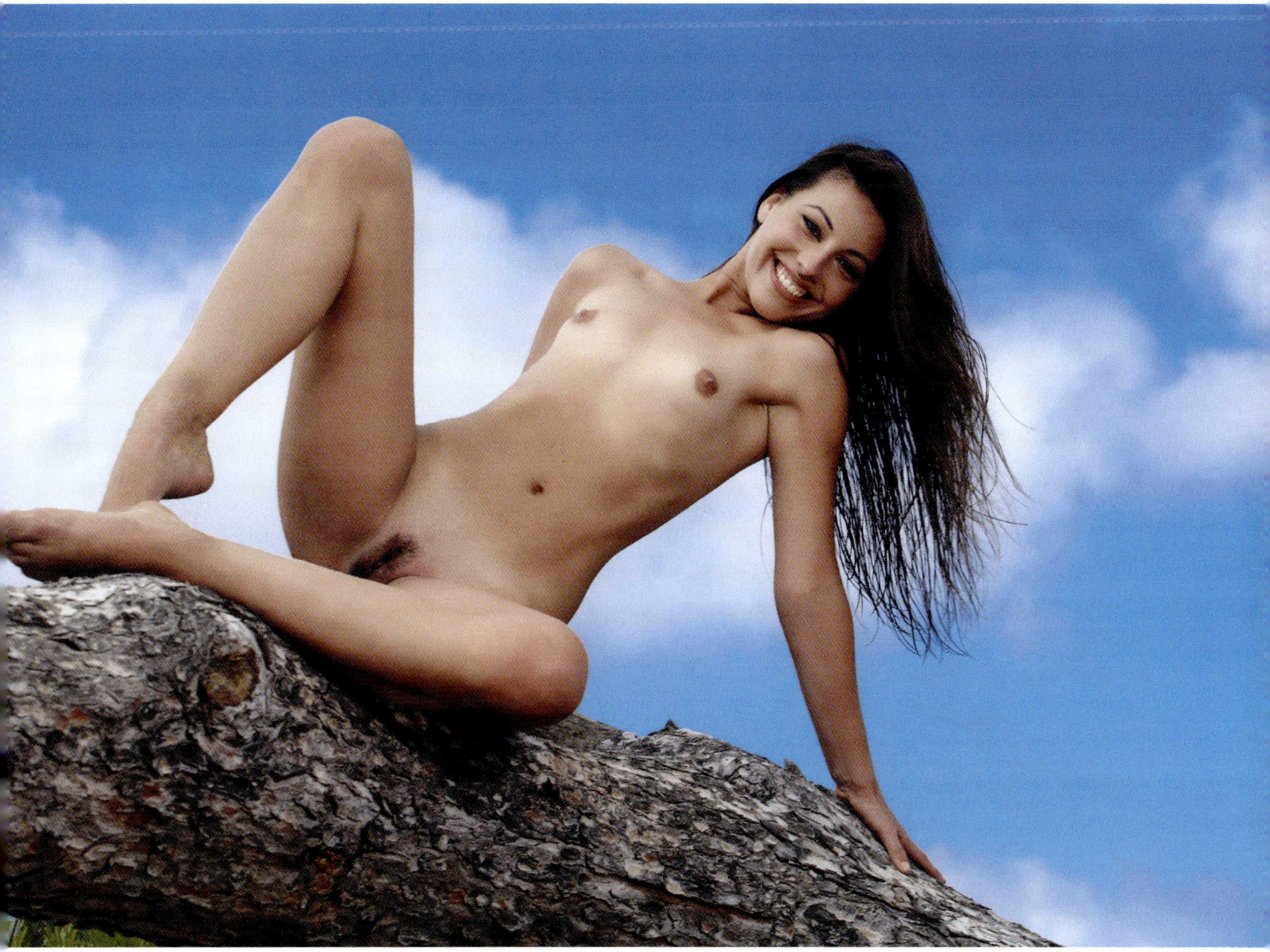

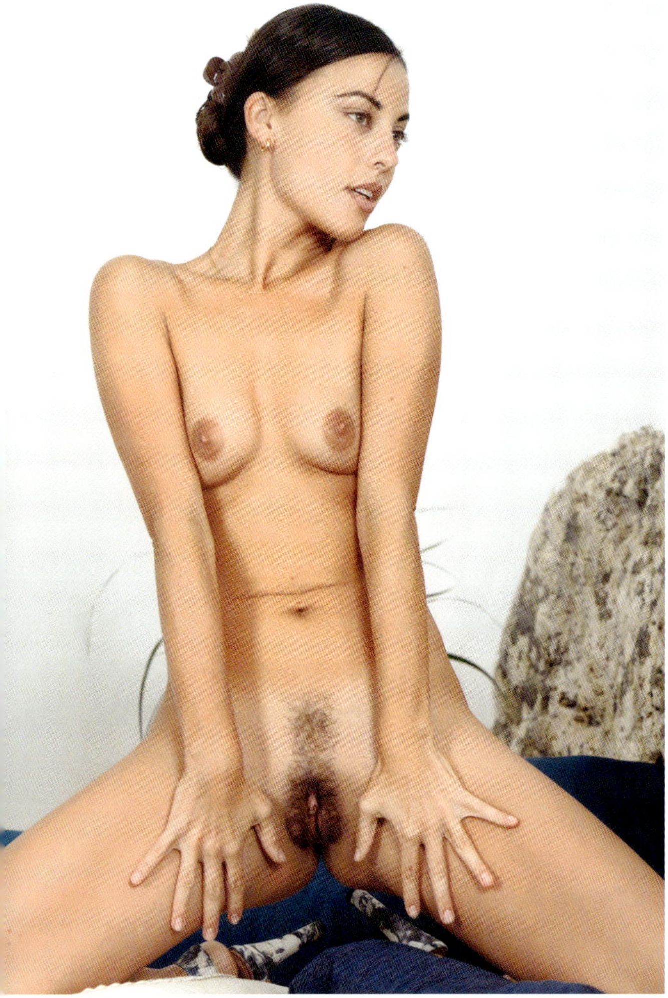

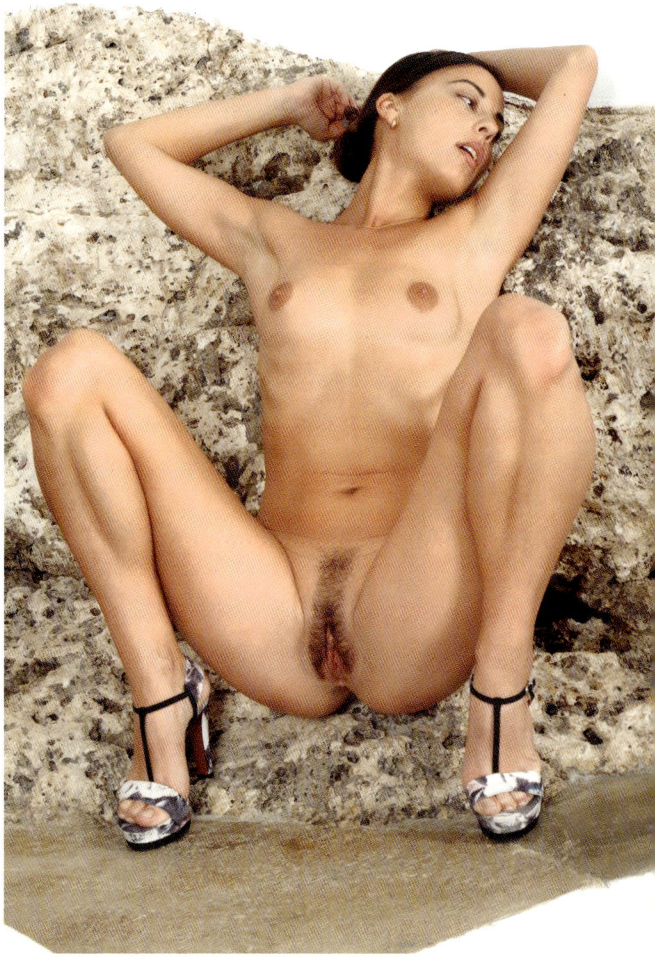

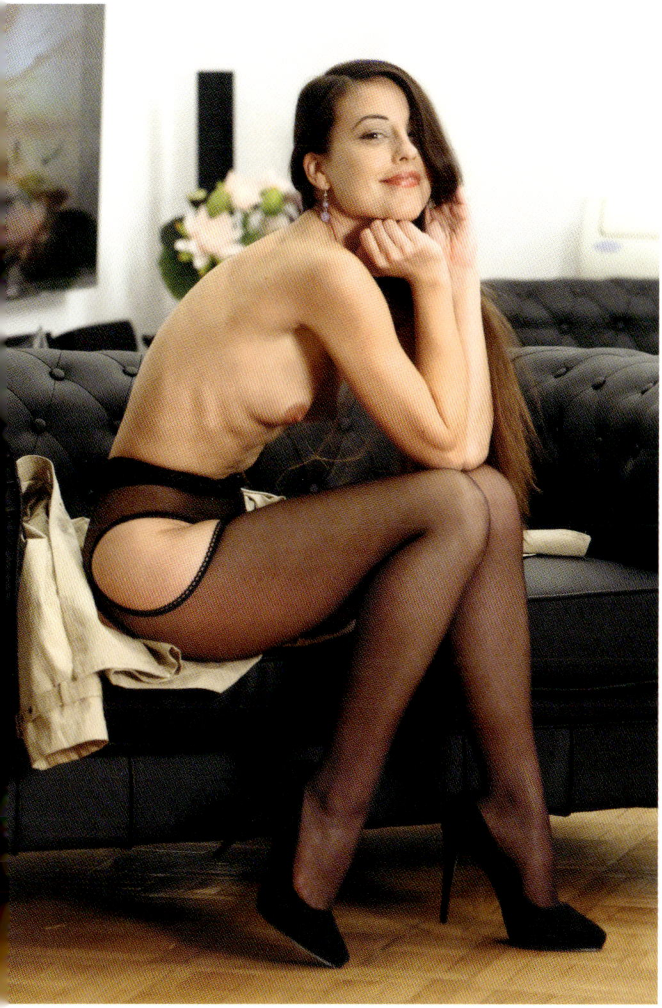

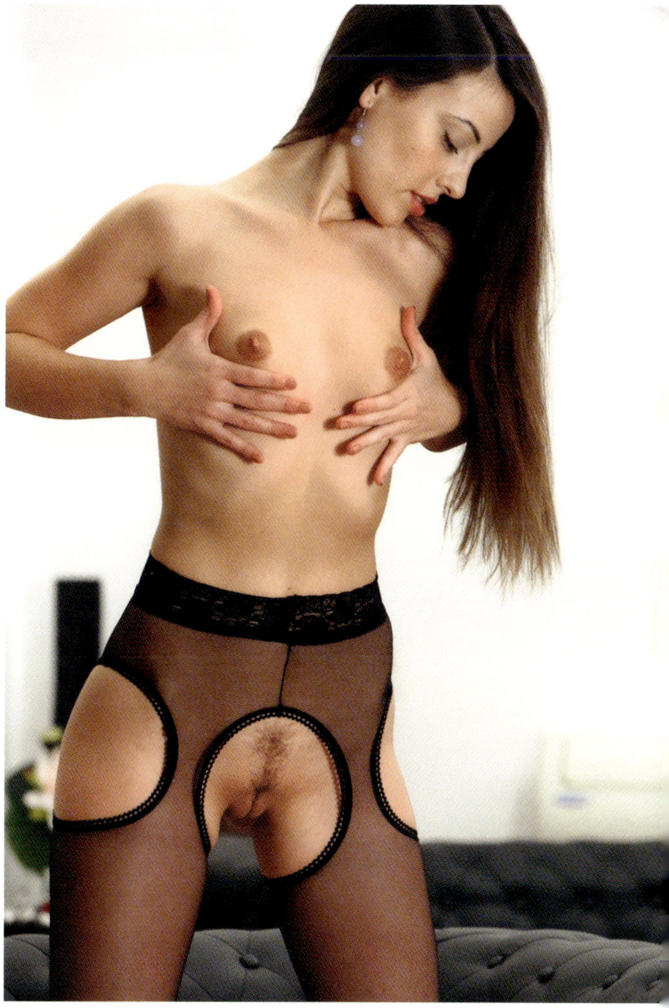

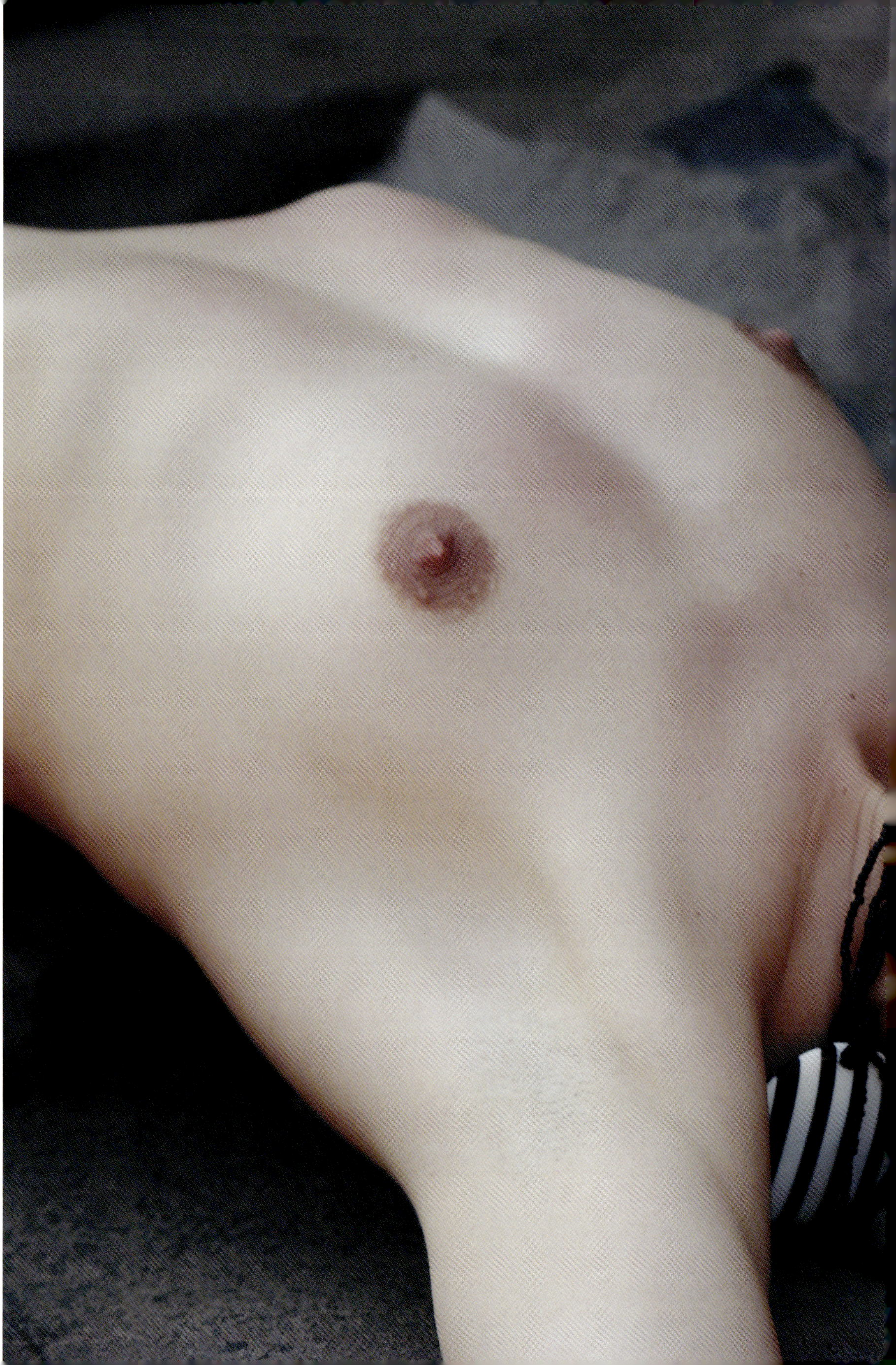

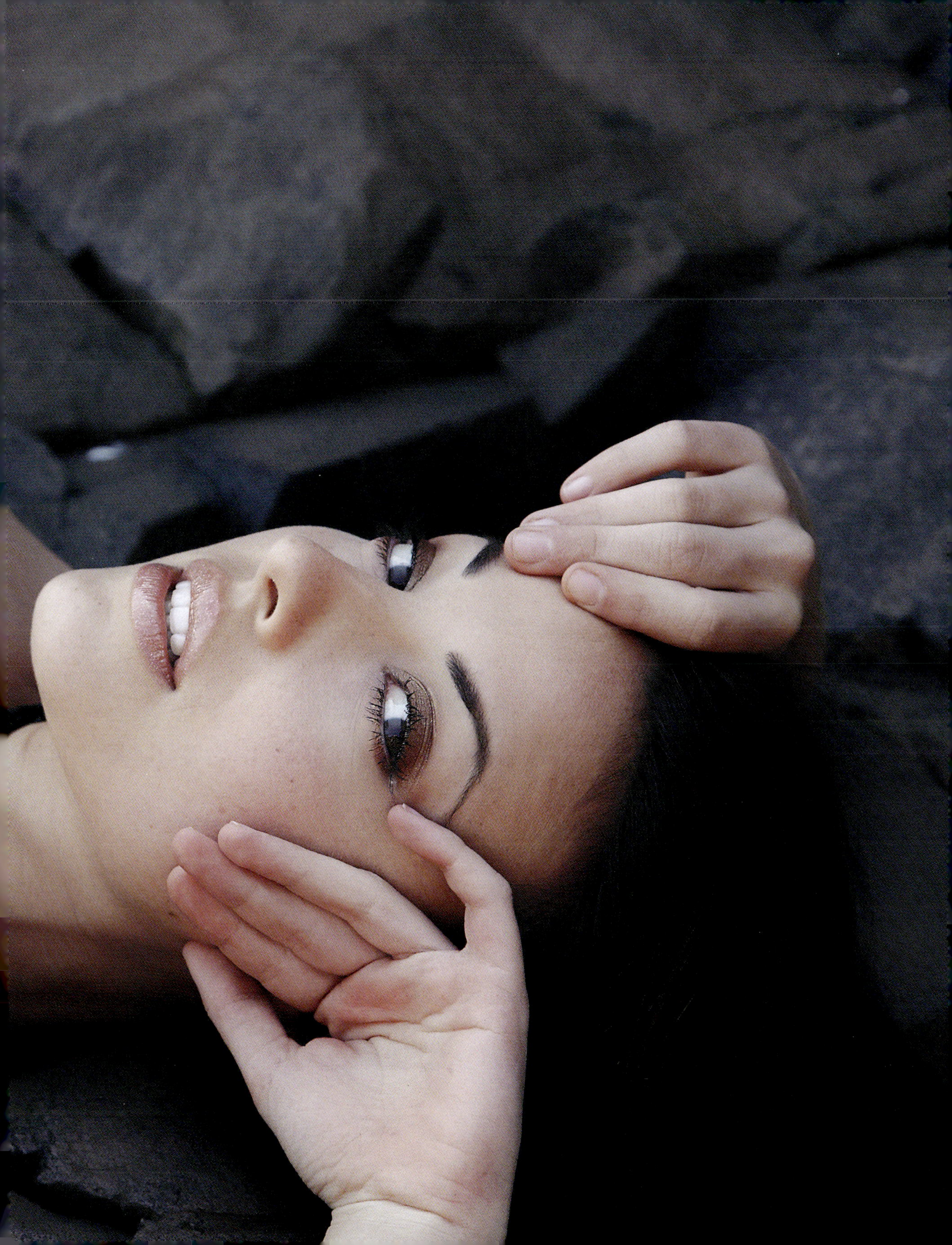

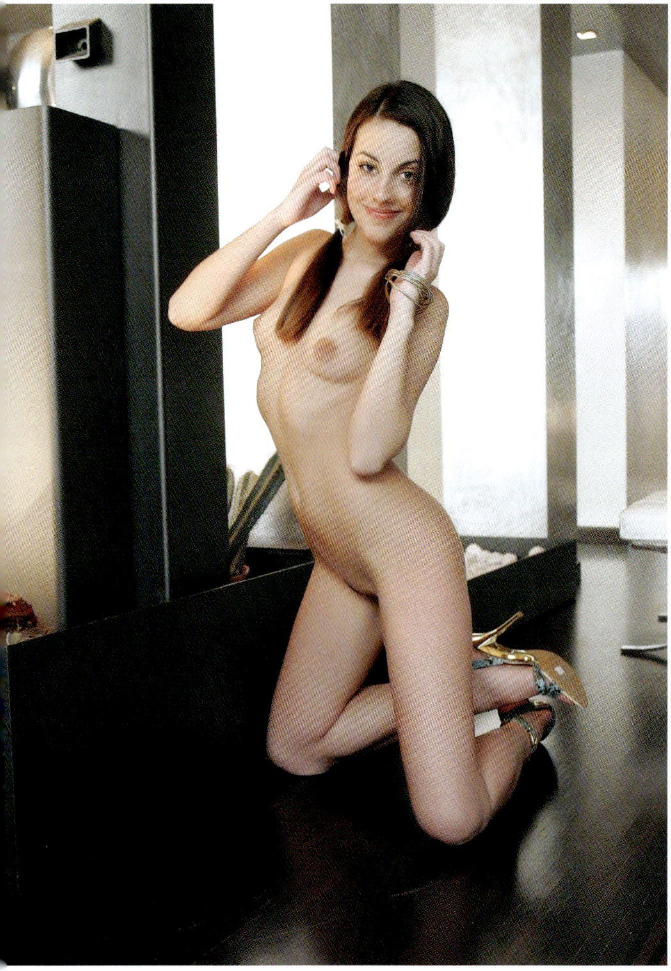

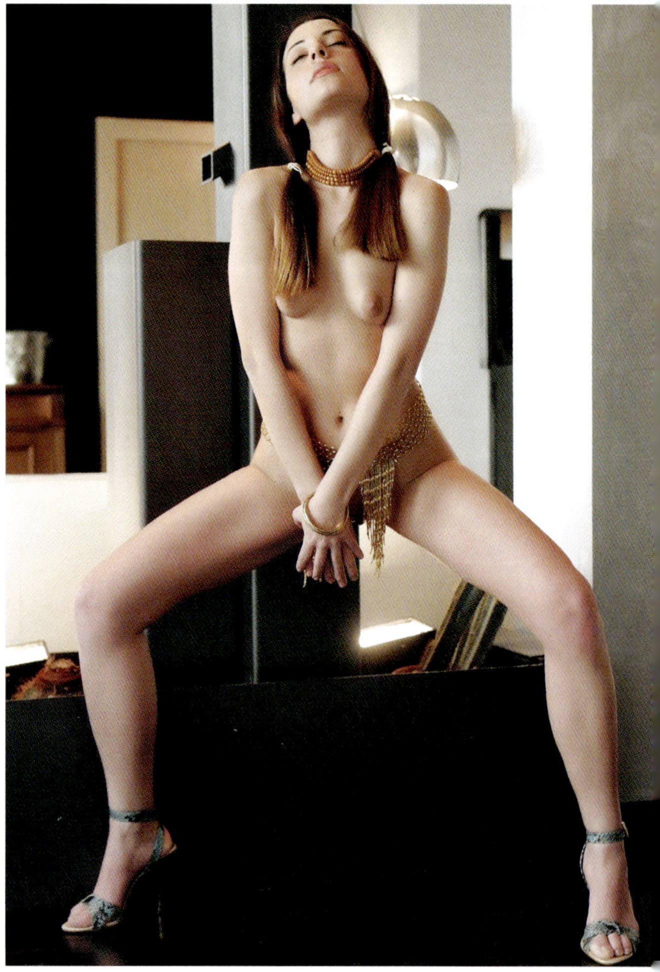

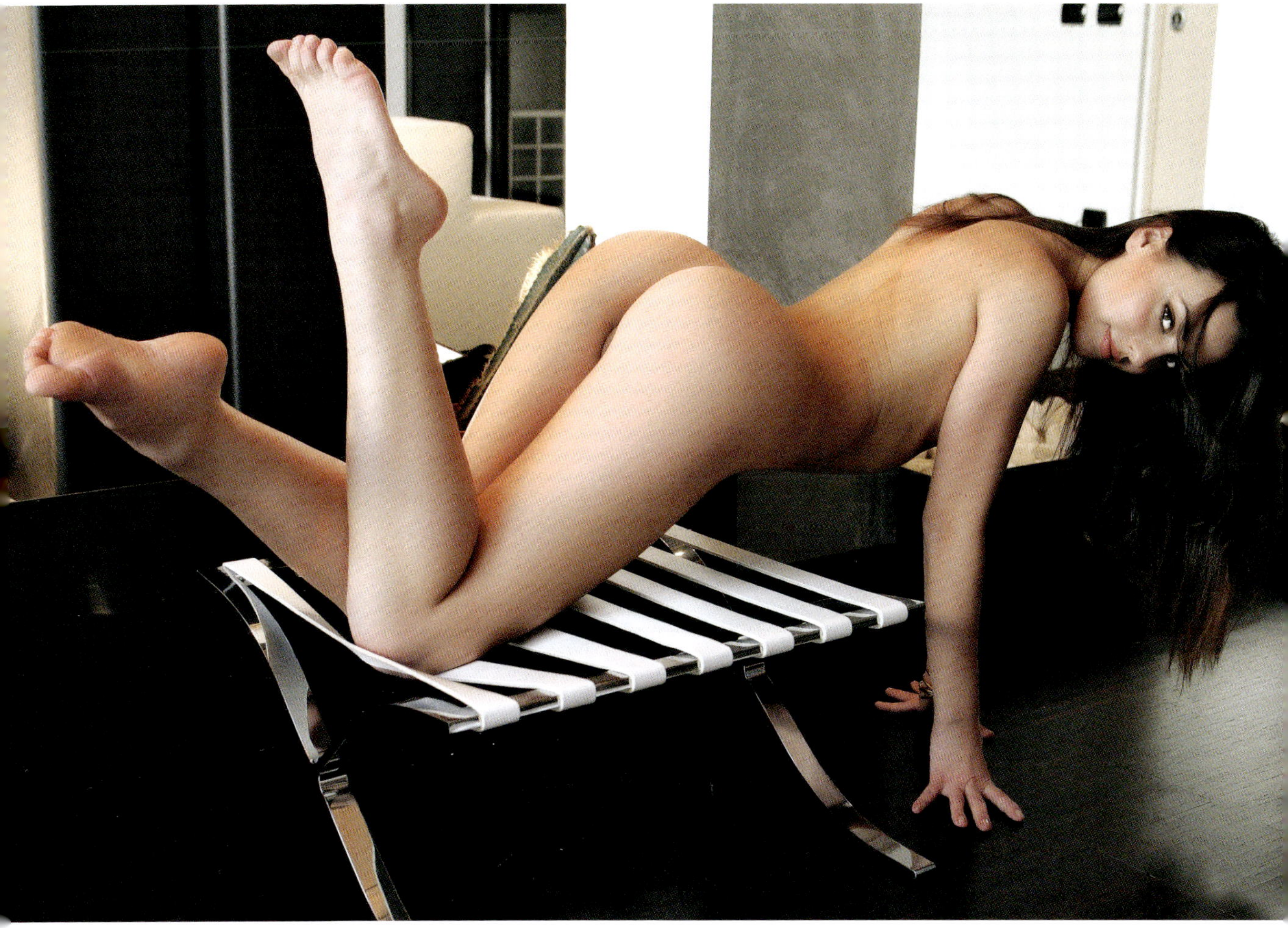

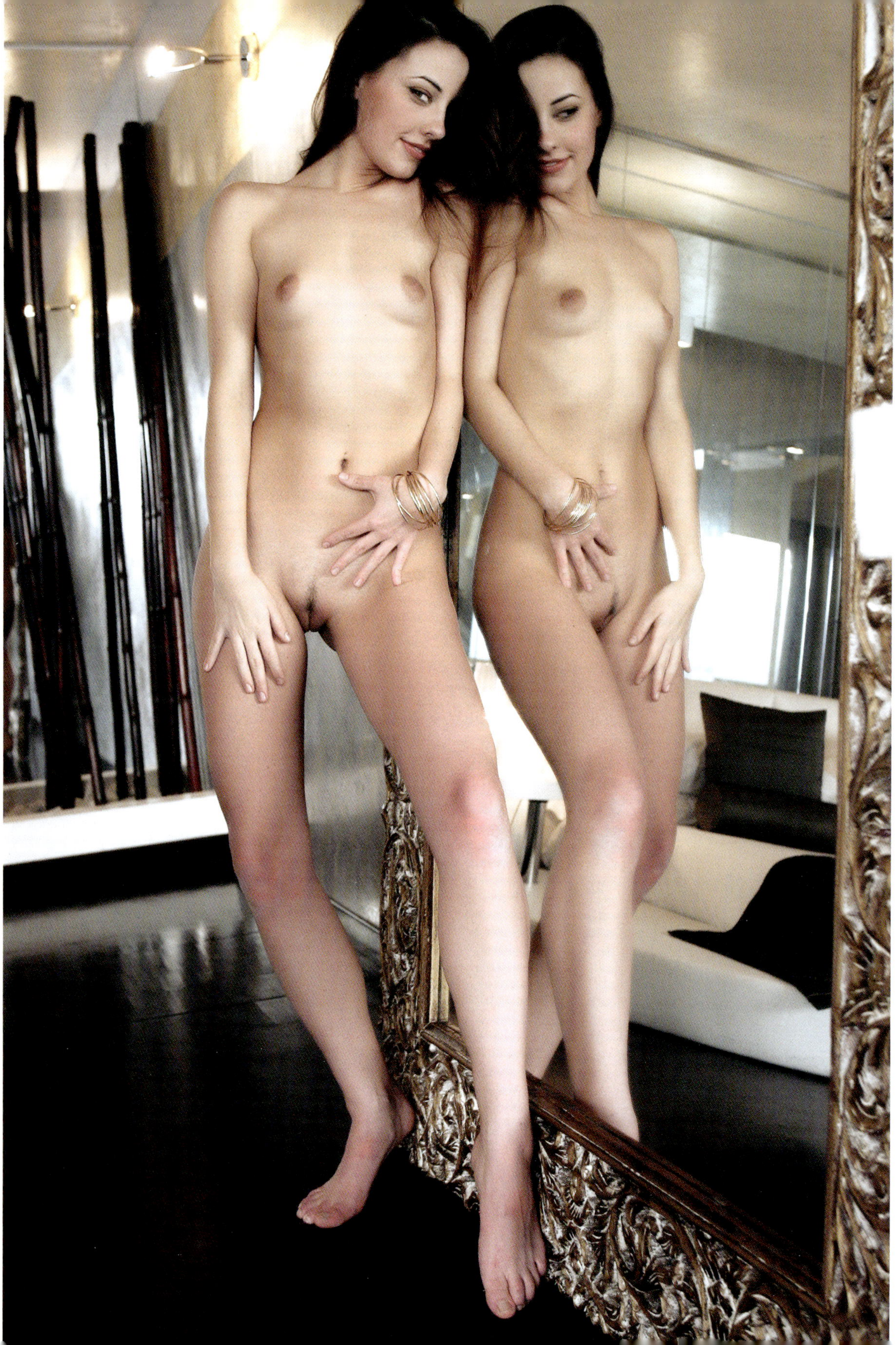

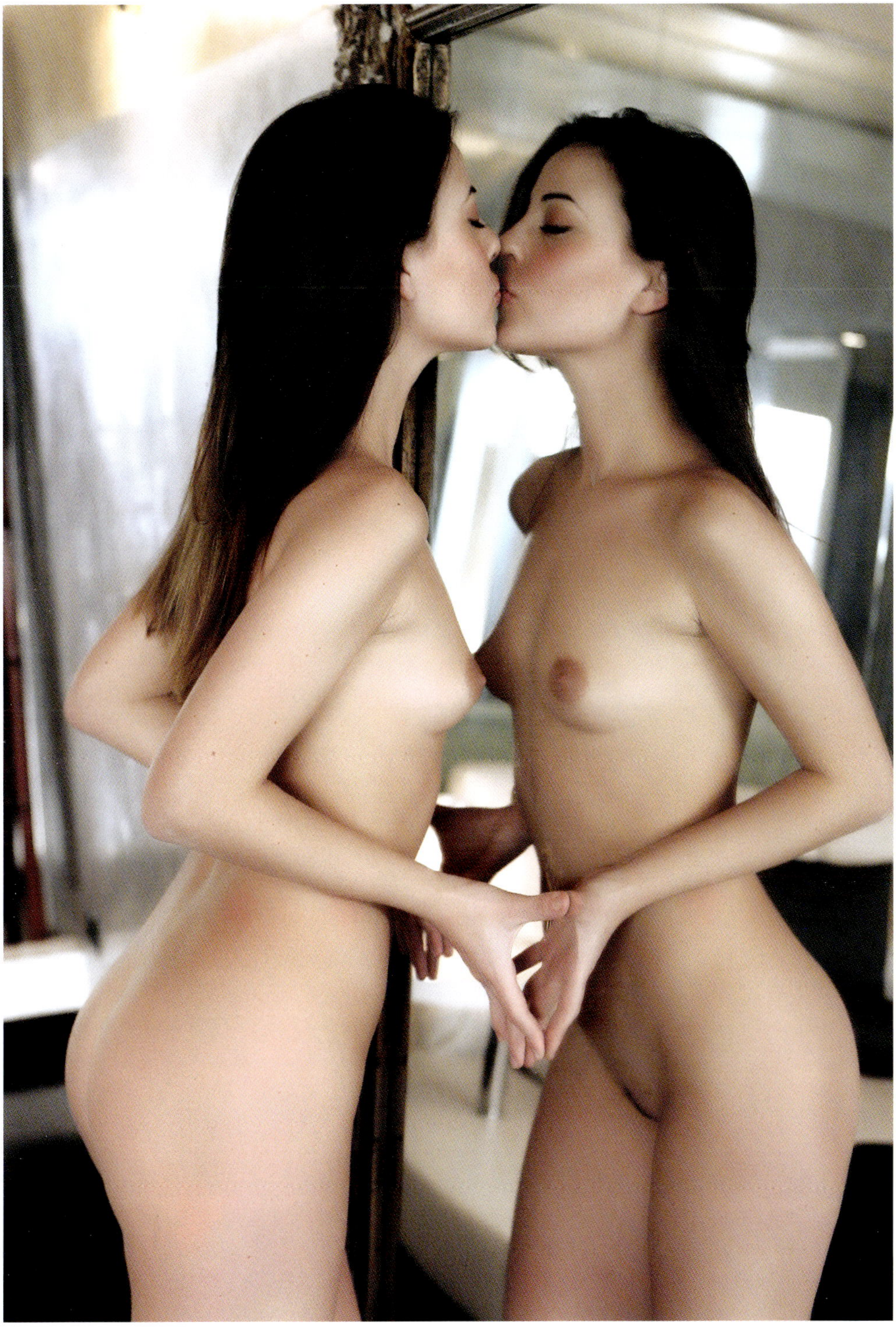

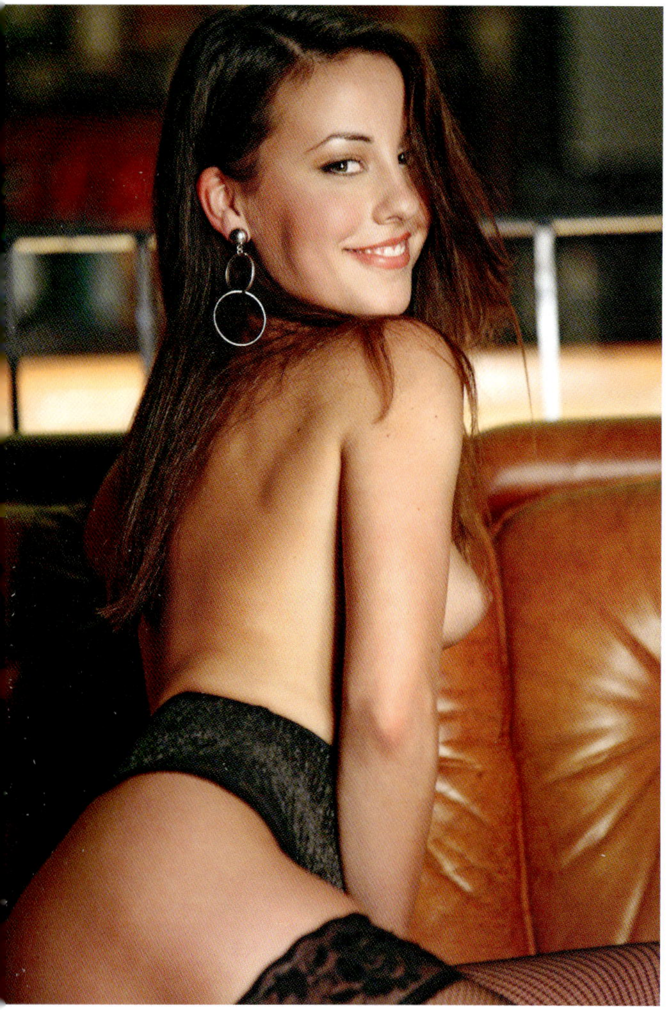
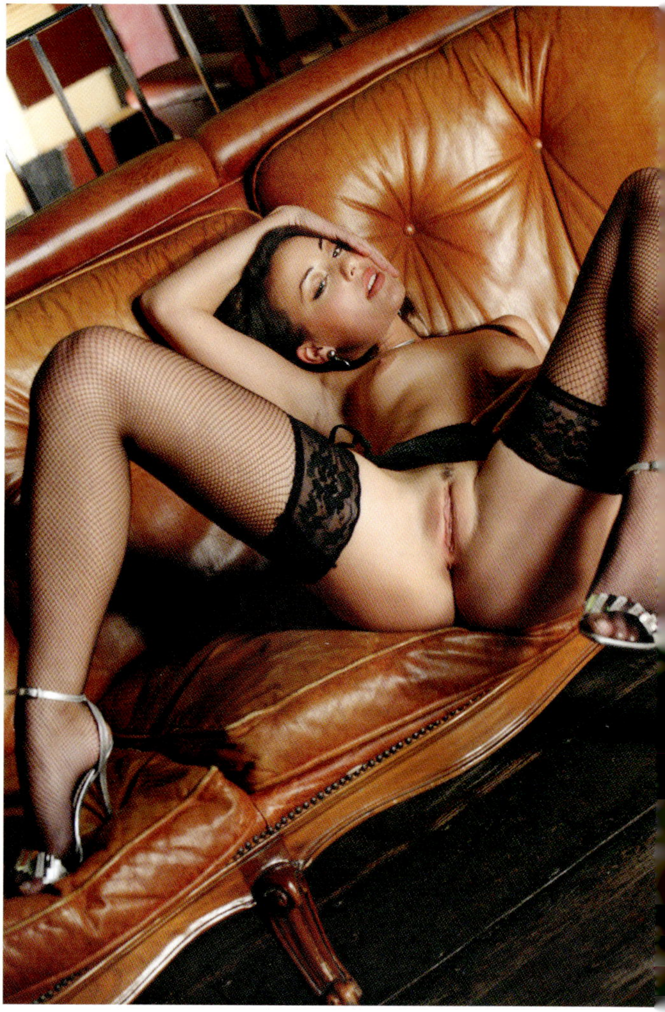

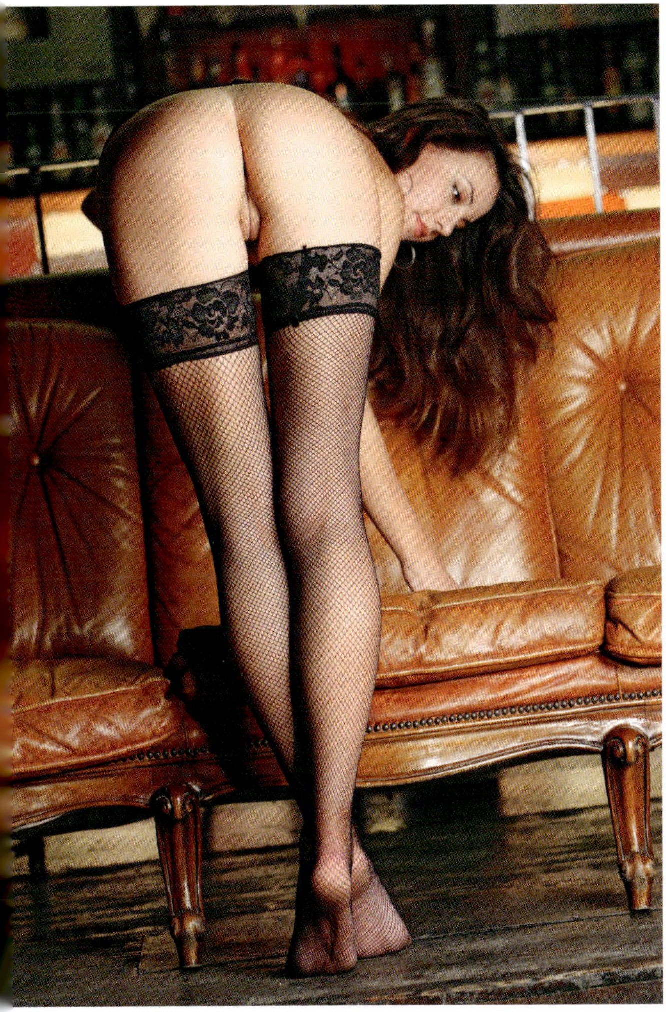

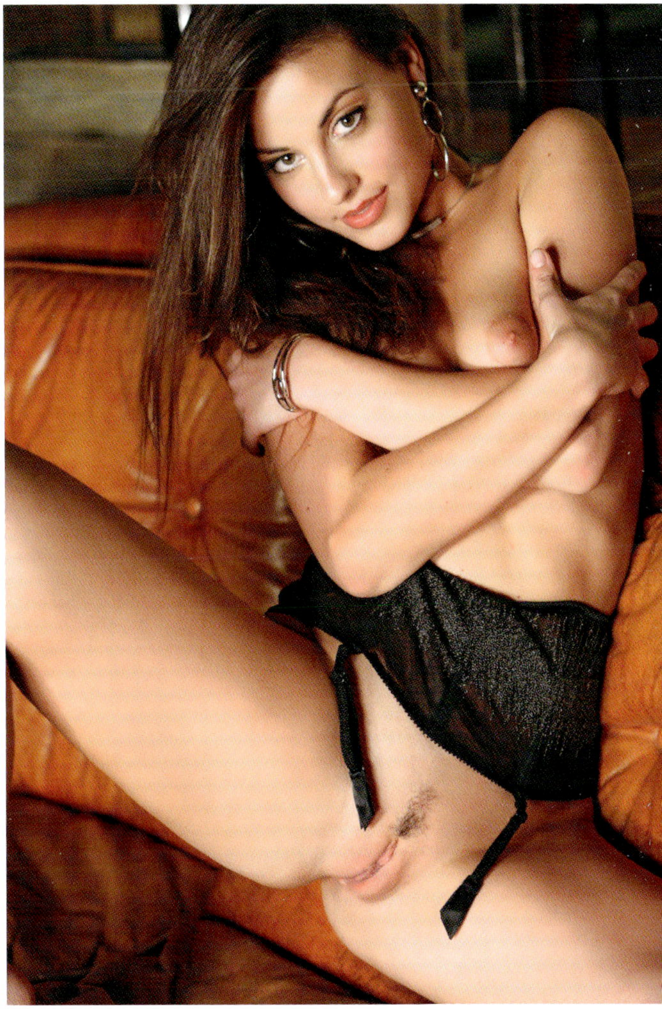

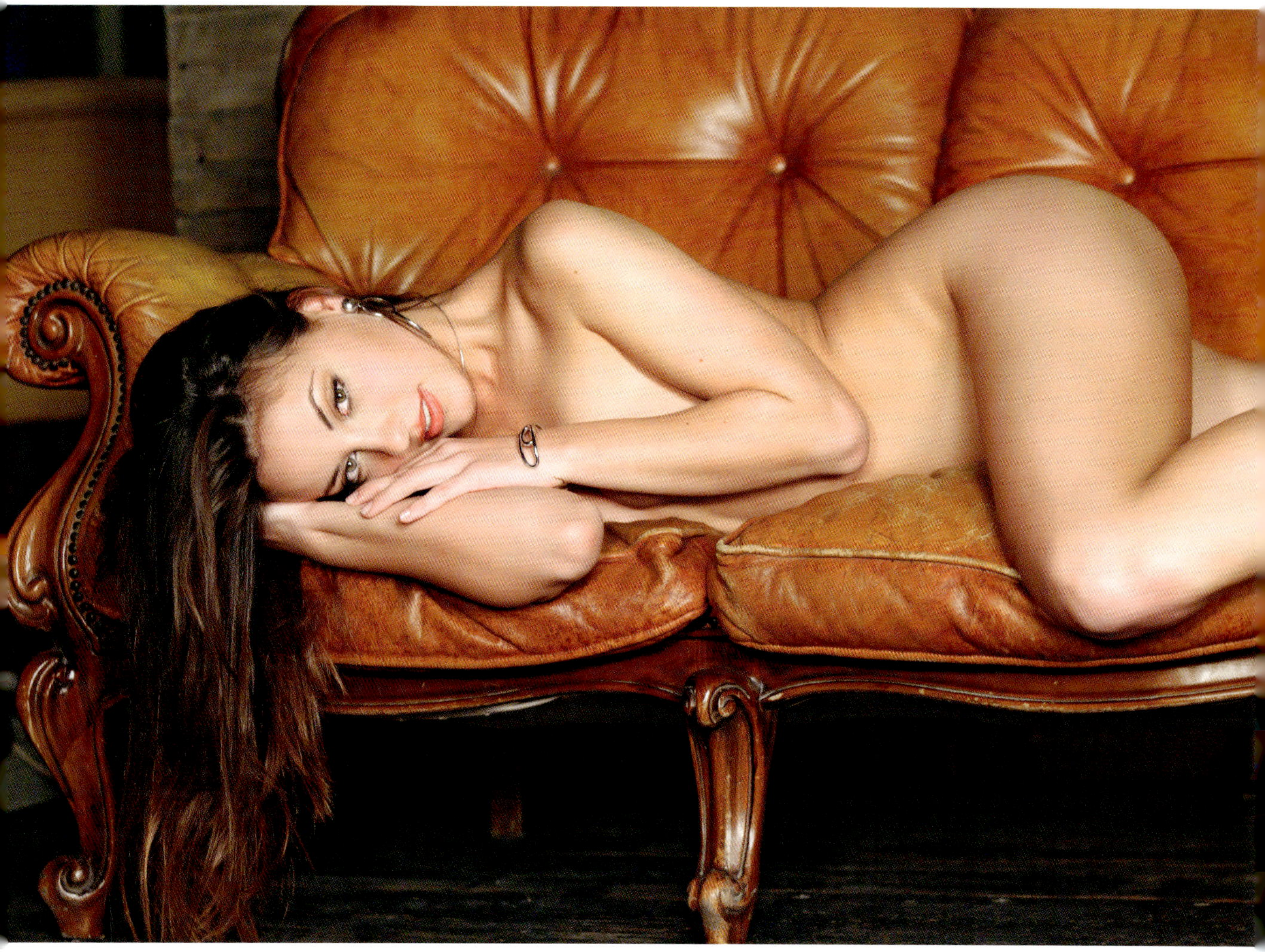

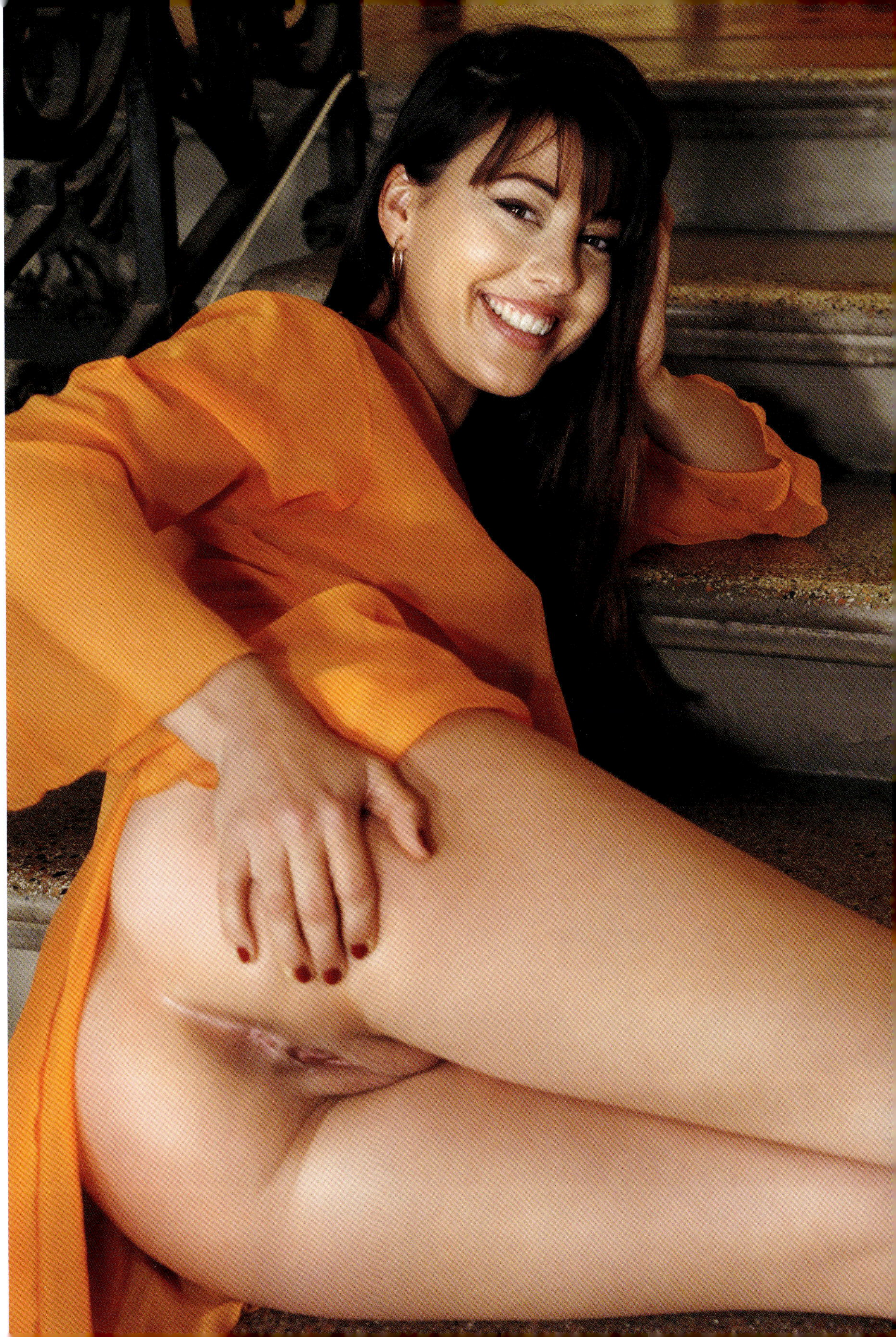

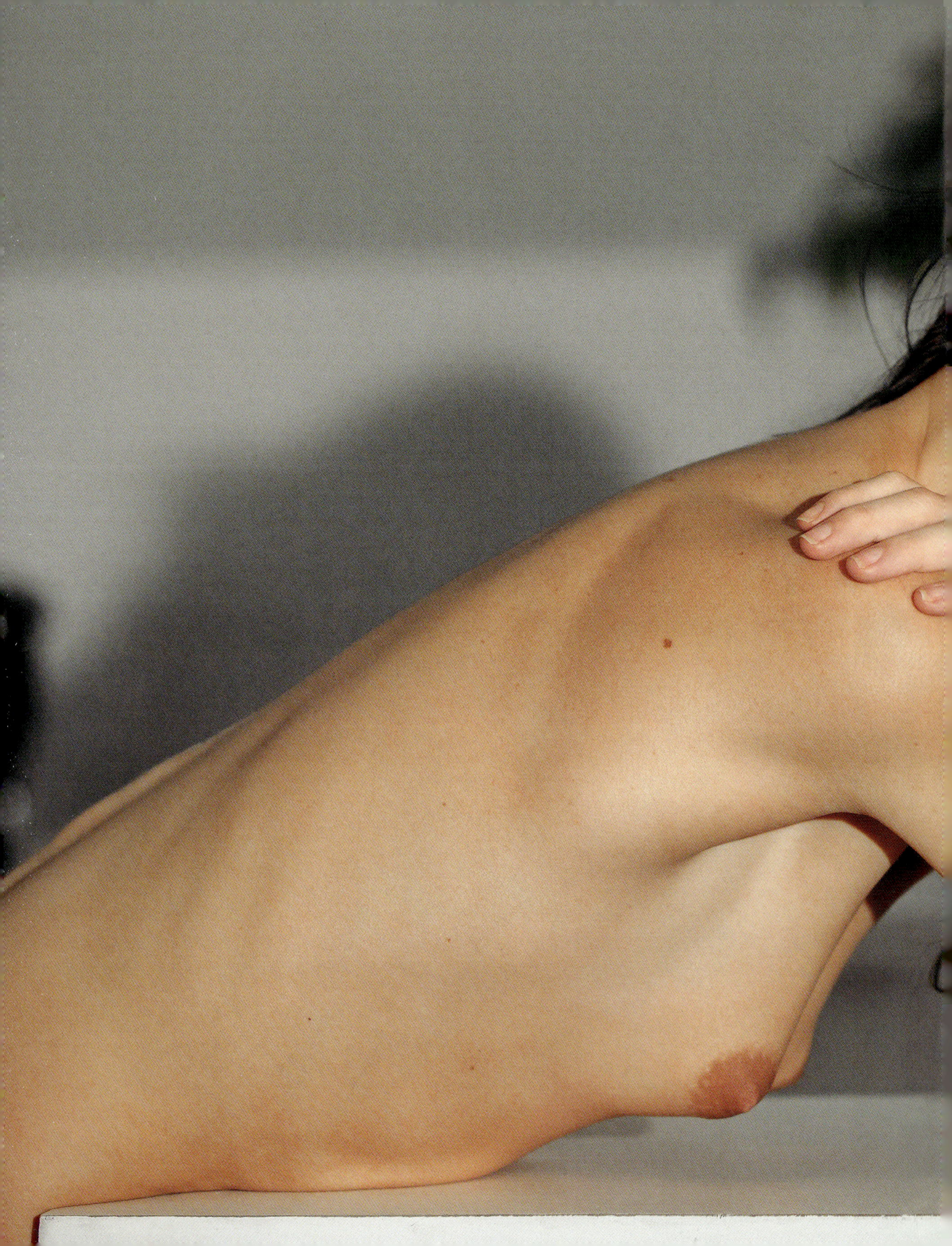

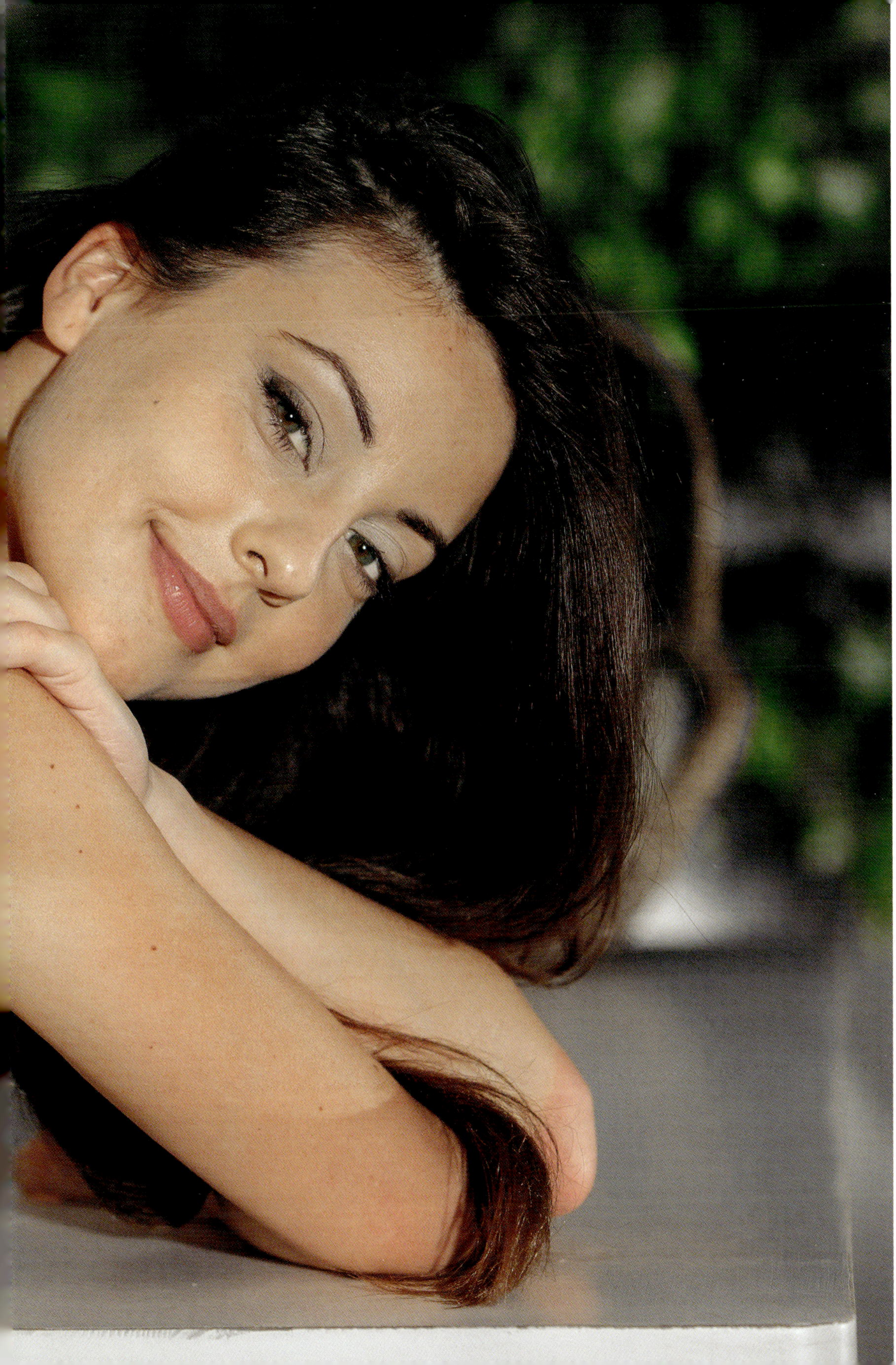

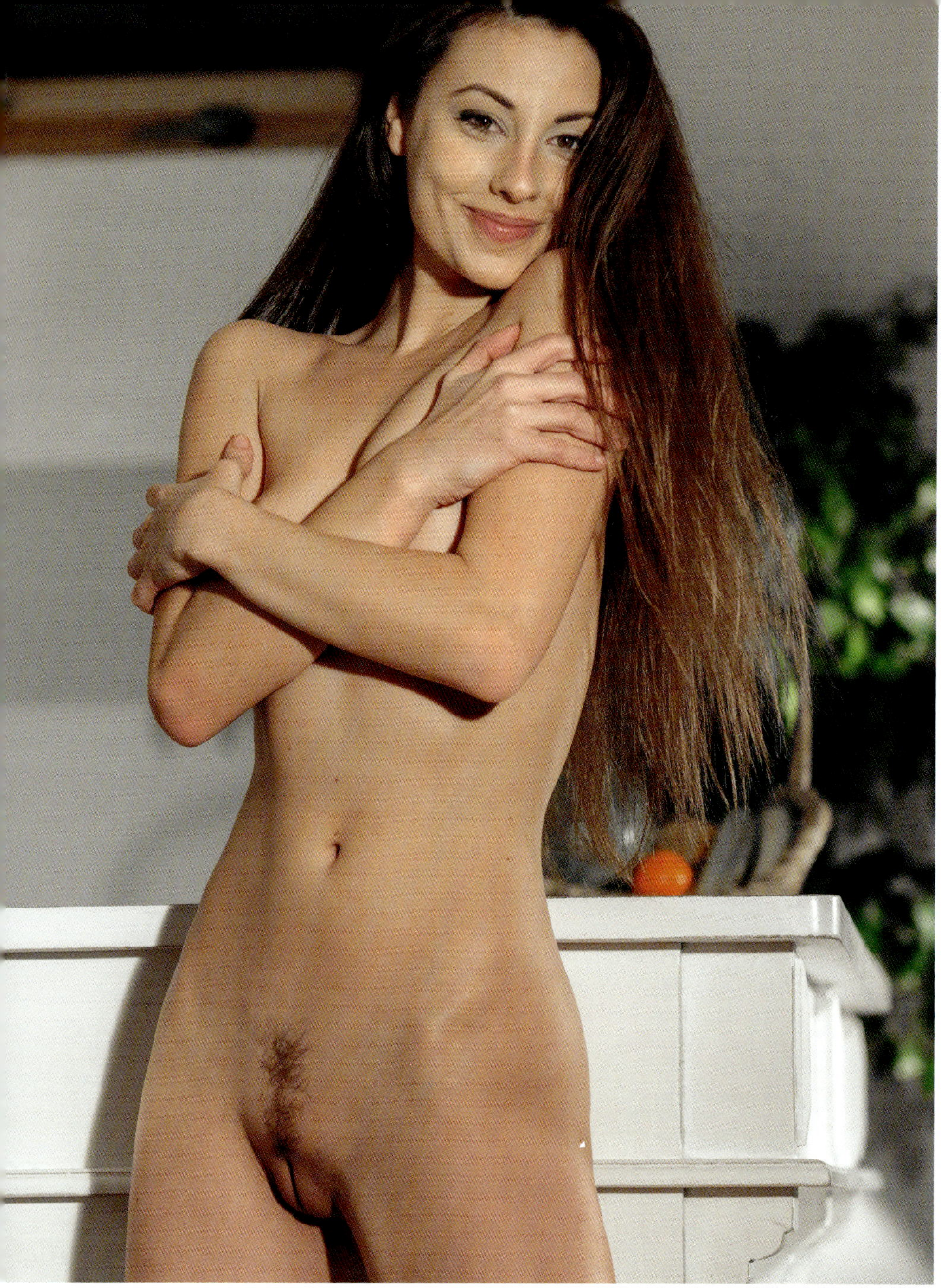

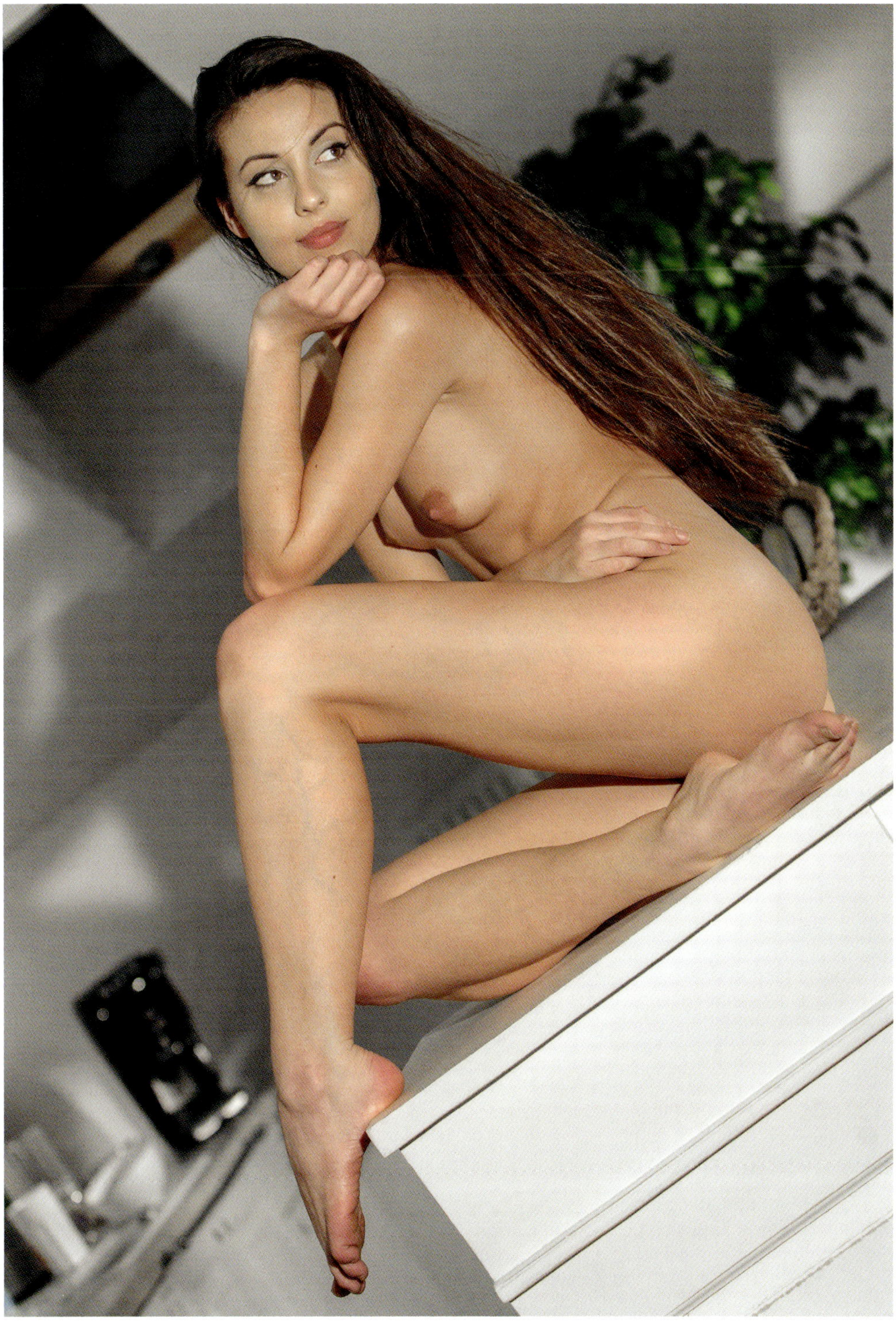

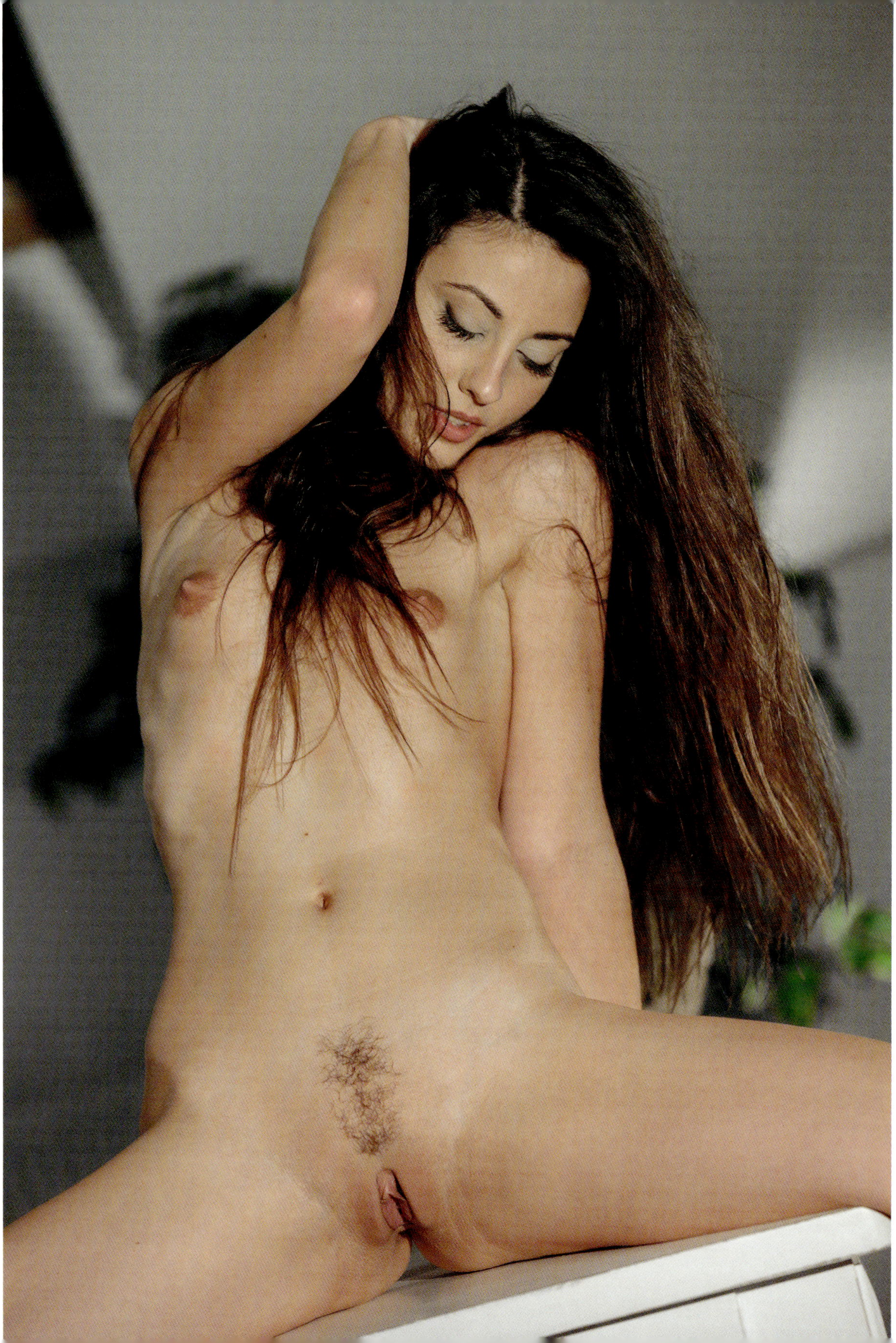

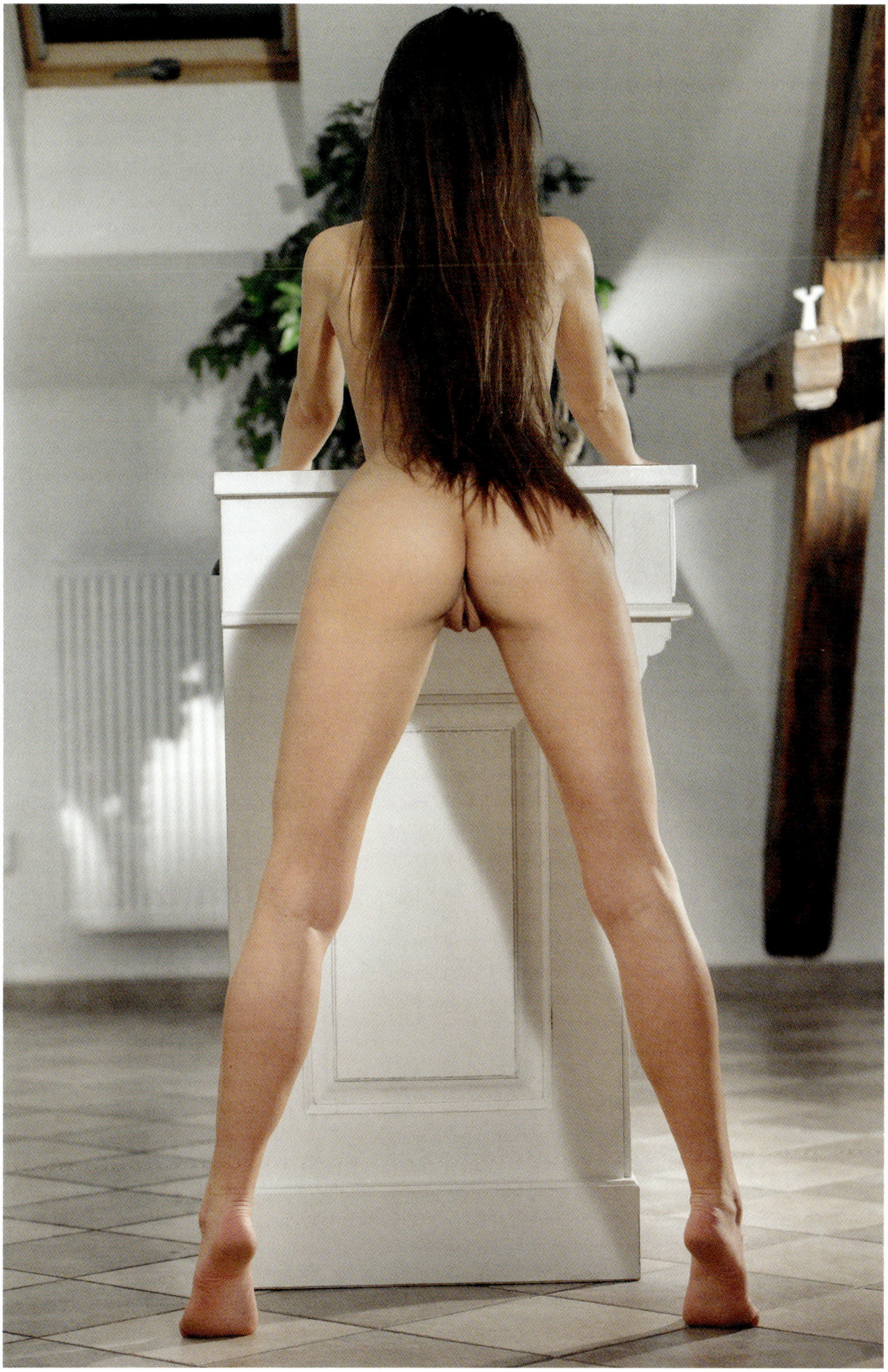

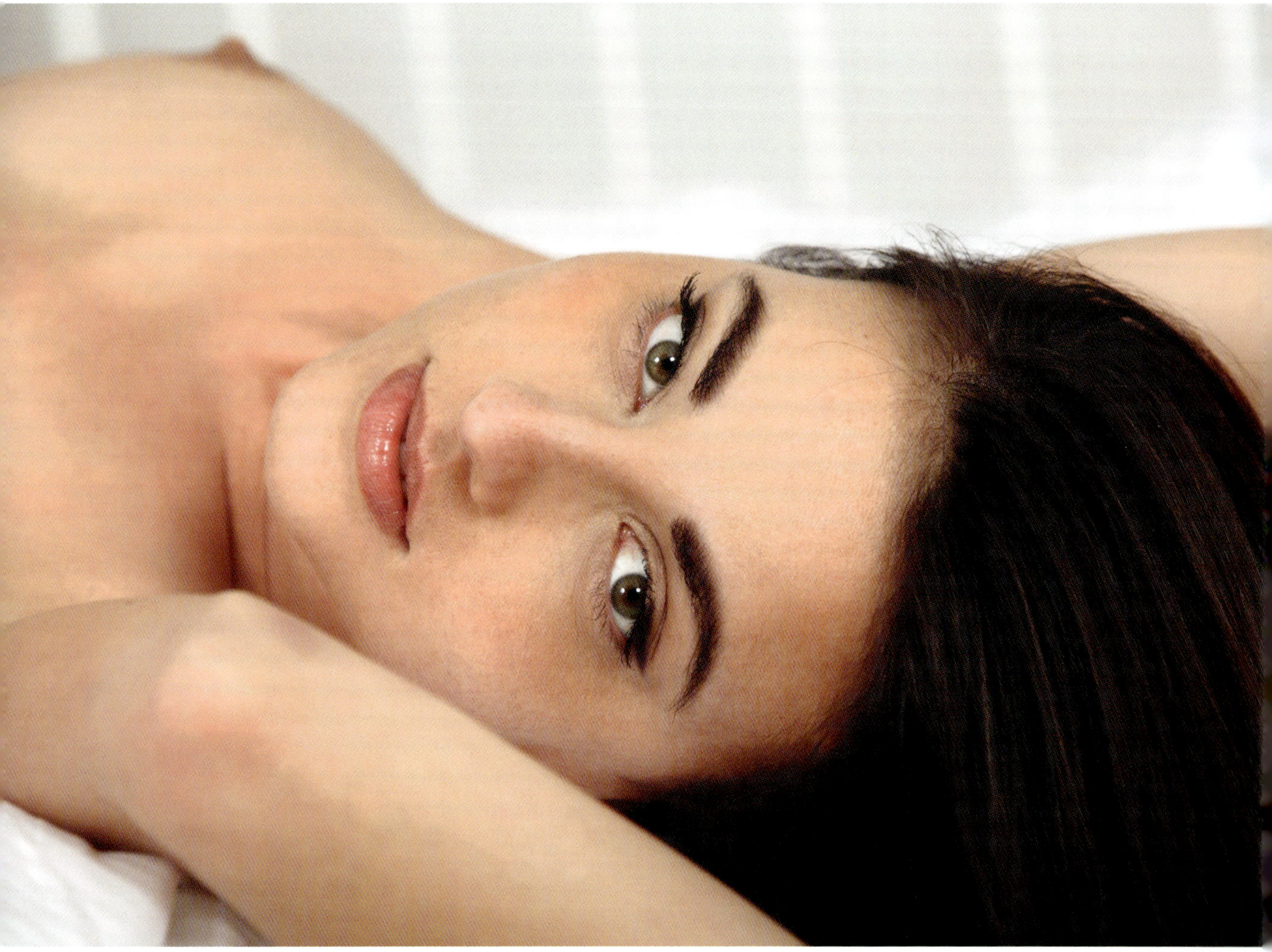

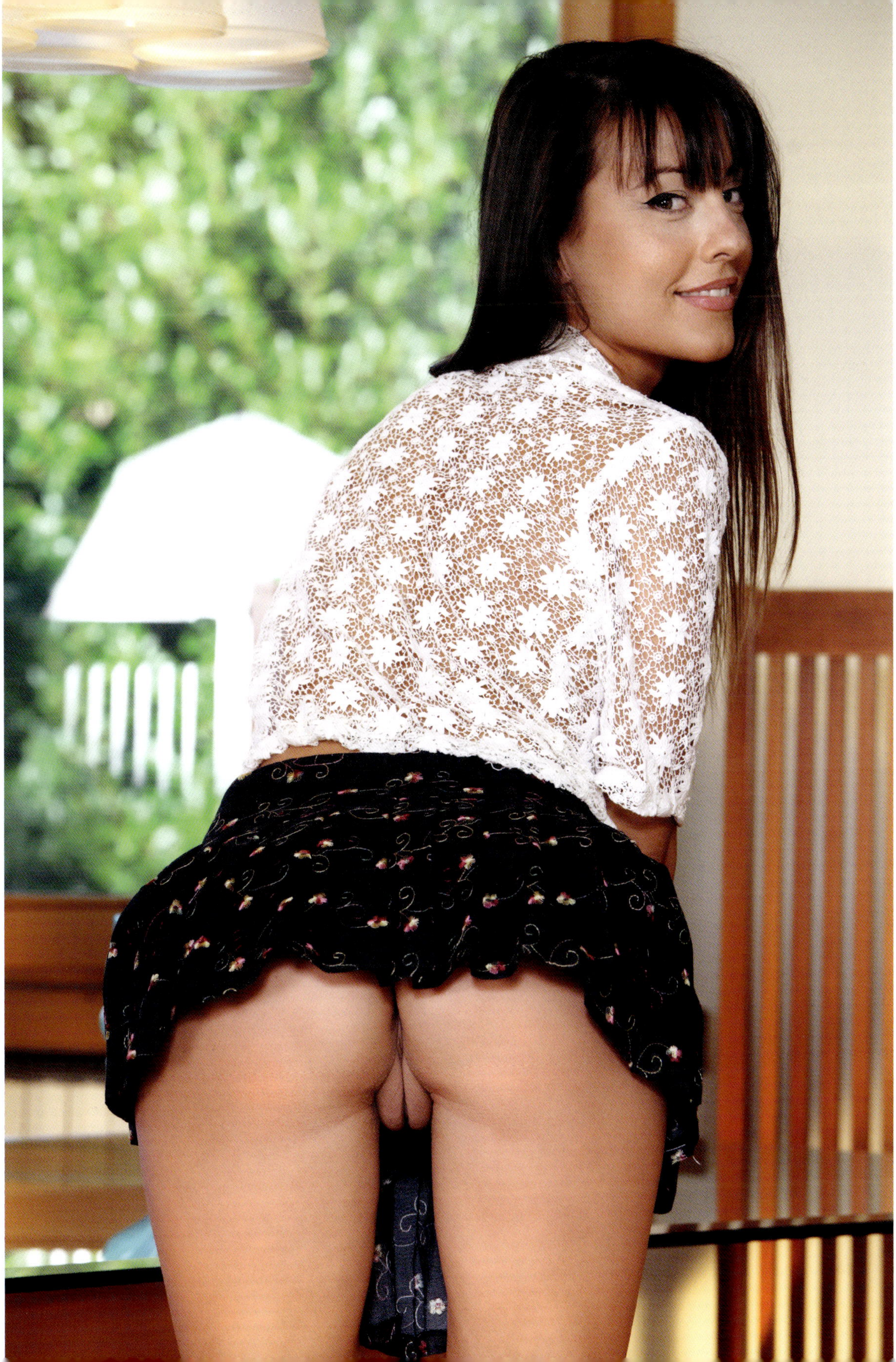

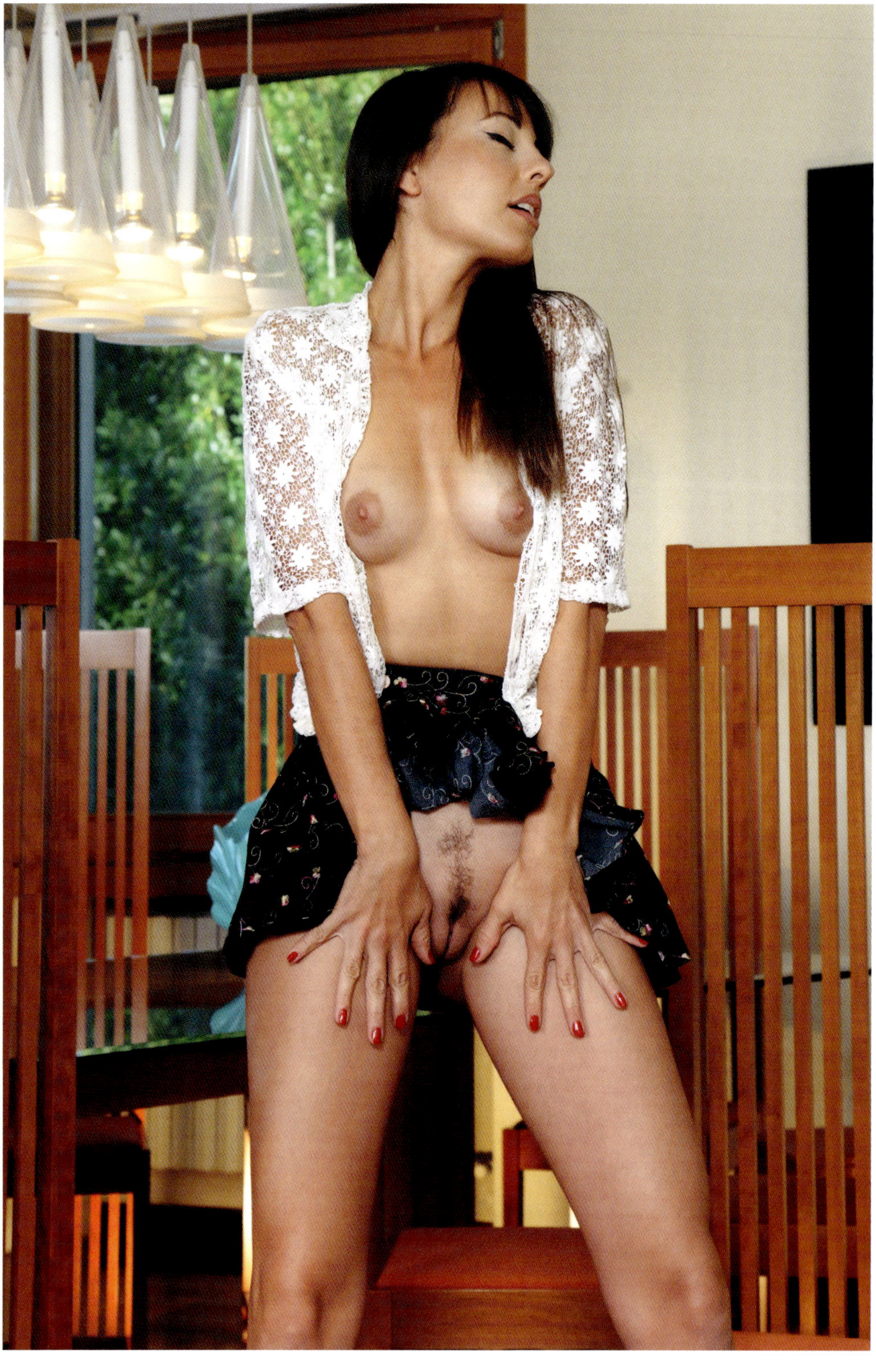

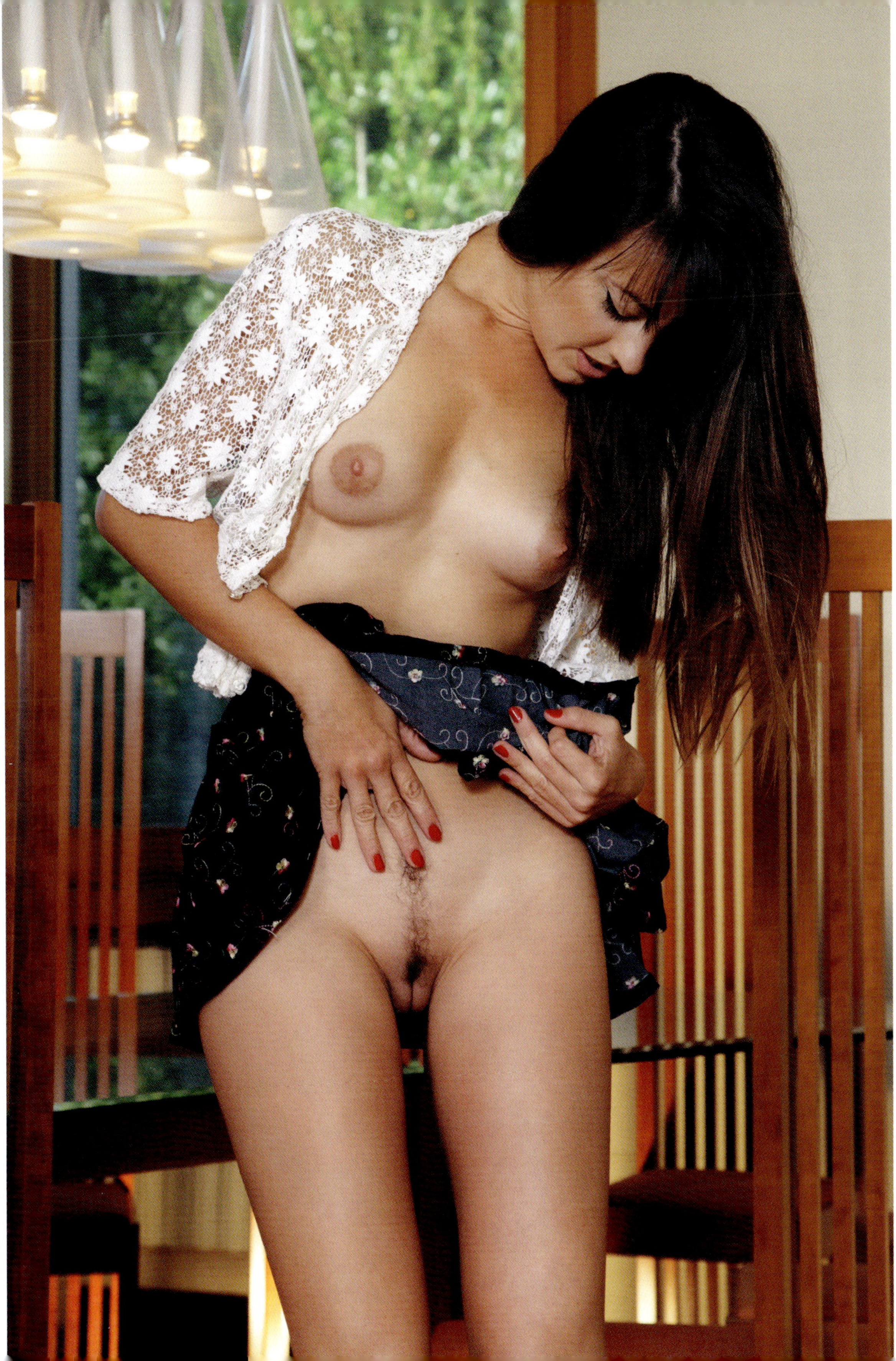

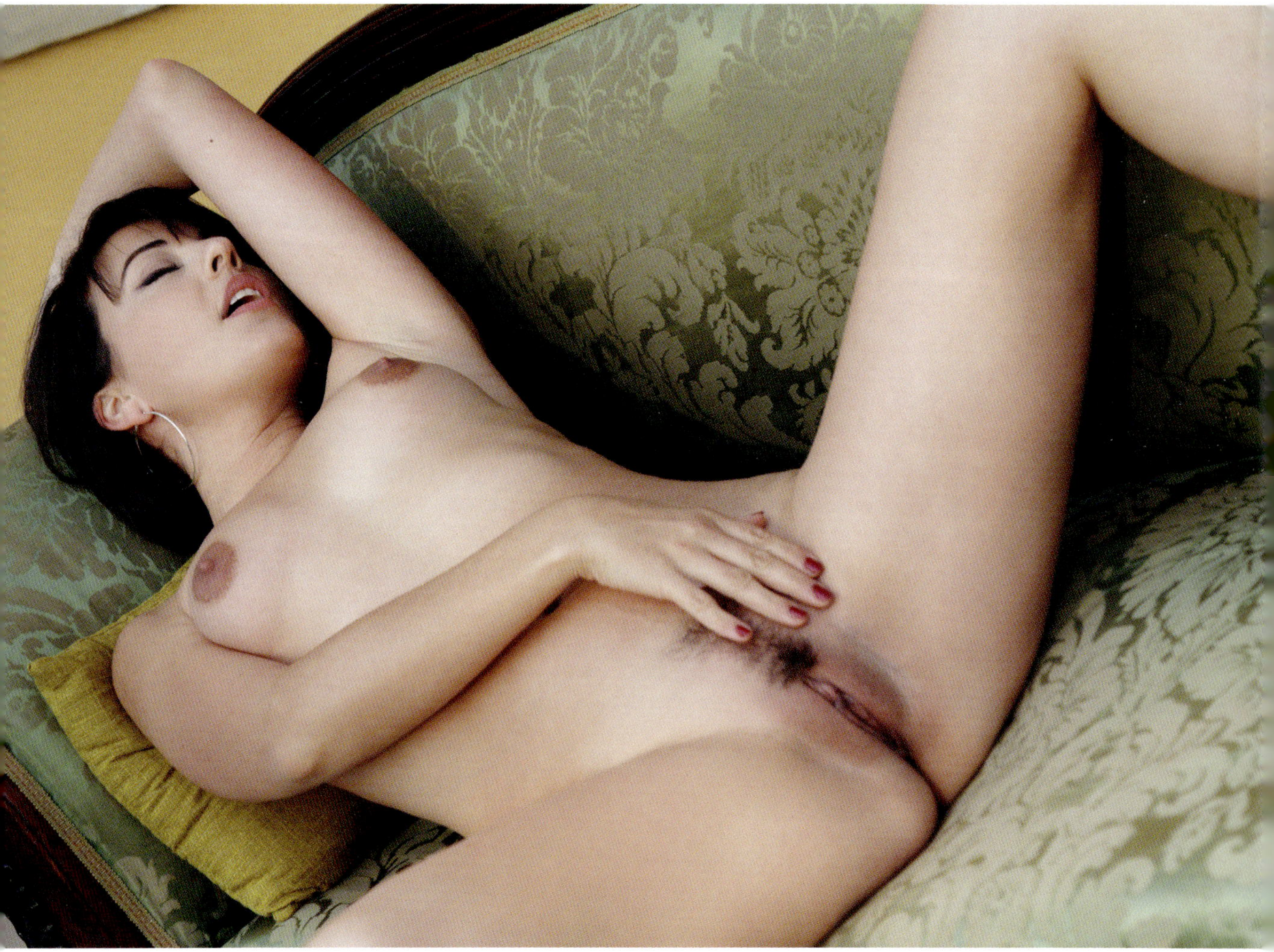

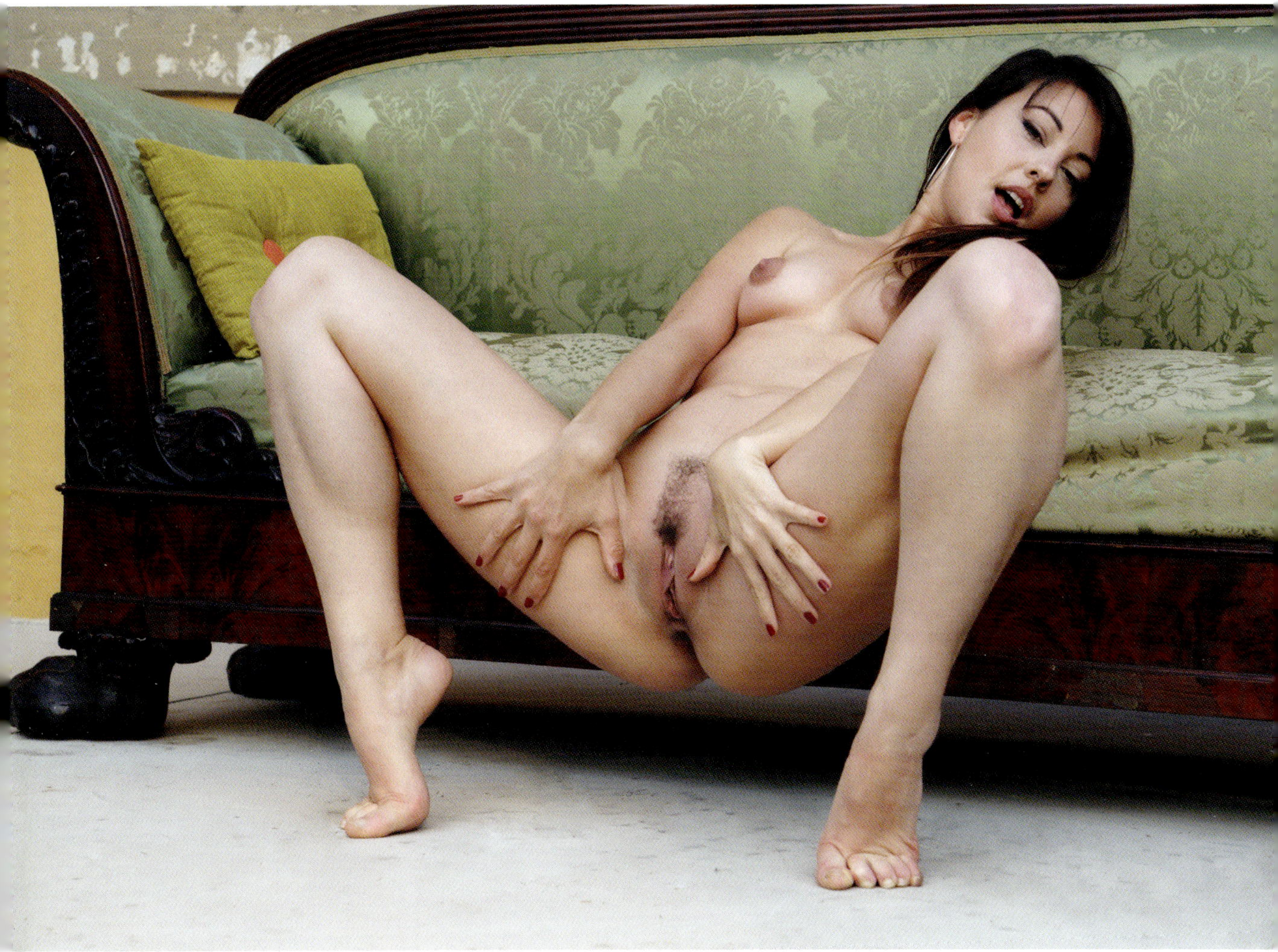

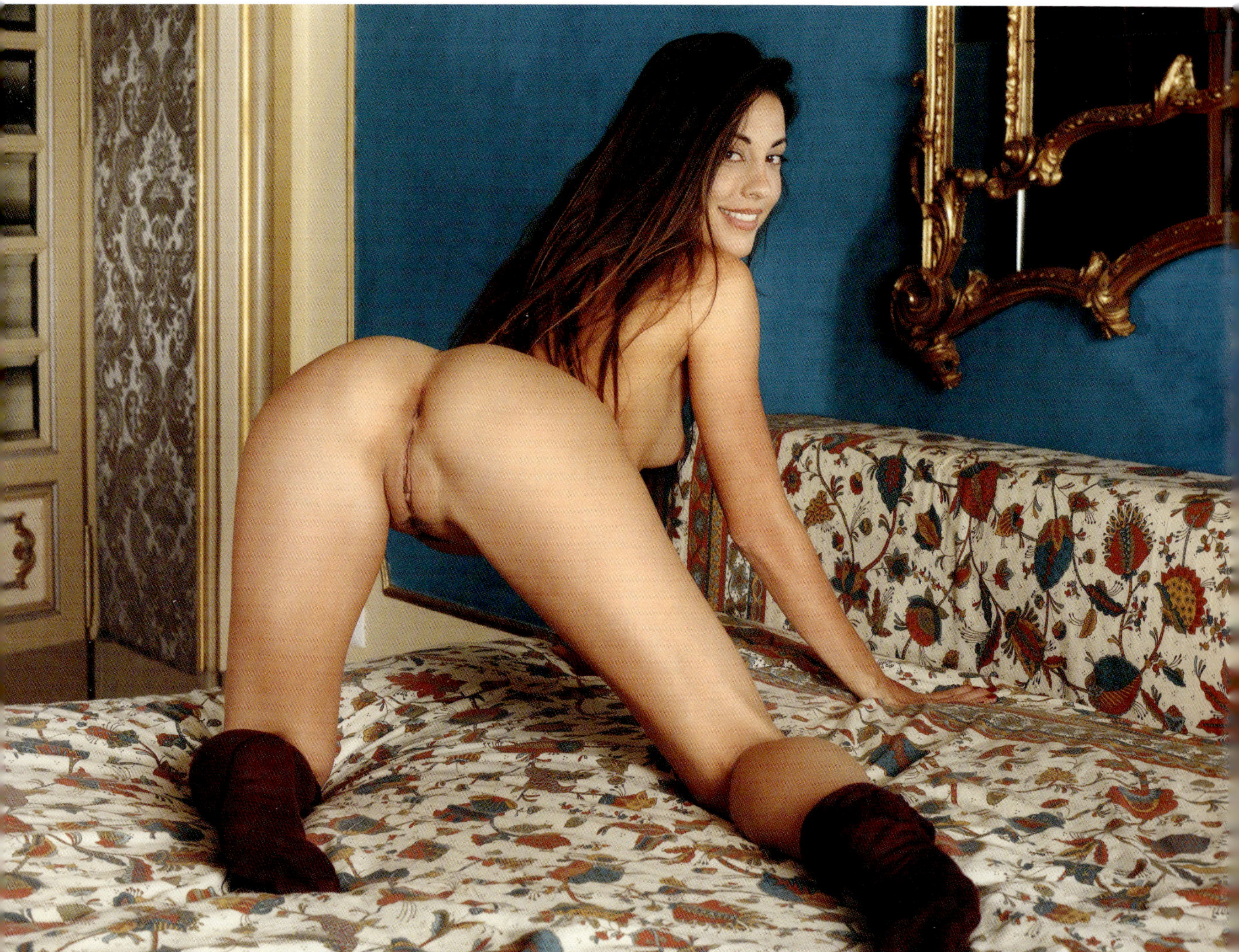

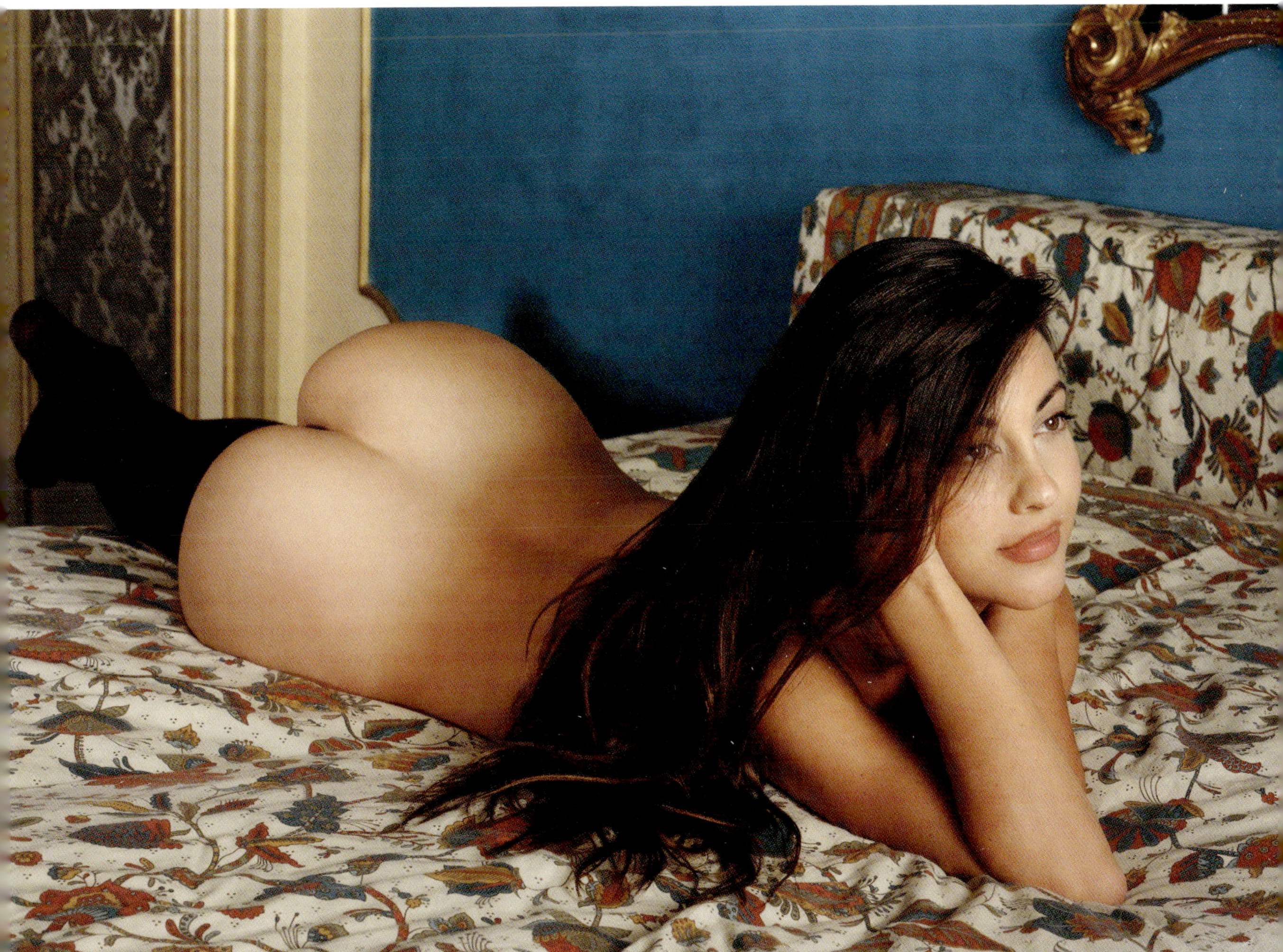

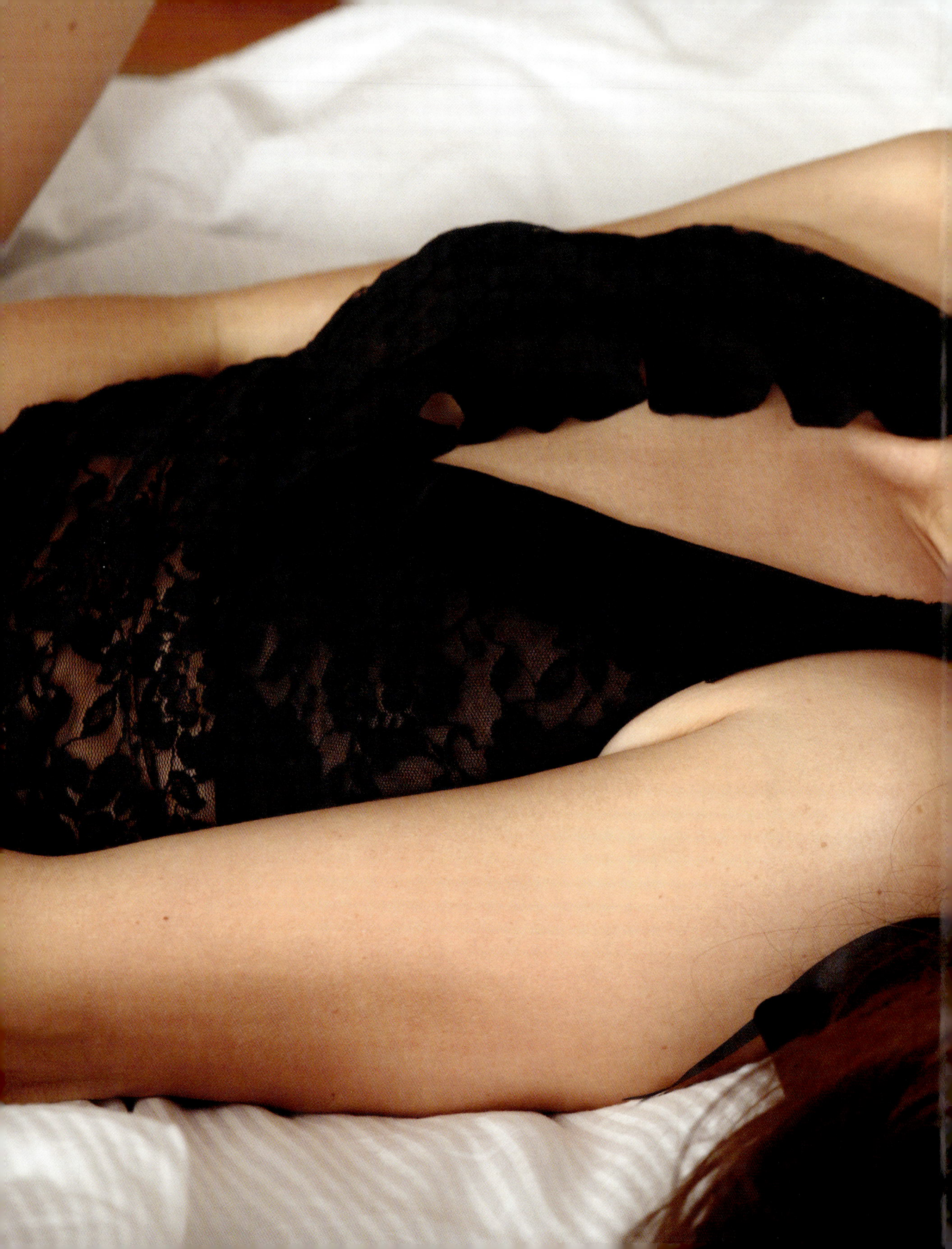

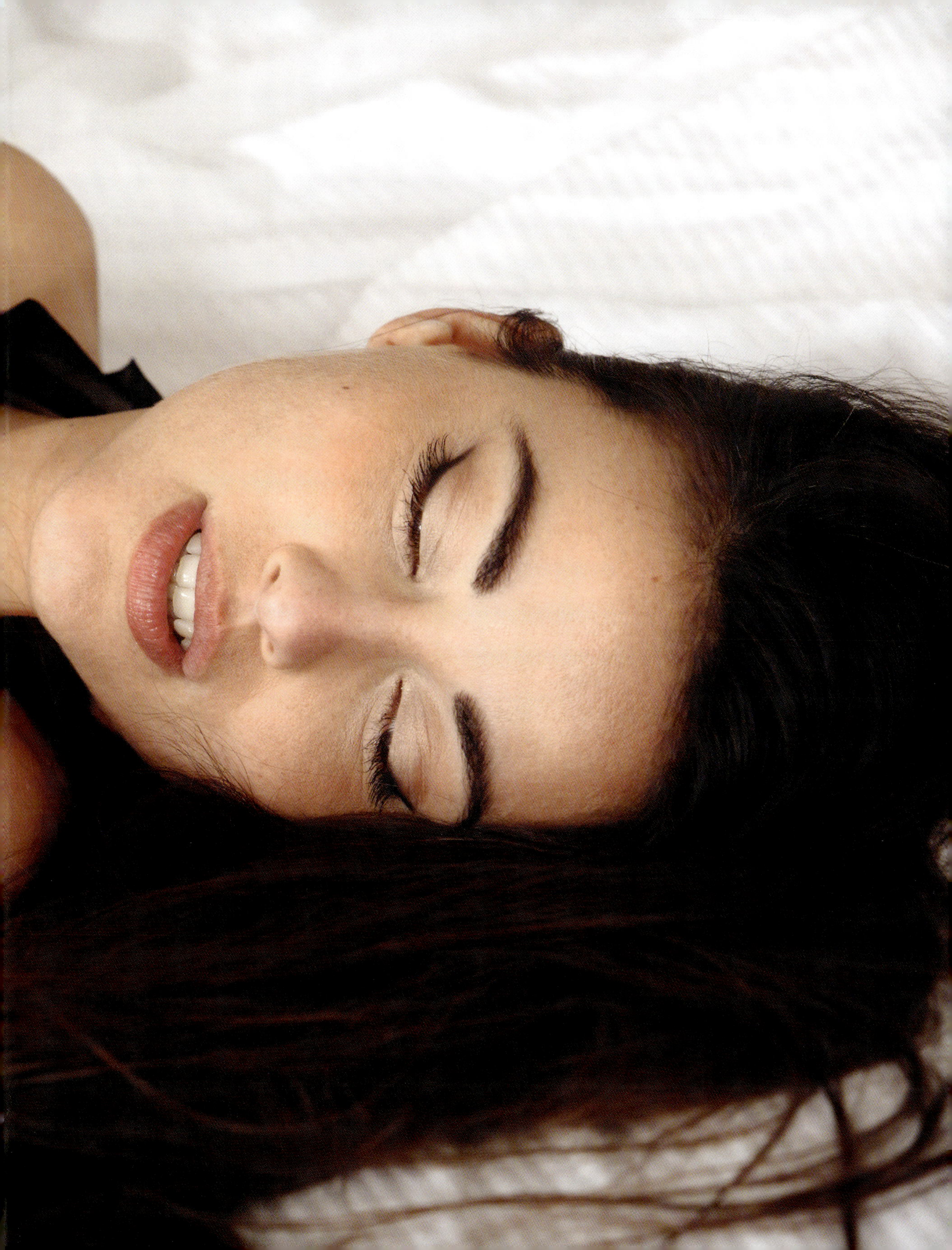

COLLECT THEM ALL: OUR MOST BEAUTIFUL

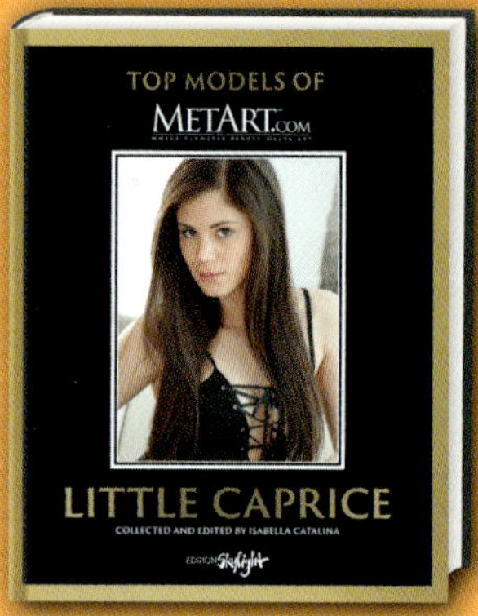

ISBN 978-3-03766-659-3

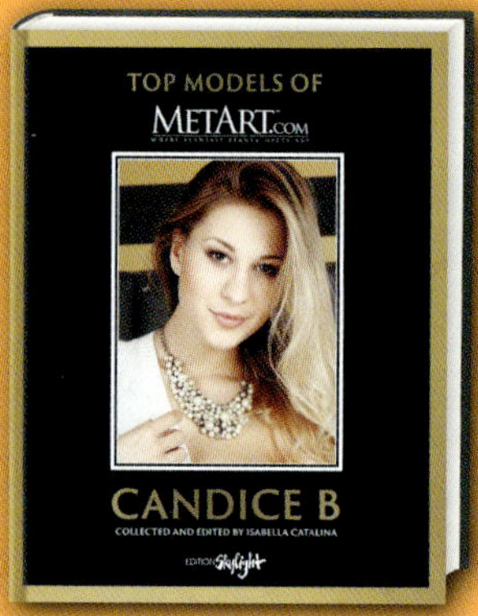

ISBN 978-3-03766-660-9

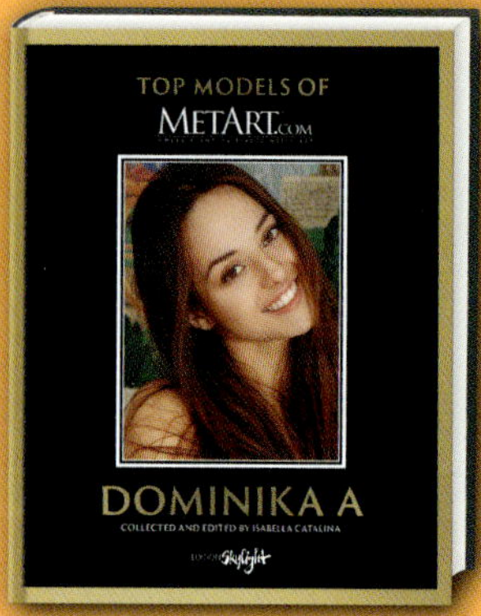

ISBN 978-3-03766-679-1

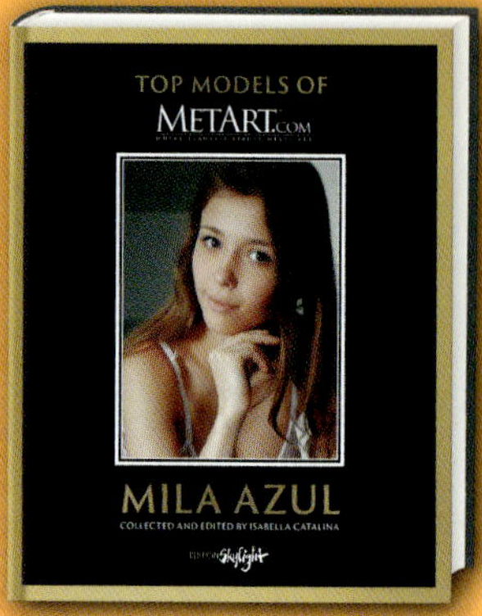

ISBN 978-3-03766-680-7

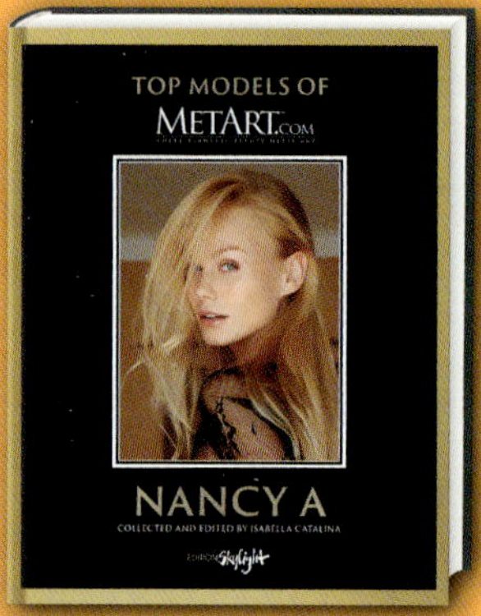

ISBN 978-3-03766-687-6

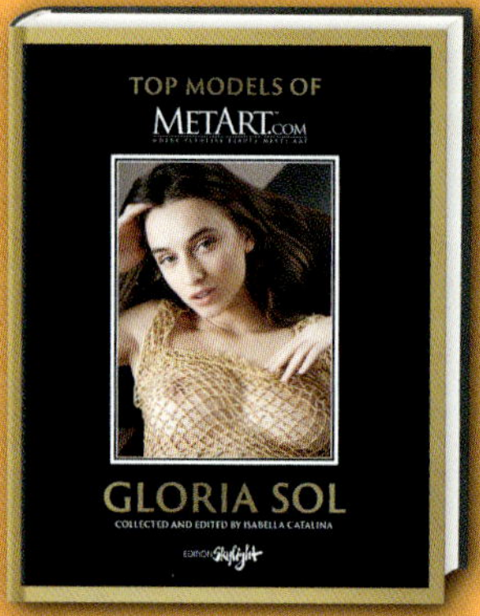

ISBN 978-3-03766-688-3

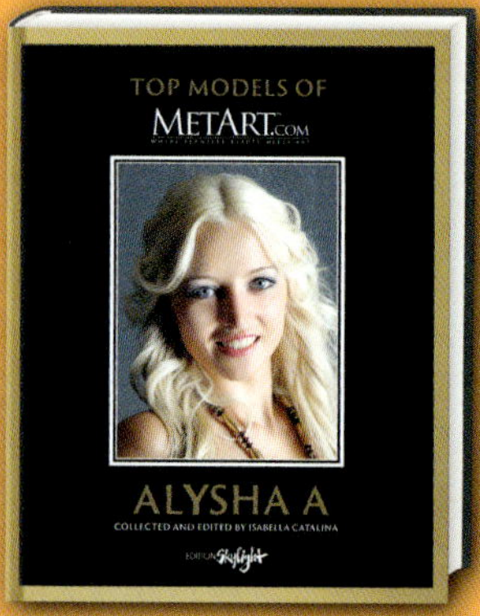

ISBN 978-3-03766-692-0

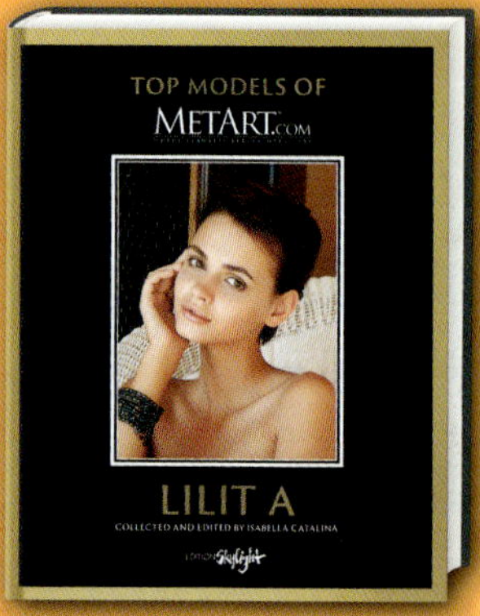

ISBN 978-3-03766-693-7

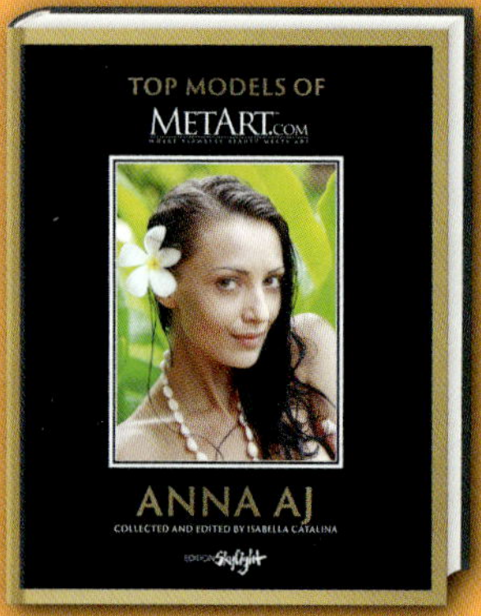

ISBN 978-3-03766-695-1

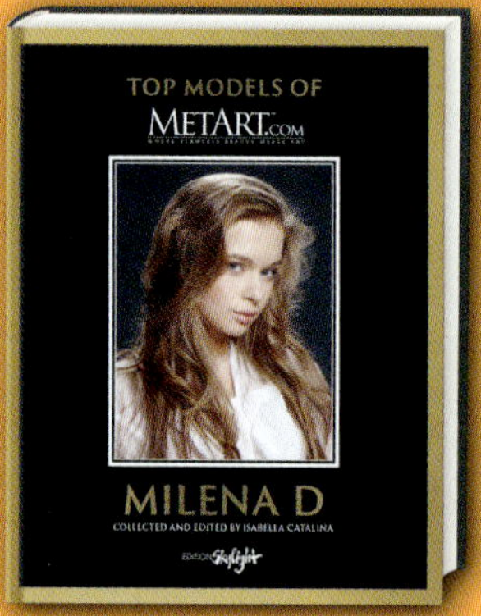

ISBN 978-3-03766-696-8

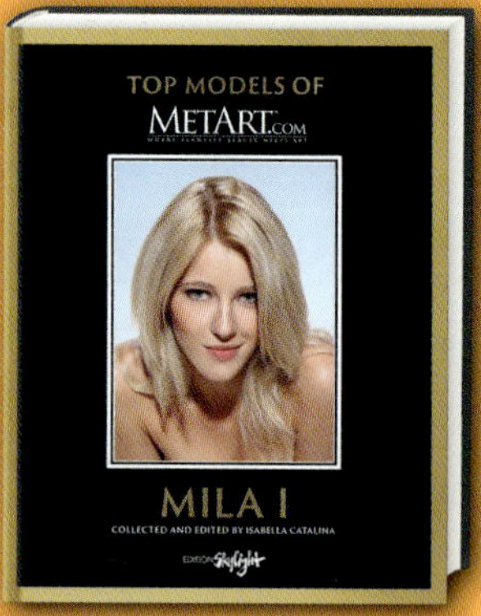

ISBN 978-3-03766-703-3

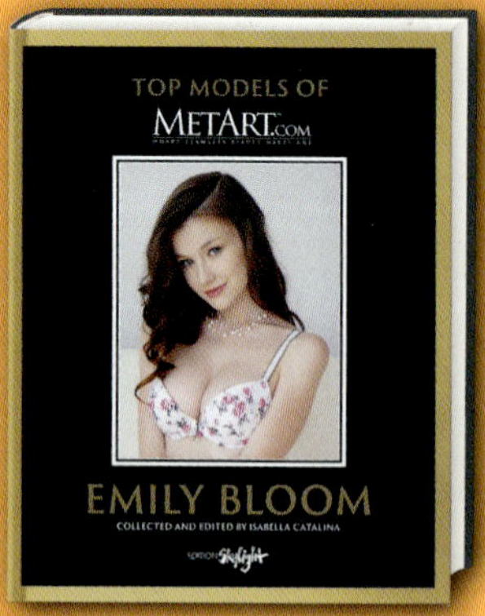

ISBN 978-3-03766-704-0

WWW.EDITION-SKYLIGHT.COM